THE CHURCH AND THE
NATIONAL SECURITY STATE

THE CHURCH AND THE
NATIONAL SECURITY STATE

José Comblin

ORBIS BOOKS
Maryknoll, New York 10545

Second Printing, May 1984

The Catholic Foreign Mission Society of America (Maryknoll) recruits and trains people for overseas missionary service. Through Orbis Books Maryknoll aims to foster the international dialogue that is essential to mission. The books published, however, reflect the opinions of their authors and are not meant to represent the official position of the society.

Library of Congress Cataloging in Publication Data

Comblin, Joseph, 1923–
   The church and the national security state.

   Includes bibliographical references.
   1. Liberation theology. 2. Catholic Church in Latin America. 3. Church and state in Latin America.
1. Title.
BT83.57.C65   261.7'098   79-10881
ISBN 0-88344-082-2

Contents

Introduction

What is liberation theology? Why has it arisen during the last decade in Latin America? Is it specific only to this time and place? Has it any validity at all? Does it threaten the very existence of the church, as some claim, or is it the authentic response of the people of God?

These are questions which I have struggled with personally for more than ten years, discussed with my students at the Harvard School of Divinity, and now dare to present to the readers of North America. But before you, the reader, spend too much time over this book, there are two caveats of which you should be aware.

The first is simply that this book consists basically of my class notes from Harvard. It is, therefore, of its nature occasionally repetitive, occasionally overexplanatory of things you may already know. It probably presents more questions than it answers. And because events are moving so quickly in Latin America today, parts of it will be outdated almost before it is off the press.

The second is more basic. The theology of liberation is very much situated in the political and economic realities of the poor, colonialized peoples of Latin America. I do not think such a theology can be directly pertinent to any North American, to any educated middle-class citizen of the industrialized West. It may not even be interesting to you because the human experience that has produced it is so different from yours. The only reason for you to read such a theology is to discover the testimony of a group of Christians who are facing the human condition in the middle of difficult circumstances. The value of such discovery comes only if other persons in other contexts first feel the deep differences in experience and then seek in their own situations the inspiration for a real theology of their own—the *logos* of God to concrete persons. This is very difficult and can be painful emotionally.

For those of you who accept these caveats and read on, another explanation is due. I have already insisted—and will do so many times again—that the theology of liberation is situated in the particular experience of those who are developing it in Latin America. More and more we are learning that theologians are conditioned by their situation, and the evolution of their investigations depends on this situation. There is no total abstract truth, only fragments, and we all collect some of them according to our own situations, which set the limits to our perceptions. You should know my own limits from the outset, and you can do so only by knowing my background and biography, my situation.

I was born in Belgium more than fifty years ago. Consequently I am a Catholic by virtue of the armed power of King Philip II of Spain, who succeeded in regaining the South Netherlands, although he failed to reconquer the Protestant North Netherlands.

I am also a liberal, owing to England's early nineteenth-century foreign policy. The machinations of the Foreign Office's secret agent, Ponsonby, in preparing and provoking the independence of the Kingdom of Belgium in 1830, led to a unique country in which Catholics have been liberal since the nineteenth century. The independence of Belgium was made possible by means of a strict and definitive alliance between liberals and Catholics; a Catholic country created a new state based on a liberal constitution. This was possible in 1830. Two years later, it would not have been possible because Pope Gregory VI then wrote his famous encyclical against liberalism, which opened a century of struggles between liberals and Catholics throughout the world. But the Belgian constitution was an accomplished fact in 1832, and it has never been revised. So I was born and raised in the unusual context of a country where the Catholics are normally liberal.

Of course, such a fact conditioned my view of the United States. The Belgian constitution was the first in Europe inspired by the spirit of the American Revolution and constitution. From a Belgian point of view, the people of the United States were the first in the world to be free in the modern sense of liberty, the first people who based their common life on the principles of the Declaration of Independence. They were the image of liberty. That image was confirmed during the next two hundred years. In the nineteenth century, the United States was the refuge and hope of 20 million Europeans, persecuted, expelled, dominated, poor, famished, from all the European countries. For them all, America was freedom and happiness. This image reached its climax in the twentieth century when the United States was twice the savior and liberator of oppressed peoples, and especially the Belgian people—in 1918 and in 1944. Such an image might be represented by the famous Fourteen Points declaration of President Woodrow Wilson in 1918.

A second important part of my experience is having been educated at the University of Louvain, where the two cultures of clear Latin rationalism and deep German *Gemüt* romanticism meet permanently. Created in the fifteenth century, the golden age of the Netherlands, within one hundred years the university was a center for humanism, with Erasmus, his Collegium Trium Linguarum, and the future Pope Adrian VI (the last non-Italian pope), humanist counselor of Emperor Charles V and victim of the intolerance of the Roman Curia. At the end of the nineteenth century, its Faculty of Theology adopted the German historical and scientific theology, following the historical method defined by Ranke and illustrated by the *Monumenta Germaniae Historica* and the famous corpus of Latin and Greek patrology, the *Corpus Beroninense* and the *Corpus Vindobunense*. These were the objects of a deep veneration, the new sacraments of the sacred scientific *Geschichte.* The school then adopted the biblical philological methods developed by German scholars in Tübingen, Göttingen and elsewhere, which finally produced Kittel's magnificent *Theologisches Wörterbuch zum Neuen Testament.* I, too, have venerated the *Th.W.* and I still venerate it. Such was the context of my education.

Eventually I became a specialist in the New Testament, and to some degree I have never ceased being one. Then a third factor intervened. Eighteen years ago I went to South America; since then I have lived and worked there—for eleven years in Brazil, seven in Chile, and long intermediate periods in Ecuador and some other countries.

Why did I go? Probably in response to an old atavistic instinct of migration common to all European peoples, like Christopher Columbus seeking the golden age and paradise lost, the myth of the good savage and a new world. My formal, rational reason was an appeal from Pope Pius XII and the Latin American Catholic Church to all the Catholic churches in the developed world (this was about 1953 to 1955) to come to the defense of Latin America against communism. (Like John Foster Dulles, Pope Pius XII was distressed by and sometimes hallucinated about the threat of communism.) But for me, I think, the problem of communism and the urgent necessity of the Latin American peoples was only a pretext; we are usually unaware of our true reasons, and our rational reasons are not so important.

In Latin America I met a new human world, totally different from my former experience. And as often happens, my meeting with this new world has been the operative principle of a conversion. It was not a conversion in the conventional, subjective, religious sense of the word, but a conversion of my whole existence—my intellectual process, my values, my understanding of life, and especially my priorities. I met a new expression of Christianity, not in the upper classes responsible for all the contradictions of these peoples, but in the ordinary people, the Indians, the blacks, the mestizos. And I found a new Christianity, the two sides of the Christian church: on the one hand, supporting established injustice and, on the other, struggling for justice and liberation more than in any other region of the world at the present moment. I had the opportunity of working near Dom Helder Camara for seven years in Recife, an experience that could not be replaced by any other. In Latin America I have been not a teacher, but only a member of a militant church, in the etymological sense of the Latin word *miles* (a fighting man).

During my first period in Latin America, I shared the hope of liberation and the hunger and thirst for justice of the oppressed peoples in twenty nations. Then I shared, as I share today, the desperation of these peoples, more oppressed after military coups than before.

I also learned to share a new view of the United States, a view radically different from the former one I have referred to. In Latin America they now speak of a third colonial system. In this view, the first colonial pact began with the Spanish and Portuguese conquest; it finished with theoretical independence in the first decades of the nineteenth century, which actually opened the door for the second colonial pact: colonization by England from 1830 to 1929. During these years of the world crisis, Latin America was practically part of the British Empire. A new independence movement began with the world economic crisis of 1929, but in the last ten years it has been destroyed by a third colonial system, the American Empire. For the peoples of Latin America, the second colonization was worse than the first. Now they wonder whether the third colonization may not be the worst of all.

In Latin America, theology cannot remain separated from the struggles of the church and the people. The real theologians in Latin America are not professors, but militants. I know many of them personally, intimately; their commitment cannot be separated from their intellectual life.

Their theology is limited: it is an inadequate theology, for poor peoples. Its creators do not aim to have it replace the whole of theology. On the contrary, they are aware of its situation and usefulness in one limited historical period of one region of the globe.

Nevertheless, I believe Latin American theology has a special value for the whole world. It puts into a concrete context a permanent, universal problem: the problem of the connections between the Christian message and the human situation. It raises the permanent, universal problem of the real meaning of the social contents of the Christian message. For Christians, even more than for the Greeks, the human being is a *zoion politikon* (a political animal). Latin America remembers the political nature of humanity and that a message needs to be meditated on by all the churches.

This then is my situation, and consequently the explanation of the ideas I present in this book.

As my experience of my situation suggests, I do not believe it is possible to separate Latin American liberation theology from politics. Neither do I believe any human manifestation can begin to be understood without some knowledge of its roots. Accordingly I begin this study with an overview of Western theological thought—its development and its uses—followed by a chapter tracing the short but full history of liberation theology in Latin America. These chapters are then balanced by a brief outline of the attitudes and practice of the church and Christians in Latin America over the centuries. Next we reach the core of the book: an examination of the dominant political theory of the day and the church's response to it, in theory and in practice. The theory of liberation is further explored in the next chapter, while the final pages discuss the practical dilemmas today's political realities pose for the church in Latin America.

Throughout the book I speak of and from the Latin American experience, as I see it after living it for nearly twenty years, though through eyes that were trained with a very different lens. Unavoidably I often focus on events, historical and modern, that may be almost unknown to the reader. (Others, more familiar, are seen from a new point of view.) And, as I have warned you, there are many questions left unanswered, many topics only tantalizingly referred to in passing. I only hope the challenges—for Latin Americans living nearly two thousand years after Christ, for all human beings now and to come—are as clear.

1

Why Theology?

THEOLOGY OLD AND NEW

Academic Theology

The theologians of my generation—at least the liberal theologians—were trained in "academic" or "university" theology. This theology found its most complete expression among the German faculties of the nineteenth century. Some schools in the English-speaking world followed them rapidly, but the Latin world has accepted this model only in this century. Louvain opened the way at the end of the nineteenth century; then the French Dominicans' Biblical French School of Jerusalem and Theological School of Le Saulchoir followed suit. Eventually it won out all over the Catholic world, in spite of its German and Protestant origins. In the time of Vatican II, even the Gregorian University in Rome and the Spanish and Italian faculties, the last survivors of Tridentine theology—theology as a defense of orthodoxy—ceased resisting. The triumph of the academic model was total; it was a result of the triumph of Catholic liberalism after a struggle of about 150 years against conservatism.

Today, however, at the very moment when academic theology seemed to be providing universal Christian thought with a new common language, a mortal suspicion is undercutting its triumph. After criticizing all previous methods and approaches, academic theology is itself the subject of a new criticism. Several new movements want to demonstrate that it was really only a particular way of thinking, situated historically, psychologically, and socially, like any human discipline. Academic theology had come to believe it was the expression of the universal thought of Christendom. Now it is being forced to consider and understand its own limits.

To understand this new criticism one must understand what academic theology is and where it came from. Academic theology accepted (and was accepted by) the program for the German university, inspired by Humboldt at the University of Berlin in the beginning of the nineteenth century. Such a program was the inheritance of the German *Aufklärung*, humanism, and, last

1

but not least, ancient Greek philosophy. In accord with this humanistic tradition—alive, active, and growing since the fourteenth century—the academic program was based on three fundamental ideas: criticism as a project; history as a method; university as place and privileged social position—the successor of the castles of the Italian princes of the quattrocento.

How did academic theology apply these three ideas?

Criticism as a Project. For the German *Wissenschaft,* criticism is the road to truth. Like its humanist precursors, German criticism thinks that lack of truth, misunderstanding, and error derive from some intellectual fault, usually prejudices, myths, or customs remaining from primitive peoples. From this viewpoint, truth is the object of an intellectual conquest: through various methods of criticism, human reason discloses the truth that has remained covered by innumerable prejudices. Human reason is a victory, an advent after the destruction of the primitive mentality; it is the decisive step to true humanity—from childish/emotive/tribal to adult/rational/social.

Not unlike the other critical sciences, academic theology also searches for a truth—the truth about Christianity. It takes Christianity as a historical subject and submits it to the critical method, accepting the suspicions of five centuries of criticism. To this criticism, Christianity, as it has been transmitted by the church as a historical whole, is not true Christianity, not the Christianity that derives from God and Jesus Christ. How could it be? The academic God is adult, rational, and social, and the truth about Christianity has been covered up by superstitions, false ideas, illusions, lies. But criticism, as an intellectual method, may be able to disclose the truth by separating it from error, and by so doing disclose the true Christianity—a Christianity expressed in the terms which agree with the ability of a rational, adult person.

Such a program is magnificent. Critical theology is not only meaningful within the general critical program of the university; it is also helpful within the church itself, because through it the church can reach the level of a rational religion. In other words, critical theology offers the churches certificates of rationality.

Of course, such a theology is totally a human work, a human way to a human knowledge of the human truth of Christianity. Therefore it has sometimes, even frequently, provoked suspicions from ecclesiastical authorities: its human, critical truth did not always agree with the official truth of orthodoxy. But in spite of these difficulties—which are usually expressed as opposition to liberalism in the Protestant churches and to modernism in the Catholic Church—radical conflicts have generally been avoided.

History as a Method. To the university (by which I mean the model of the German university of the nineteenth century), science is, above all, history. In it historical criticism, initiated through several centuries of humanism, has reached its climax. All human sciences have been transformed by the historical method, just as the natural sciences were transformed by the idea of evolution. The historical method provides all the human sciences with a definitive criterion for disclosing truth and unmasking lies, mistakes, mystifications, illusions. In this way the history of an entity takes the place of the ancient idea of essence or nature. Searching for a scientific "explanation" of something is equivalent to discovering the historical process of its occurrence.

Under this model, theology becomes historical criticism applied to Christian documents. The Bible; the origins of the church; ancient, medieval, and modern theology; doctrine, liturgy, and institutions; and so on are inexhaustible material for historical criticism. The theologians of "scientific" theology think that by disclosing the innumerable mistakes of the past, the illusions of the Bible and other Christian documents, they are disclosing the truth of Christianity. History allows them to show the countless false interpretations of Christianity in the past by comparing its original documents with many historical stages of the church or the Christian way of life and revealing the differences and contradictions. More especially, history allows them to show the relativity of present orthodox, official theology in order to demonstrate that it is an interpretation of Christianity relative to certain cultural conditions. This is important, because historical criticism intends to compel the church to come back to its original documents. Academic theology believes that returning to the origins of Christianity—in other words, to the original documents of the church, as they are explicated by the historical method—is the only true road to the truth about God, Christ, and Christianity.

The recent history of the Catholic Church shows the triumph of this approach. It can be said that Vatican II was led by historical theology. Indeed, in some ways its program has been the program of historical theology itself.

University as Privileged Position. The university is sure it is at the center of the spiritual life of humanity, in the place where the spirit becomes flesh and history. The university is sure it is the presence of the permanent truth, that it is above all the struggles, the conflicts, and especially the interests of particular individuals. Academic teachers regard themselves as completely objective, as absolutely impartial conveyors of the universal principles and values of human reason. They do not allow opinions, prestige, interests, emotive reasons, or prejudices to guide them. For them the university is the temple of criticism where the disciplines of the historical science are discovering the universal truth. Obviously such persons—individually and as a group—are creatures of privilege. Perhaps society does not shower them with material rewards (although it rarely lets them starve, either). But it is a greater privilege to avoid the common human condition: struggle, emotions, passions, political considerations.

Academic theology has thoroughly assimilated the way of life of the university, which is its home. It also lives inside the privileged place. Far from all prejudices deriving from contact with practice, university theologians often believe that they are the only persons possibly able to distinguish the truth about Christianity.

Critique of Academic Theology

Such were the ideas of the nineteenth-century university; there is undoubtedly a continuity between the academic theology of that time and the dominant liberal theology of this century. Interestingly, those three typical features of the German university—criticism, history, and university—are precisely three of the major objects of the more radical criticism that is being made by the new generation.

The University. Some individuals are not sure that the university can be the ideal place in which to discover the true meaning of Christianity. If the matter of theology is the message of Christ, they are not at all sure the university is the most appropriate place in which to understand it. For some modern theologians, especially those from Latin America, the university is not and never has been the universal place in which truth can be contemplated outside any contingency and relativity. The university is a particular place which, like all other places and all human institutions, is conditioned by the sociological context of its presence. The critics call attention to two principal limitations of the university: the separateness of its place and the false purity of its privilege.

As to place, today's theologians, like the scholars of several other disciplines, are less and less sure that being far from any action is the best condition for discovering the reality of anything. On the contrary, they are inclined to think that sharing in action is a necessary precondition to discovering the reality of anything. They do not doubt the value of the academic contribution to the better understanding of human beings and their Christian calling. But they believe that the academic viewpoint leads more to a "formal" knowledge than to a "real" one. This is important to remember when the subject is theology. University theology may be mainly accurate when it refers to the formal aspects of Christianity (for example, its language or patterns). But such formal knowledge does not show the reality of Christianity as a way of life. University theology is even able to show the formal or external continuity (or discontinuity) between Christ's teachings and some Christians' way of acting today. But only by sharing action itself is it possible to reach a suitable position for grasping the reality of the gospel, the real or inner continuity with the evangelical inspiration.

What is the action that must be shared in order to grasp that inner reality? If the matter of theology is Christianity and the message of Christ, action consists of announcing God's salvation through words and works. In the Christian vocabulary, this action is called *mission*. The new theologians think that only an active presence in the mission of the church can give an individual access to the privileged room from which it is possible to understand the reality of the gospel today. Consequently they think that a mere academic theology cannot focus on Christianity. Such a theology will constantly make comments on the peripheral particulars, the outer shell of Christianity, but it will not convey the deepest meaning of Jesus' revelation.

As to the university privilege of objectivity and separation from the world, the new theologians doubt that it exists. No member of a university is a pure soul. No one lives in the abstract world of ideas; people live among the social classes; belonging to one, allied with others. All human beings share the competitions and struggles of their classes; their ways of living and thinking are conditioned by their class and their class interests. The academic professors of the German university are heirs to the humanists, the first intellectuals in the Western world who have wanted to live far away from the problems and struggles of humankind. The humanists and their heirs regarded themselves as independent from all parties, thinking and living above all classes. (This is why they often regard themselves as ideal peacemakers.) But actually, the humanists were not outside class: they were dependent on the princes and noblemen who were called to support them. Later the German universities came to depend on the states, or governments, which were also organs of the upper classes. Now, in Germany and elsewhere, the members of the university have become like members of the upper classes in prestige, but they can never forget that their economic and social condition depends on the favors of the privileged classes. So as of this moment, the university is strictly linked with the bourgeoisie.

Under this condition one may ask whether the "universal thought" of academic science is anything other than the ideological "universality" of any dominating class. Every bourgeoisie attaches to its interests a universal meaning and regards the set of its prejudices to be as worthy as a universal wisdom. In virtue of its social position, the university has to acknowledge that its universality is also particular and reflects the specific condition, way of life, and goals of a given social class. (Today that class is probably the dominating class of the national state.)

The limitations of such a "universality" for theology and Christianity are obvious to anyone living outside the university itself. Academic theology has been able to gather great knowledge and to rectify innumerable mistakes. Its major achievements have been with the elements that are prior to knowledge of the Christian message: method problems, hermeneutics, auxiliary sciences, language. In these and every other science related to the introduction to Christianity, it has succeeded in reaching a remarkable objectivity. But its approach to Christianity as a way of life in the actual reality of everyday life has been superficial. Thus its universalism is abstract and unreal; its objectivity does not reach the Christian message for our times in itself and so it fails to disclose what God's presence means in the world of today.

Many Christians now think that the viewpoint of a theological group trying to avoid any ties with the real world and actually linked with the dominant social class or system is unavoidably partial; it should, at least, be completed or corrected. They remember that God's wisdom has been revealed to the poor, the ignorant, the weak, and the rejected, and they believe that this statement is not an abstract fact to be contemplated, but a program to be applied. They believe that the Christianity of the upper classes is unavoidably marked by features that might be called idealism, artificiality, lack of depth. Only the poor are able to feel what salvation, hope, justice, or justification are; only those who have felt throughout their lives, and are presently feeling, what suffering, oppression, and injustice mean are able to hear God's promise and God's liberation. Only the person who has been rejected is able to understand what God's mercy means. In this sense, the experience of the poor is the starting point of a true knowledge of Christianity.

The Historical Method. The new historical schools themselves have shown the limits of the historical method. The absolute objectivity of the historical method is a myth. There is no universal viewpoint; historians are not outside history, are not able to look at history in some universal way. Historians are not some incarnation of pure intelligence. Historians are inside history, parts and authors of the events which they look at; their own appreciation is a part of the event as an element of human culture. Consequently, any historical vision is partial (in both senses of the word). All historians develop knowledge of the past according to their own intellectual evolution. Generally every historical vision is partly individual and partly classicist, reflecting the worldview of its author. Hence there are many historical views of the same events and processes. All historians view the past according to their cares and understandings in the present. Each body of historical work is an attempt to destroy some other views of the past and to make evident a new prospect, a new interpretation.

This does not mean that history is helpless or absurd. On the contrary, human intelligence cannot proceed without a certain view of the past. History is the reflection of the present, but such a reflection is necessary because our minds are unable to grasp present occurrences, concrete reality, immediately. Memory, the ability to distinguish, is the condition of any intelligence. The present is conscious (or self-conscious) only when compared with some other realities of the past and perceived as different from them. The present exists as a new reality only if we can distinguish it from the past.

This means that we cannot possibly know the revelation of God for the present time if we do not know what it was in the past. Therefore a certain form of history, a certain knowledge of the past is unavoidable.

But what past? And what history of what past? The first question is easier. In order to understand Christianity as a task for today, obviously what we must know is the past of true Christianity, the past of faith, hope, and love.

But what history—or more accurately, whose view of history? The academic historians project into the past their human and Christian interests for the present. Consequently the criterion that allows us to appreciate the value of their knowledge of the past is the relevance of their interests for the present Christianity. Their academic position is not a privileged condition, because academic history is not an absolute viewpoint. Its starting point is the historian's own understanding of life and the world according to his or her own situation and behavior in society. Therefore the academic historian reflects, to some extent at least, academic values and the academic way of life. But it is not certain that the academic way of life is more objective than any other way of life, especially when it comes to faith and Christianity. History is a mediation necessary for everyone, not a privilege for a few special scholars. Some theologians suspect that for such mediation a point of departure that is more important and relevant to the understanding of the present meaning of Christianity may be the memory of the people, the poor and ignorant, even if it is not objective according to scientific methods.

We may draw the conclusion that the academic theologians' understanding of Christianity is worthy or worthless according to the value of their non-scientific starting point; the way they live their own Christian life determines the worth of all the conclusions of their historical, scientific works on Christianity.

The sense of history as a science, indeed the sense of science in itself, presents another problem. Science has its own goals and its own methods. Although the nineteenth century accepted the idea that the scientific method was a privileged starting point for any human wisdom, including a right understanding of Christianity, that "conclusion" was really only a postulate. We would be unwise to continue to accept it as a demonstrated truth.

Criticism of the Criticism. Academic criticism has taken every human being and social institution as subjects of its discussion since its inception. But only in the twentieth century has it begun to take itself as an interesting subject for research. Yet it is necessary to criticize any criticism, including the academic one. Such an academic criticism is conditioned by its historical context. Any criticism starts from the struggle for values. The values for which academic criticism has struggled have been freedom of conscience and expression, freedom of religion and philosophy, freedom from any irrationality in religion, politics, economy, and social life. To gain these it has tried to destroy various prejudices and irrational factors in religion, culture, and society. It has sometimes succeeded. But the freedoms for which it has fought have been primarily freedoms for the intellectual and the upper classes. The universities have forsaken the struggles of the common workers for freedom, have ignored the liberation of the oppressed classes; therefore their criticism has disregarded irrational factors in social relations and social structures. They have forgotten the material conditions of life; therefore their Christianity has been oblivious of the material condition of human persons—the daily problems of eating and working, the fact of being rejected or humiliated. They have also become oblivious of the fact that, to a certain degree, their

own Christianity—our own Christianity—is a luxury of a developed civilization, and the price of such a luxury is paid by the working class.

The new theology, however, has been quick to learn that the ability to
criticize relies on the insignificant work of thousands of workers performing
innumerable meaningless gestures that allow some expressions of luxury.
Criticism has to be criticized for ignoring such conditions. (It seems probable
that any civilization is, to some degree, a luxury product, which raises the
very serious problems of producing luxury and of the place of science in
society and church. Unfortunately there is not space to pursue this very
involved question here. But clearly we may not think that a condition of
luxury is the better viewpoint from which to understand the evangelical
message.)

The people of God are not made up only of intellectual elites who are able
to express themselves through the best notional and rational forms. The
people of God are also made up of common persons who never have any
opportunity of searching for such sophisticated expressions of faith and love.

There is another problem for the criticism of criticism. Thinking is not
merely a spiritual activity. It uses words; and words, like all cultural expressions, are power. By means of words, human beings are able to influence
other persons. Within the complex transmission system of a given culture,
these operations are not disinterested: the words are used as powerful
weapons in order to overcome in class warfare, political competitions, and
other means of capturing more power.

Here it is important to remember that power does not result only from
material weapons, military superiority, or financial capability. Human beings
are not guided solely by fear and interest, so power also results from seduction and persuasion. If someone wishes to achieve or defend some social
position, to organize a meeting or group to overcome one's enemies or
promote one's friends, words are always necessary and often successful
without the least show of force. And even when a military or financial threat
is concerned, there is always a certain mediation by means of words. (At the
very least, the threat has to be communicated by means of words.) So the
person who is able to control words or make speeches is a helpful, even
necessary collaborator for any power.

Theologians are among the persons who are able to use words. They are
the professionals, the specialists of the sacred words, and to some degree they
have a monopoly, or at least control, over the sacred words. Such words give
power and open various opportunities. By means of their words and
speeches, theologians can charge someone with a crime of superstition, of
endangering the faith and orthodoxy, heresy (the modern words are "subversive," "communist," "progressive," "conservative," "fundamentalist"); they
can defend, protect, or denounce a group; they can strengthen or challenge
the power of the authorities within the church or the whole society; they can

bolster the establishment or the revolution; they can divide or unify. And they can promote the position of their class within church and society.

Nothing entitles us to think that the practical function of words remains independent from their use in thought. On the contrary, the human sciences are presently showing that there is probably a strict connection between action and thinking. The academic theologians of the nineteenth century, like most contemporary scholars, believed that they were only men of thought, indifferent to power and power relations. Today we know that such an idealistic condition is impossible for any human being. So, may theologians remain indifferent to the repercussions of their words?

Two major questions in the Latin American church today follow logically. Does the theologian actually use the power of words in order to help the power of the people of God (in the church or in society)? Does the theologian give the power of the sacred words to the people or to the social classes which presently dominate the people and control most other sources of power? These questions articulate a problem for our times. It has never been raised by university theology.

The Theology of Continuing the Past

So far I have spoken about only one aspect of the education of the older theologians: their grounding in the academic, critical, and historical theology inherited from the German university model of the nineteenth century. But the theologians of my generation had another tradition added to that. If they were Protestant, they were also educated by the dialectical theology of Karl Barth, Emil Brunner, Friedrich Gogarten, and so on; if Catholics, by neo-Thomist or neo-scholastic theology. What is interesting here is not their differences but their similarities. For each group the tradition was a project in self-consciousness, a tie to the theology of a former ideal era, an attempt to immortalize a definitive expression of the word of God.

I shall talk mainly about how neo-Scholasticism affected Catholic theologians, partly because that is of my own heritage, partly because what has happened in Catholic theology is of more immediate importance to the Latin American experience.

Neo-Thomism. The restoration of medieval Scholasticism, particularly the Thomist system, occupied Catholic theologians for almost a century, from Vatican I to Vatican II. Although I think there are positive values to creating a certain continuity with medieval theology, as a witness to the Christian tradition, this project was in some ways a strange idea. Indeed, in several aspects it was really anachronistic, especially insofar as it was a part of a more general attempt to restore the medieval church. During the late nineteenth century, neo-Scholasticism became a part of the romantic movement that involved almost the whole Catholic world and culture. (One need not restrict that statement to the Catholic world. Next to scientific rationalism, romanticism was the chief movement of German culture, by means of which it spread throughout the culture of all Europe and beyond.) Neo-Scholasticism meant returning to the past, opposing "modernity" and all the modern trends of rationalism, liberalism, and scientism. In some ways it was an attempt to answer the needs of the time, for returning to the past seemed to be the answer to the challenge of the new century and its self-confidence.

For the Catholic Church, returning to the past was necessarily a restoration of the thirteenth century—the climax, the most perfect age, the first reference. It was seen as a movement to return to the most perfect stage of the history of the church, to undergo a conversion to the ideal. But I suspect that behind such an idealization of the Middle Ages was the nostalgic wish to struggle against time, history, and death, to maintain the church in its golden period, to fix it in its most "perfect" stage. Church leaders and theologians wished to begin church history again in connection with its ideal past. In order to make possible the continuation of the past, they tried, to a degree, to ignore the historical changes that had occurred since the thirteenth century.

Why did they attempt such a project of fixing and immortalizing the "most perfect expression" of theology? There are various possible interpretations of the fact, several of which may be true simultaneously. I suspect that theologians were thinking that theology, as a logical set of sentences and arguments, had to be the most total expression of God's word. Their logic may have gone something like this. God's word is eternal; it has always the same worth for all the generations. Theology has to express the eternal meaning of God's word; therefore, the stability of its language and system must be the right expression of the eternity of that word. The stability of Thomistic theology over the centuries ought to be, to a degree, the image of the fixity of God's word. So, consciously or not, these theologians were trying to express the totality of God's word. They had the illusion that they were continuing the complete expression of God's word: that their theology was, in its formal stability, the right expression of God's eternal word; that their activity allowed God to continue speaking to humanity. They had the illusion that their thinking was inside divine thinking; that the product of their investigations was the true expression of God's revelation; that, at least to some degree, they were discovering the secret of God's thinking, as a scientist discovers the secrets of matter and nature. Just as scientists might think that, by understanding the universe from its principles, they can grasp the viewpoint of the Creator, so theologians might think that by understanding the process of salvation from its principles they have been placed in the viewpoint of the Savior and the word of God.

Of course, all Thomist theologians knew perfectly the human and historical origins of the ideas and words of their theology. They were completely aware on an intellectual level of the difference between formal connections and real union with ideas. But once the old concepts and words entered into the Thomist system, they became, to some degree, idealized, fixed, and immortalized; under the halo of a golden age they became the image of God's word forever. All the Thomist theologians wished to contribute to the definitive expression of this definitive theology. By expressing, however imperfectly, such a definitive theology, it was psychologically easy to get the impression that they were speaking in the name of God, that they were persons who especially knew what God thinks. So the theologian became "the one who knows what God intends to do."

Of course, since these were Catholic theologians, such an impression depended greatly on the reactions of the hierarchy and the control institutions of the Roman church. But for the neo-Scholastics, the control of the Roman church has not cut down the impression of speaking in God's name; on the contrary, it has provided a guarantee and a support.

Dialectic Theology. For most Protestant theologians I believe that dialectic theology accomplished a similar function. For the Protestant, the ideal time of the church is that of the New Testament as read in the light of the experience of the Reformation. The theology of the New Testament is the definitive image of God's word. To some degree, Karl Barth's work is an attempt to immortalize simultaneously the theology of the New Testament and the intuition of the reformers. Note that I do not say "the New Testament," but rather, "the theology of the New Testament," in other words a system of ideas and sentences drawn from the New Testament and transformed into a fixed logical system. Such a system carried out the function of a new Scholasticism. By expressing either system, theologians thought that they were expressing the word of God, that their thinking was the expression, the continuation of the word of God.

A Critique: The Purpose of Theology. And many theologians, Catholic and Protestant, who have worked in these systems still believe this. Such a belief is, of course, an overestimation of the theologian's mission. Theology is human work, nothing more. All thinking is human work. A theological system is by no means the reflection of God's thinking; it is the answer to certain human cravings, intellectual needs, or sociological trends. Just as science expresses some psychological need of humankind (for example, the need of curiosity, of demystification, of solving the puzzles of nature and life), a doctrinal system may be an answer to a psychological need of security, of stability, or of self-justification into a privileged position. We cannot know exactly what are the unconscious goals of intellectual operations because their movers always have rational arguments for them. But the rational backgrounds of intellectual operations are often, one suspects, ideological, covering up the actual reasons (which may be quite irrational).

Theology is not the means by which God speaks to humankind. Theology is not mediation between God and human persons and communities. Theology is not the continuation or the presence of God's word. God does not use the speeches of the theologians in order to make himself understood. God has always used and continues to use other means. God speaks by means of the poor, the rejected, the oppressed. God speaks among the communities of poor and ignorant people. True wisdom has not been revealed to the learned; it has been revealed to the simple. God appears under the guise of a Samaritan, a foreigner, a pagan, a tax collector, or a prostitute. God has his own representatives inside the church—they are the poor and the simple. They are the ones whom God has chosen to communicate with humankind. Therefore, theology cannot be the word that guides the Christian church; it cannot constitute the theory of a Christian practice.

Consequently, what does the desire to build and establish forever a whole ideological system as a theology mean? Such a theology does meet several positive goals: to some degree, it may be necessary inside the church, and it does protect Christianity against the evident and permanent dangers of subjectivism and irrationalism. But it is also risky. It is very easy to make such a theology a way of dominating the Christian people or the whole society. Today, as in the past, such a theology, under the mask of communicating the word of God to humanity, can offer to ecclesiastical, civil, or military powers the ideological help they need to submit the people of God to their own projects.

Of course, we may not deny the evident positive values of the scientific or systematic theology. Both protected certain aspects of Christianity, both were answers to particular historical situations. But the value of those protections and those answers lay in setting up certain boundaries, a task not nearly so ambitious as the projects of the theological movements of the nineteenth century (movements which still determine theology today). We must never forget, as did the theologians of those movements, that the mission of theology is not to offer God communication with humanity.

Theology is a human work, a human speech, with human goals. It is conditioned by all the factors that normally condition human actions. So it is natural that in the last decades all theologies, like all cultural expressions, have been submitted to the criticism of the human sciences. Sociology, psychology, anthropology, ethnology, and linguistics, among others, have shown the relativity of any theology. Such analysis is justified because theology is indeed a human science, not a sacred work.

In fact, I ought to note here that, among all the human sciences, theology is the least scientific. It is by no means the ultimate synthesis the medieval theologians had thought it, the superscience that includes all other sciences. On the contrary, submitted to the analytical study of the various criticisms, theology has to acknowledge that it is a typical case of eclecticism. Theology has created no methodology; its method is a blend of all the methods used during the last four thousand years. Theology is the result of a long history in which have been joined the contributions of many historical periods and cultures: oriental religious thought, classic Greek philosophy, Roman law, and attempts at modern scientific concepts, as well as many other sources.

The most systematic of systems cannot cover up such an eclecticism.

Far from being a reproach, I think that theology's eclecticism is a token of faithfulness. The more theology becomes scientific and submitted to one method, inspired by the dominant science or fashion of the given period, the more independent it becomes from the true message of Jesus Christ. Jesus Christ did not give to his disciples any scientific method whereby to understand his message. The Spirit does not act scientifically or systematically. So rather than "correct" the eclecticism of traditional Christian theology, we probably ought to increase it by adding to it new methodological principles which derive from the new approaches to reality common both inside and outside Christendom today. (Indeed those from outside the Christian countries might be especially helpful.)

Since theology is not based on a revealed method, it may, like any discipline use, all the available methods. Consequently, theology always comes after the scientific development of the human spirit. Theology is continually searching for its method by adjusting the methods of each new culture it meets. That is the reason theology is unable to guide the way of life and the spiritual problems of Christian people: theology comes after the problems, not before. That is also the reason the Marxist principle of "theory-practice" is not suitable for theology: theology does not come before, but after, faith and action.

A fuller discussion of the role of theology will come later in this book, but a few principles are already obvious. The target and the meaning of a good theology result from its methodology: offering all the approaches of human intelligence to God, putting all the capability of human thought at the disposal of God. Thus the eclecticism of any theology may be the consequence of its own mission in Christianity. In other words, theology may be the relation of all human knowledge to God's revelation—the shifting and sublimation of human science in contact with the word of God. The deepest meaning of theology may be the complete opposite of the idea of God—needing the collaboration of human science in order to speak to persons and peoples; its true movement may be that human intelligence wants to offer God all its forces in order to convert human intelligence itself. In such a view, theology does not mean the revelation of God, but the conversion of human intelligence and human sciences to the word of God.

If such is the right movement of theology, we cannot say that theology has always accomplished its true mission.

THEOLOGY AS A CONVERSION

Following this argument further we see that the major problem of theology is its own conversion. The truth of theology consists in converting theology so as to become faithful to its own mission. The truth of theology is its struggle, and the aim of the struggle is the liberation of human intelligence.

The Struggle Against False Theology

The enemies of a true theology are in itself; theology is a civil war, a constant struggle against itself. In facing God's revelations, any human intelligence confronts a dilemma: Should it use God's word to win prestige and opportunities of directing and manipulating other human beings by means of an ideological system covered over with the weight of God's word, or should it offer all its forces to serve God's will and Christ's salvation? Such a dilemma may be conscious or unconscious (the unconscious condition is probably worse).

Within this dilemma is a right theology and a wrong theology. For a Christian the fact of making a theology is not important; what is important is the distinction between a right and a wrong theology. There is, of course, no right or wrong theology as an absolute and eternal definition. But in any human situation, in any debate, there is a right statement and a wrong statement, a right attitude and a wrong attitude. The right theology is the one that leads to a right attitude. The right theology is the one that is of service to God and the people of God. The wrong theology is the one that is helpful for some human interest, such as security, fear, prestige, control of the state, control of public opinion, control of the people.

There is often great difficulty—and danger—in distinguishing the right and the wrong theologies, especially when the dilemma is unconscious. Sometimes in the church there is a dream of unanimity, of a common theology, the *theologia communis*. Such a dream is a dangerous illusion. Throughout the course of church history, division and struggle have been permanent. The truth of theology has been its patience and steadfastness in struggle. In each period, besides the innumerable but unimportant *quaestiones disputatae,* there has been a major debate, a chief controversy around the central problem of Christianity in that time; each period the truth or untruth of theology in that period was always in reference to that debate. But according to our dilemma, there is no eternally right theology or eternally wrong theology, only a right theology for the present moment.

There is another aspect to the dilemma: the right and the wrong theology often do not oppose each other like Yes and No. There is not always explicit contradiction; civilized persons such as theologians usually avoid contradictions. So the opposition between the right and the wrong theology is usually rather like an opposition of word and silence. The wrong theology is often a system conceived and built and closed in order to avoid some problems, some words that are precisely the expression of Christianity. Each of its statements is right; each of its sentences is true; its language is faithful to the Bible and the church. But the whole is wrong because it intends to exclude the major debate of the moment. In each period of church history, the truth of Christian theology does not depend on its formal faithfulness to the

Christian language, but on its attitude in the major debate.

The wrong theology is a silent theology about the chief problems of the moment. To some degree it intends to enclose Christianity within its past; it is a closed culture, an adaptation of the past to new conditions of human life. Such a theology is able to provide a solid instrument of self-defense for the upper classes, the clergy, the ecclesiastical hierarchies; often they can even extend it to the lower classes because they control the dominant culture and they have such power of communication.

On the other hand, the right theology is the one that wants to face the primary problem of its time. Many of its particular statements may be wrong or inaccurate; but the whole is right if it serves God's word at a particular moment by dealing with the decisive problem of the time. Such a theology is a service for the people of God.

For example, I think the theology of liberation is lacking in a serious scientific analysis in the historical knowledge of church history, in biblical exegesis, and in several other areas. But if I compare this theology with the others that oppose it today, right and wrong become very clear. The other theologies are right in all their statements, but the important one is missing. They remain silent about the major problem of our times: the domination of the whole world by a small minority, which submits it to the false god of today, economic expansion, with the complicity of Western culture and the Western churches themselves. No theology is entitled to remain silent before such a condition of the church and Christian thought.

Here it is worth remembering the struggle of the true prophets against the false prophets. The false prophets were those who did not want to express the new word of God about the present moment of history; they constantly repeated the words God had pronounced in the past, leaving the people of God in a false security based on formal continuity with previous days; they resisted the new step of God's history. The false prophets preferred the security of the past and announced to the people the permanence of the present, that is to say, the continuation of the past. They did not ask for a conversion facing the new conditions of history. They spoke abundantly, but their many words only covered their silence. And they wanted to compel the true prophets to the same silence. Therefore the struggle of the true prophets was first an attempt to break the will to silence. The true prophets are the ones who denounce the plot of silence. Their voices rise amid a universal silence. Theologically a lie is not always the contradiction of truth; it can also be a continuing silence when truth should be spoken.

Of course, theology itself is not the prophetic voice. The theologians are not the successors of the prophets. The New Testament is quite clear: the new prophets are not a group of scientific specialists but the people of God. Within the people of God some individuals appear with prophetic charisma in a more specific manner than others; these are not necessarily the theologians. Theology is only putting human intelligence and science to the service of the people of God. The people of God is the voice which must break the silence. And theology is called to serve this people. But with what service?

Here the key figure of the people of God intervenes. God is present in the world through Jesus Christ his Son, and Jesus Christ is present through his body, which is the church, the people of God. This body is the people as a people; any institutional system of the church has to remain subordinated to the people themselves.

So a true theology is a service to the people that is Jesus Christ's body, a service lent to the church as a people in order to undertake its role in the world as the people of God. Any theology that would not lead to a deeper responsibility and ability of the people of God as a people is wrong and false; it is a pagan theology using Christian language.

To put it another way, a silent (and therefore wrong) theology is the one that prevents the Christian people from accomplishing their responsibility in the world. One way of preventing it is to cover up the problems of the moment so that the people of God remain unaware of their present responsibility. But there are other ways of doing it. Think, for instance, of a theology that supports the privileged role of some elites, a theology that submits the people to a dominant ecclesiastical institution, and by means of that institution to a dominant state (the false prophet of Revelation 13).

A true theology, on the other hand, intends to liberate the people of God from the false theologies that reject them, separate them from their responsibility, and reduce them to the condition of a pagan people. This is the crux of the struggle: there are theologies that separate the people of God from their mission in the world and there are theologies that help them undertake it.

There is a practical test to distinguish between the two. If a theology claims to be a system in which God's word is completely explained so that the people have only to listen to it and obey, that is a false theology of silence. Such a theology is an expression of power, the ideology of the privileges of a class of mandarins or doctors of the law. Such a theology shuts in the word of God by means of a technical language so that only the doctors of the law may understand the secret of its mysteries.

Almost all religions, including the Christian church, have used such a process as the basis for clerical supremacy at some time or other. Let us examine Catholic history, for instance. In the Middle Ages, theology and the university were the basis on which the clergy maintained their privileges as the first order in society. "Cleric" was a synonym for "scholar." The result was the existence of two levels of Christianity: educated Christianity for the clergy and monks; ordinary popular Christianity for the laity. Only the clergy had the key to the true religion, theology. Theology was used to exclude the laity from reading the Bible and intervening in the church. Theology was not to be communicated to the people. Some of its conclusions (the more useful ones) were translated into a common language for the common people, but theology itself was a reserved science. And since the laity were not able to understand it, they had no capability to discuss the reasons of the clergy.

In the eighteenth century, and even more in the nineteenth, the official theology had to face the rebellion of the laity, the secularization movement of all Western civilization. In response, ideology shifted and theology became apologetic. Since that time, the task of official theology has been to defend the ecclesiastical system against secularization; in other words, it became apologetics against liberalism, rationalism, socialism, Marxism, and so on. By means of an apologetic theology, the clergy have tried to put the new intellectual methods, sciences, and techniques at the service of their old system; they have tried to use the reasoning of modern thought against the basic movement of that thought in order to strengthen the old system of values and ideas. They have not faced the new occurrences as an entire system or movement that required a conversion of the church itself.

Apologetics, however, has never changed anyone's mind. It is helpful only for the theologians themselves, who use it as a means of self-defense. By apologetic arguments, the clergy defend their own security, strengthen their intellectual resistance against the seduction of new ideas. Through their apologetic theology, the clergy speak to themselves, try to defend themselves against their own temptations. Such a theology is a kind of solipsism. To some degree, it can save an institutional system, but not the faith of the people.

Theology as Public Property

True Christian theology, therefore, is a struggle against false and basically pagan or pharisaical theology. If theology becomes the privileged language of the clergy, it becomes the ideology of their dominant position, a way to avoid any question that might endanger the establishment. History teaches that in the past true theologies never succeeded without a previous struggle against an established theology; then they themselves become a new established theology. Such a struggle is authentically Christian if it intends to restore the use of Christian words to a voiceless people.

Thus, to some degree, the movement of right theology is exactly the contrary of the movement of human science. The sciences work by becoming ever more technical and specialized; their language becomes more and more abstract, more and more different from common speech. In this way any human science gives rise to a new elitist class. Indeed, we now realize that science, far from unifying persons and peoples, divides and separates them by making elites, a result that the nineteenth century was spontaneously convinced would occur.

On the contrary, by virtue of its final goals and aims, Christian theology may not be enclosed inside a technical, elitist language. Its aim must be the liberation of the Christian people, or, to put it another way, the liberation of the word of Jesus Christ through the liberation of the voice of the Christian people.

Note the difference between means and end, method and aim. Theology is never in itself a popular voice because it entails the use of the technical categories of many disciplines and methods. But that technical system is not properly the object of theology. It is only an intermediate stage. Theology has no worth in itself; it has no meaning in itself. Its only true goal is serving to promote the voice of a free people.

The human sciences proceed from simple, ordinary, empirical knowledge, criticize it, and go on toward an abstract language; each advance takes them further from the common understanding of the ordinary person. On the contrary, right Christian theology proceeds from a complex system of technical terms and seeks simplification in order to increase the understanding of God at the level of the people. Theological knowledge of God's revelation is never better than popular knowledge. The faith of the simple and poor is better. And the aim of theology is to liberate such a faith, not to shift it. The knowledge of God in the poor has been and remains oppressed by the sin of the world, which often finds complicity among the ideologies of domination supported by the upper classes and often by the clergy and the theologians as well. Theology reaches its goal when it contributes to liberating the faith of the poor from the intellectual sin of corruption, from the ideologies of domination, as well as from the false theologies linked with these ideologies.

The starting point of theology is not the word of God, although those who use it to support the ideologies of domination like to think it is. Theologians have received no special revelation from the word of God in order to study; they have not received any special intuition of the word of God in his people. Rather, God has revealed his wisdom to the simple and the poor. It is they who proceed from God's word. Any theology proceeds from another theology and all the auxiliary sciences, from two thousand years of Christian theology and probably from thousands of years of underlying pagan theology. A bad theology confirms and continues the ideological functions of previous theologies without criticizing them. A good theology opposes such ideological trends and intends to rediscover the simplicity of the gospel. In short, the gospel and words of Jesus are not the beginning but the end of theology. Theology has accomplished its mission when it may remain silent because the people of God have met the word of Jesus and the wisdom of God. Its true aim is to give back to the people the Christian gospel that the elite and ideologies have taken away from them.

Jesus addressed his words to the poor and the masses. So often the religious (and social) elite have taken the interpretation and understanding of the gospel away from the masses, and theology has furnished the process with an ideological basis. Then another theology has to save the gospel from the hands of the elite and give it back to those to whom it was first addressed.

Announcing the gospel is the task and responsibility of the poor and the simple, but how can they fulfill this mission if they have lost the right of understanding the word of God, if they dare not speak?

A theology is Christian if it succeeds in converting the church to the language of the Bible—not to the formal and literal language of the Bible *(kata sarka)*, but to the spiritual language *(kata pneuma)*. God talks about simple realities: love, truth, peace, justice. Such realities are the hope and the problem of the poor; they disappear under the sophisticated culture of dominant classes. A true theology does not want to ignore the problems of the world at a given time; it does not attempt to be a refuge for persons who somehow live outside the world. Rather, it wants to restore in the world the hope of the poor so that their voice can be heard again.

SEARCHING FOR MEANING

The Problem of Meaning

The same conclusions can be reached from another starting point.

Like any science, theology uses language, and all language is situated between formalism and meaning. Language can be used to reveal or to cover the reality of life.

The temptation of formalism is especially strong in the case of theology. A spontaneous movement toward orthodoxy is very strong in any religious group, and it always leads theology toward some sort of formalism. Orthodoxy does not intend to use words to reveal the reality of God, only to confirm the continuation of the past, to signify that the past continues, that there is nothing new or dangerous. Orthodoxy gives rise to a system of ideas in which logical connection or structural unity prevails. The connection of religious ideas becomes more important than their meaning, and all the concepts are finally defined by the other concepts of the same system—each concept is defined by the place that it occupies inside the system. In this way each concept comes to express the structure of the whole by representing some figure of the whole rather than a reality. If this approach is taken to its logical conclusion (as in structuralist philosophy), reality no longer exists, only structures; words themselves loose any contact with reality, and survive only as signs of a structure.

There are some theological systems which suggest such a structuralism. For instance, we have all encountered some theology books that define the Christian ideas like this. "What is God? God is the creator of the world. What is the world? The world is the result of God's creation. What is creation? Creation is God's action. What is the action of God? God's action is creation." "Who is Jesus Christ? Jesus Christ is the Savior of mankind. And what is the salvation of mankind? Salvation is Jesus' work." "What is salvation? Salvation is forgiveness of sin. What is sin? The act forgiven through Jesus Christ. Why did Jesus die? Jesus died for the forgiveness of sin. What is sin? Sin is the fact that caused Jesus' death." And so on. All the concepts of a theological system are defined without ever coming out of the system itself. Each word connects with other words and suggests this connection. Each word appeals to other words and nothing else. Such a theology is shut up inside a perfect circle. Since it lacks any contact with the real world of men and women, there is never any room for problems or discussions.

In such a system, there is no possibility of discussing one concept without endangering all the others. This is the best position for any orthodoxy. Those who accept one of the ideas are led to accept all the others without difficulty. More important, they cannot deny one of the concepts without giving up all the others. There are no alternatives other than absolute faith and absolute skepticism. So the fear of skepticism becomes the major argument of orthodoxy.

This fear can rely upon the call to security. The feeling of truth, subjective fact, is often mistaken for security. Human beings have a psychological need for security, and one important form of security is feeling one knows the truth. The feeling of truth, subjective fact, is often mistaken for security of knowing the truth. Many people get a feeling of truth when the ideas seem clear. And what ideas seem clearer than those that have a clear connection with some other ideas? If a system shows an entire set of strict logical connections, the impression of truth and obviousness is complete.

Thus the strength of an ideology, especially one backed by a theology, does not depend on its truth, but simply on its logical connections. A logical system offers to the intelligence a feeling of rest and stability—security, which is mistaken for truth.

Most human beings probably do want security more than truth. Truth is generally complex, defective, full of contradictions because of the deficiencies of words, the inadequacy of informing, and the multiplicity of the approaches necessary. So truth makes people insecure and many reject it because it does not feel true, especially in contrast with the obviousness and security of a closed system.

When the aim of theology is maintaining this security, what is called "theological development" or "theological study" is actually nothing more than showing some new connections between the same words, or putting some new elements into the system by connecting some new words with it. When a new connection or a new element has been placed in the system, people feel some impression of happiness. They test the truth of the new development by its logical connection with the system.

That is precisely the process which we often denounce in the Marxist way of thinking. But many theologians use exactly the same method that they criticize in another ideology. For them the solution of a theological problem is to be found through a process of perfect deduction from previous knowledge. I am not making a mere theoretical objection here; such a system has very pragmatic results.

With such a theology, God, Christ, the church, and so on become factors of security: they are the parts or the figures of a whole system without problems, symbols of a world without problems. God and Christianity cease being really mysterious; on the contrary, they are obvious, with no meaning for an unknown world. They have their meaning and function in themselves— being the basis of psychological security, personal or social. The system excludes any difficulty; indeed, it is a whole system of excluding difficulties. It does admit new problems because they are helpful in making apparent new connections within the system, in making the obviousness of the system seem clearer and more brilliant. All problems give an opportunity to show that there is no problem.

We know that the major difficulty of any science of reality is acceptance of a new perception, some new data as new reality, and being ready to shift the whole system because of this acceptance. Many individuals, even many scientists who pride themselves on their objectivity and adaptability, prefer to replace a new reality with new words which they can then invest with a meaning that is nothing other than a connection with the whole old system. That is much more secure than dealing with difficulties, than changing the system, than facing truth.

That is precisely what has happened since the theology of liberation appeared. It is an innovation and consequently a factor of insecurity. So several theologians have tried to do away with the feeling of insecurity it provokes. Their method is always the same: by deducing the concept of liberation from the system and reducing it to the logical connections of the system, the problems disappear. "Liberation" then does not say anything more than what the system has always said.

The theologians of the system of orthodoxy want to "protect" or "defend" God's revelation from any touch of contingent realities, which certainly do provoke feelings of insecurity. When someone tries to apply Christian concepts to an event or situation in the world or—worse still—to a decision or movement in political life, the theologian-protectors of the system immediately answer: "We may not apply God's word to such a particular event because God's work may not be reduced to any particular reality. God remains above all particularities; God's truth is true for everybody in all countries and at all times. All the concepts refer to an abstract eternal human condition without allusions to concrete events." Such a system gives up any meaning.

And that brings us to the question of meaning. What do God, Christ, the Spirit, salvation, the church mean? Surely they are not merely the signs of an ideological system, words that may not touch contingent reality.

Any meaning is a reference to life, human life. According to the message of the New Testament carried and lived by the church, the people, the poor and simple, these words do have a meaning. The meaning of Christianity is the new person, God's presence in the new human existence. This presence is not formal or objective, it is active. God is present inside the action of the disciples, an action that is a new humankind. The last meaning of Christianity is charity, love, agape.

It is sure that the truth of the Christian concepts is not entirely contained within any particular action. But, on the other hand, this truth can exist only in particular acts. The truth of God is multiple. What derives from his truth, what reveals him, is the multiplicity of acts of love, not a universal sentence about the concept of love.

The transcendency of the Christian realities does not mean that they are not present in particular acts. On the contrary, it means that they can be present in countless circumstances. Christian love does not exist *in se,* only in multiple applications. Theology must not seek the essence of love *in se,* but the multiple applications of it, and especially the application of today in the circumstances of today.

The theological problem of the meaning of the biblical concepts is not the problem of their sense for all humanity in all times; such a sense would be empty and meaningless. The problem of Christian love is not the problem of a concept of love; such a concept would not be original. It is not the problem of the understanding of the first disciples, although such a knowledge may be helpful. Rather, the spiritual meaning of Christian love and action is always particular. God's word does not reveal what charity and love mean for all people in all centuries, but simply what they mean for us just now in virtue of the specific circumstance in which we are.

In short, Christianity must always be situated, or it is empty, meaningless. For instance, outside the practical circumstances of human life and action, Christian mission and love, Jesus Christ's death is meaningless. Certainly, even without meaning, it can be helpful as a religious experience, in the way that the death of Osiris, the death of Timat, all the myths of a dying god are helpful. But it becomes meaningful only when one actually undertakes the death of Jesus Christ in one's own life, in a personal or collective action. The meaning of Jesus' death is its call to a similar condition in similar circumstances.

From that we must not deduce that the meaning of the Christian concepts is merely individual, any more than that it is abstractly universal. In a sense, the personal appeals are individual facts, but a Christian is not called to live as an isolated person, far from other brothers and sisters in faith. All vocations inside a given context belong to some collective calling. Any Christian may rely upon the help of many others in order to understand the meaning of Christianity in his or her own life. So the meaning is, to some degree, collective. The Christian concepts are neither abstractly universal nor strictly individual; they are common. Together we are searching out our vocation within a particular condition of the church and the world; we all are facing the same challenges. Theology is not a universal language but a common language for a common searching for a common calling. And that common language, common searching, common calling must always be in touch with the facts of contemporary life in the world. Today some individuals think that the renewal of the church can be based just on a new understanding of the old system of the whole of Christian thought—in other words, a shifting of the previous system. They believe that if the theologians would only carry out such a modernization of the whole system of theology, the church would be able to begin again with confidence and enthusiasm. Unfortunately such a task is impossible. It is impossible to build a new system adjusted to the present conditions.

Authentic theological work has always been an approach to going back to the particular vocations. The theologian starts from a system (or various systems), and goes ahead by seeking the particular vocations of his time. He works from the universal to the particular. In Latin America, for instance, theologians are wondering what God's call to the church in the present circumstances is—not in any circumstances but in these particular circumstances. What are love, charity, conversion, here, just now? What is God's will just now? What is the sign of the kingdom of God here? After the military coup in Chile in 1973, a Chilean bishop asked: "And now what do we do with Medellín?" He meant: "How can we apply the spiritual meaning of the bishops' conference at Medellín in the new circumstances? This is an aspect of the general problem: what do we do with Jesus' gospel now?"

Of course, no theology has an adequate answer to such a question. It is not the role of the theologians to find the answer. That is the mission of the people. But within the people of God theologians may be helpful, as I have already pointed out.

Theology and Action

The problem of theology and action (in the Christian sense of the word) is very complicated, and I can only introduce some aspects of it here. First, there is never complete correspondence between thought and action. That is the reason most thinkers have rejected action as an illusion, a dream, an impossibility. In many ways they are right. Action, however, is the human condition and Christian vocation.

The problem is that our action is never totally conscious. We remain at least partly unaware of the practical, concrete processes in which our action interferes, and consequently we are not able to control our action completely. No one is totally aware of one's own action. We do imagine some idea or figure of our action, but our idea is not an exact representation of it. Indeed, it can even happen that what we imagine is just the contrary of what our action actually is. We can think we are preparing for socialism when we are really preparing for fascism; we think we are preparing for peace when really we are preparing for war. Generally, however, what happens is not such a contradiction, but an excess of imagination. We attribute to our actions an excess of efficiency or value; we overestimate them. (The opposite situation is also possible.) But the task of defining a Christian action in the world is not rendered impossible by such mistakes; they only show that all our decisions and choices are risky and precarious, which is the human and Christian condition.

Such mistaken ideas of action may be individual or collective. The collective images of action are myths. There is a real historical action, and the mythical representation of this action. When it comes to theology and action, the major problems come from those myths.

For example, there is the myth of the unity of action in Western civilization. The Western scientific and technical culture teaches that there is no possible action outside the laws and channels of the whole system, and consequently no possible action can shift the system as a whole. Thus revolution is impossible and all people have to find their places inside the system and to share talents and rewards according to their own specializations. Submission to the system is the rational law of science and technique the condition of any efficiency. Now if such a system is dominant, the unavoidable conclusion is that any possible action inside the system necessarily shares in and strengthens the system itself. By acting inside the system we unavoidably confirm and maintain it. The only conclusion for either the First World or the Third World is that any revolution is impossible, a conclusion that is born of the despair of leftists and the cynicism of rightists.

From this major myth of our Western world derives another, opposite myth: the myth of the total action that is able to destroy the whole system and to build another, radically different society. Such a myth is unavoidable in today's Third World.

It was the myth of Latin America in the 1960s, the myth of the guerrilla, of the *foco guerrillero,* of total revolutionary action. It is the myth of absolute violence able to make a total renewal of the whole society. Of course, such an idea is a myth and a dangerous one. The danger is twofold. Historically, violent total revolution as a universal way has met the terrible resistance of the established society, and many persons have died because of such a myth. Moreover, this mythical representation of action leads to a radical lack of action. Many persons await the historical opportunity of carrying out such mythical action and the opportunity never occurs. Sometimes many individuals wait ten years, twenty years, or more and do not act at all.

Because of such myths of action, many Christians cannot see how Christianity can be concerned in any manner of action in the world. They realize they cannot enter into either the myth of scientific efficiency or the myth of total revolution, so they assume their Christian mission can have no connection with action.

Such an assumption is strengthened by the realization that the role of theology is sometimes mistakenly taken to be providing an ideology for one of these mythical actions. Of course, using the sacral power of religion to strengthen a mythical action, either scientific or revolutionary, is not the task of a Christian theology. But if Christians see it being so used, their belief in the myth is increased.

The whole problem of myths can be solved only by placing them beside real historical action, which cannot be reduced to myth. Then we can see that action is not necessarily mythical, and that theology does not have to support any myth of action. On the contrary, theology is able to follow and to help the people of God as they search for the true action within the real conditions of human existence today.

The Meaning of God

This should be sufficient to show that various aspects of the Christian message remain meaningless outside concrete action. We should not forget that a trend to gnosticism has often been present in the past. All Christian dogmas can be understood within a gnostic system: the orthodox criteria are rarely sufficient to distinguish Christianity from gnosticism. The sole final criterion between the two is precisely real action in the real, material world. Gnosticism remains within the person and does not lead to concrete action in the concrete world. Accepting matter and materiality as a true place for faith, conversion, and love is surely the definitive criterion of true Christianity.

Within this view of Christianity, what is the meaning of God? And what are its implications for Christian theology? The first subject, and to some degree the sole subject, of any theology is, of course, God. But if Christian theology is nothing more than a doctrinal statement about God, or a logical system of ideas about God, it remains a simple cultural statement, without meaning, at least without a Christian meaning. Clearly the salvation of humanity does not depend on the interest of the people in such a doctrinal system. The difference between accepting or not accepting such a system of ideas about God cannot be of importance concerning the future of humanity.

It is interesting to note here that according to the Bible the enemy of God is not the atheist, but the false god, the idol. The atheist is a fool, but not dangerous. The idol is dangerous. The contrary of faith is not atheism, but faith in a false god, idolatry. This is so because the problem of God is not theoretical, but practical—true worship or false worship.

Atheism may be ignorance of the true problem about God. Atheism may be indifference; the present-day message of the churches often leads to the idea that the problem of God is not important; that it does not concern human existence in its serious aspects, and that consequently it is an artificial problem. (Such a position often derives from the triviality of preaching, which does not succeed in conveying the essence of the problem of God.)

Atheism may be the denial of one god in order to defend another, in which case the atheist becomes an idolator. For instance, Marxism denies the Christian God, asserts another god, the lord of the revolution against the present society and its god; he is called "History," or "Matter," but his qualities are those of a pantheistic god, and for many nonintellectual Marxists he is transcendent. Atheism may even be silence, an inability to speak or think before God's mystery, overtolerance, an incapacity of asserting.

In the context of this discussion, it does not really matter what leads people to atheism. What is important is that according to the Bible the atheists are fools, but not enemies. The enemies are the false gods. In a way, the whole of biblical history is a description of the permanent and historical conflict between the true God and the idols. Consequently, the theological problem today does not consist of the struggle against atheism, but against the false gods of our times.

The ancient religions of the oriental empires introduced a monotheism that was the background and the support of all kinds of domination. It is with us still—domination of the father in the family, of the teacher in the school, of the state in society, of the employer in enterprise, of the general in the army. This God, one and alone, isolated from any dependent being, eternal, self-sufficient, and impassive, is power. He is given the name "the Almighty," the source of all power. Such a God is awe-inspiring, terrifying, an overwhelming "I," who is permanently asserting "I am," which implies "and you are not." Such a God is the source of any vertical authority, any imperial power, and all those who would dominate others ask for his support and protection.

Such a God is partly rooted in the psychology of every human being; he is the "superego" who oppresses the guilty individual. The transcendent monotheistic God is the loneliness of a big "Myself," the big selfish one, the image and reason of any individualism. Such a God means will, law, judgment. He is the exact contrary of the God of the New Testament, but he is frequently the God of the common person. This God is sometimes condescending with the poor victims of a competitive society's struggles, but it is he himself who founds these struggles and rewards the winners. Consequently he is very welcome in individualistic societies based on dominance. Military dictatorships especially like transcendent monotheism, because such systems find their pure image in monotheism.

This God does not need to be demonstrated to anyone; his name is written in the hearts of all human beings, in their fear and guilt, in their search for security and submission. Law and domination all over the world are a clear demonstration of his existence. Order in world and society—especially order with force—is a permanent witness of this presence.

The monotheistic God divides the world into two categories: his friends and his enemies. His friends are those persons who accept his will and obey; his enemies are those who do not accept submission and obedience. The greatest sin is lack of submission. And the really devout and religious persons are the supporters of their God against his enemies, the persons who defend his friends and attack his enemies.

A Christian theology must liberate God from all this historical monotheism which has been—and still is—the principle behind the ideologies of so many kinds of oppression and domination. We now realize that any idea of God supports some way of life. Consequently, the meaning of an idea of God is precisely the way of life it supports—the kind of social relations, relations of the person with self and nature, ideas of life and future that are based on it.

If the monotheistic God is the basis of the selfish "I," or the powerful "superego," the very reflection of selfishness, Christians are called to seek the meaning of God elsewhere. This means avoiding the way of interiority, of inner experience, because the human being's inner experience does show a monotheistic God. Rather, Christians must follow the word of Jesus, who said and showed that God appears in the other: the poor, the rejected, the Samaritan, the sinner, the sick. God's appearance is the appeal of a powerless person. God is creator before being lawyer: indeed, he is not a lawyer at all. God gives rise to life, peace, justice to the person who needs it. When he wants to accomplish something, he does not command before he gives the Spirit; actually, his law is nothing but his gift.

This discussion of the meaning of the idea of God has been an example to show how important it is to examine every part of a theology in relation to its effect on human existence. This is the only way to distinguish a right theology from a wrong one. All aspects of the Christian message must be submitted to the same sort of investigation I have used here on the meaning of the idea of God. Various other elements of the problem will turn up in subsequent chapters. The important thing to remember is that no element of religion or theology can be discussed apart from its situation, its connection with historical reality, in a particular time and place.

2

The Theology of Revolution

The theology of revolution has been out of fashion for several years, which makes it possible to speak of it with more serenity than formerly. And it certainly should be spoken of, for neither the theology nor its problem—the problem of the underdeveloped world and the international system—has disappeared. Indeed, it might be more accurate to say that, in many circles, the problem is recognized as a problem and that the theology of revolution is now out of the spotlight of public opinion because it has grown into an ordinary subject for Christian ethics. It is no longer a strange visitor whose behavior scandalizes; it is now a member of the family whom theologians may mention without passion, preconception, or bias.

Negative Definitions. Before defining the theology of revolution (which can be done only by tracing its history), it is a good idea to be clear about what it is not. Such negative definitions can clear up a lot of misconceptions.

Revolution itself is not simply a new "case" for moralists, one that could perhaps furnish a new chapter for a treatise on social justice. Consequently, the theology of revolution is not a new theological statement to be added to preceding statements. It is a change of perspective, another viewpoint, which provides a new insight into the whole of theology, or at least the greater part of it. Indeed, once one recognizes the facts of revolution in history and in the life of humanity at the present time, one is forced to take a look at society, and thus also at human beings and their salvation, from another perspective. From this new viewpoint appear new meanings for several biblical themes; one can perceive aspects of the Christian message long forgotten or never before disclosed.

Further, the theology of revolution is not a doctrine that can be explained logically and in an orderly manner. It is, rather, a "problematic," a concern, a collection of problems around a basic question, a gathering of soundings, suppositions, and questions around the following subject: What is the connection, the relationship between Christianity and modern revolutions? (Even if one answers that there is no connection at all, the reply still gives a direction.)

Why was the phenomenon of revolution absent from Christian theology and ethics until recently? The explanation lies far back in history, probably as far back as the Greek philosophy that provided the frame and the basic topics for Scholastic theology. Working from this basis, classical theology presupposed a fixed society and aimed to define rules of action from inside that established order. It regarded changing the whole of the society as outside its perspectives and ability. For example, when dealing with the virtue of justice, it took as its subject matter human action within society but not the action of human society as a whole.

But in recent years, the long silence has been broken, the presupposition changed. Today even the most moderate authors accept the theme of revolution. For instance, the French Jesuit Pierre Bigo, who wrote in 1965 a classic work on the social doctrine of the church, published in 1974 *The Church and the Third World Revolution,* which is a good summary of the main topics currently used to explain the problematic of revolution in the underdeveloped world.[1]

The theology of revolution is, however, not a sudden new creation, but the convergence of several streams of Christian thought that are connected to a number of practical present-day movements in the church. It is not to be expected that the theology of revolution could actually be fixed inside a theological system, either at present or in the near future. It is only a moment, a very short moment of about five or ten years, in a long process that cannot be stopped. This process is still being born, still coming to life; it has not yet entered the historical museum of past Christian events. As it continues to grow, the forces that have now produced the theology of revolution will almost certainly generate new reflections and precarious new theologies related to other concerns or issues (for instance, black theology, Christians for Socialism, prophetic theology in Latin America, African theology of authenticity, and so on). The theology of revolution is not complete, but this does not mean that it is useless. It has already changed Christian theology as a whole as well as every one of its parts; it has also influenced every possible theology in the future.

Two Warnings. Before beginning an explanation of what the theology of revolution is, two comments or explanations must be made to avoid confusion. In the first place, the subject matter of a theology of revolution is sometimes misunderstood. Its problem does not consist in determining the legitimacy or illegitimacy of the revolution itself. Neither does it consist of a search for the abstract conditions of a right revolution; it is not an attempt to develop a theory of "just revolution," like the "just war" theory. In practice, almost everyone accepts the legitimacy of some wars without going through a lot of theological analysis; for example, few people questioned the rightness of the war against nazism. In the same way, few Americans would question the rightness of the American Revolution.

Of course the theology of revolution does not intend to approve one kind of revolution or condemn another. It is not intended for living in the nontemporal world of eternal ideas, but neither is it meant to legitimize any party or political movement. Undoubtedly, it will be so used by several parties; historically all theologies have been so used, especially the so-called nonpolitical theologies. But that does not invalidate its true purpose. The theology of revolution connects the words of divine revelation with the present condition of the peoples searching for the signs of God's judgment on the world of today.

The second misunderstanding that must be cleared up arises because Latin American theologians of liberation are often somewhat overinsistent about the difference between their theology and the theology of revolution (which they call "European theology"). Actually, the movements are different, but there is an evident line of continuity between the two theological insights. Although the Latin Americans try to avoid European theology, they frequently use European arguments. For example, Hugo Assmann discusses problems using the arguments of Johannes Metz's disciples against Metz himself. Gustavo Gutiérrez takes over the arguments of several French theologians, such as those of Paul Blanquart about the connections between Marxism and Christianity, utopia, and faith and science. Enrique Dussel uses the topics of Emmanuel Levinas and Paul Ricoeur against Hegel, whom he considers the most representative European theologian. Consequently, the theology of liberation can be seen as a particular and original path within a more general theology of revolution. Latin American theology is really one mode of European theology; it is not another, different system of thought, as is, for example, Greek oriental theology, whose concerns and processes are radically different.

THE ORIGINS OF THE THEOLOGY OF REVOLUTION

Since the theology of revolution is more a movement than a statement, it is best analyzed by seeing where it comes from and in what direction it is going. Its origins will be discussed here; its causes are partly reflected from its origins and will become even clearer in the later chapters of this book.

In the history of ideas, isolating and enumerating sources or separate cultural units is always conventional and approximate. But however artificial this isolation may be, one cannot discern the cultural and historical processes without isolating cultural units. In view of this necessity, let us consider six sources of the theology of revolution, which are like six streams meeting at a certain moment in history. Despite the limitations of any arbitrary selection, I think I have not failed in objectivity by isolating the following six sources: (1) the problem of development and its historical evolution; (2) Metz's political theology; (3) the new theology of freedom and its consequences for Christology, anthropology, and ethics; (4) the new trends in the interpretation of church history and religious sociology; (5) the dialogue between

Christianity and Marxism; (6) the new interpretation or method of theology as a ministry in the church.

The Evolution of the Problem of Development

The problem of development appeared in the 1950s. Since then it has known two different stages, and the emergence of a theology of revolution was connected with the transition from the first stage to the second.

The First Stage. After World War II, two simultaneous events or changes brought about a new phenomenon. New understandings in the science of economics and a new climate of public opinion in the Western world resulted in the movement to forward development among the underdeveloped peoples.

In the 1950s, economists began to understand that their subject matter was not (or not only) the arrangement of economic variables and their links inside an abstract, theoretical, and historical societal pattern; rather, it was a movement, a dynamic within a changing society and among several dissimilar societies. Soon afterward, the very traditional distinction between "irrational noncivilized" and "rational civilized" countries disappeared and was replaced by a new distinction between "underdeveloped" and "developed" countries. At this point both categories were considered as belonging to the same whole, as two different stages of one evolution. The "uncivilized" peoples were seen as beginning to become "rational" (although retarded). Accordingly, said the economists, the "underdeveloped" peoples could also become "developed," that is, like the "developed countries," their metropolitan sovereigns for so many centuries. To accomplish this they had to go through a process called "development."

Just at the moment when economists were defining their new ideas about development, Western public opinion was becoming aware of the way of life in those parts of the world that were mostly in process of decolonization. Generally the West had thought that those people were living under the colonial protection system happily, peacefully, and blissfully unaware. The image of colonial ideology was truly a product of the eighteenth century—childish peoples, "good savages." Suddenly after the war it became known that those peoples were mostly living in extreme misery and poverty and under domination such as the white peoples could never imagine. This situation aroused sympathy in the West; it also caused much uneasiness. The rebellion of the colonial peoples against Western domination was obviously a logical possibility, since misery and revolt were known to be preconditions for revolutionary unrest. Consequently, confusion, desperation, and anarchy could be avoided only by radical change in the former colonial world (now called the Third World).

In this context, the development theory was received as a providential salvation and a universal solution; development became not only possible and desirable, but an urgent and unavoidable necessity. The churches of the developed world responded with distressed appeals and urgent warnings such as the encyclical *Populorum Progressio*. Pope Paul VI expressed the perturbation of the Western conscience in the face of this new reality that seemed intolerably shameful. Development became evident as a duty in justice to all peoples. Development was social justice applied to international relations, said Pope John XXIII; it was the new name for peace, said Pope Paul VI.

To develop? Certainly yes, but how? The Western world felt reassured because, as usual, Western rationality had found the proper answer. The economists of the Western world had found the development formula: it was self-evidently that which the Western world had followed. This would not be difficult; all the underdeveloped nations had to do was to go through the same process the developed nations had gone through for two centuries. The countries of the Third World were behind but they could accelerate, especially if they received a little help from Western know-how. Western economic science was thus the most valuable gift the rich nations could give the poor nations. So taught and wrote Walt W. Rostow and his colleagues in the "developed" universities all over the developed world, as did several of their Third World pupils whom they adroitly educated and returned to the Third World. (These disciples are now leaders in economic management in their own countries, thanks to the current military governments and to American aid.)

Rostow and the other accepted economists of the day also taught that the development process could be speeded by "aid" from the stronger nations. This aid could be provided in two ways: by the intellectual aid of transferring Western technology and methods to the underdeveloped nations, generally by aid missions through which economists and other experts gave "technical assistance"; and by the material aid of capital investment. The greater the aid, the faster the underdeveloped nations could reach the development level of the West.

Following the same reasoning the churches began teaching that developed peoples had to collaborate with the poor peoples' development programs by means of aid. Aid became a Christian duty based on Christian ethics, charity, or social justice. The churches even built their own aid institutions. But although these organizations constituted a new chapter in the churches' social-assistance program, they entailed no conflict with civil authorities. (Indeed, they were quite parallel to what the civil authorities were doing themselves.) Consequently, the churches had no need to change their theology; aid-work offered no threat to the stable framework of the whole of Christianity. It was the logical extension of recognized theories of social justice.

The Second Stage. During the 1960s a radical change took place in development consciousness. The reason was simple: after ten years the condition in the Third World was worse than ever. Neither development politics nor aid programs were succeeding. According to statistical and socioeconomic analysis, the gap between rich countries and the poor countries was widening considerably every year. The inequity in the distribution of wealth inside the underdeveloped nations was also increasing. The upper classes were concentrating the major part of the gross national product in their own hands. Rural conditions were worsening continually, while hungry masses of workers were crowding into the marginal shantytowns of the new megalopolis. Sickness, unemployment, illiteracy, malnutrition, slums—all were increasing. So were social uneasiness and various kinds of disturbances. Political instability was growing, which seemingly could be overcome only by setting up dictatorships and military governments. These governments were supposed to maintain order and security by means of an overwhelmingly rigid repressive system maintained by huge police forces. In short, it seemed that only the police structures, armaments entrepreneurs, and a few elite individuals had profited from a decade of Western aid and development policies.

What had happened? There was something fundamentally wrong with the accepted idea of the development process. A few Christian thinkers, such as Louis Lebret, François Perroux, and Colin Clark, had been publishing severe and well-founded warnings about the idea since the late 1950s. In the following decade, a new comprehensive explanation of the problem of development, its nature, and its evolution was made, chiefly by experts of the United Nations Economic Commission for Latin America. Later this explanation was adapted by Arab, African, and Asian economists, as well as by several enlightened Western experts, scholars who were able to free themselves from their own countries and their countries' interests.[2]

The new view of the development process may be summarized in the following statements:

1. Underdevelopment is not belated development at all; on the contrary, it is nothing less than a secondary effect of the development of the developed nations. Development of one part of the world has produced underdevelopment in other parts as the result of the interaction of various factors. (One analogy sometimes used is that of a good kitchen, which produces excellent dishes and necessarily a lot of leftovers. Underdevelopment is the waste product of the developed world.) The developed nations' economy invaded the whole world, taking control of the trade system throughout, using the production sectors that could forward their own prosperity and destroying the economic sectors that did not favor it. The result for the less developed nations has been a complete disruption in their social and economic structures, extreme neglect of their peoples, terrible problems of unemployment or underemployment and, last but not least, powerlessness in solving national problems because all power belongs to stronger foreign nations, which have no interest in changing the present condition of international relations. Within each poor nation there is a privileged sector, usually the former

dominant class, which has been absorbed into the system of foreign domination. This group finds a real gold mine in the system and exploits it without considering the despair of its own poor. Without needing to work (or "develop") it acquires more wealth and power than before; any social solidarity disappears.

2. Consequently, the relationship between developed and underdeveloped countries cannot be thought of as one between advanced and primitive countries, nor as one between "aiding" and "aided" countries. The best way to explain the world condition is as a set of relationships between "dominating" nations and "dominated" nations. A true development process would really be a process of liberation.

3. No development is possible if a radical change in structures and processes does not take place in the underdeveloped countries themselves. Formerly it was believed that international trade and the free market would be the motors for development, with aid as a booster. The new economists, however, now believe that the present system of trade and the free market are the main obstacles. Even aid presents obstacles to development rather than promoting it. It appears that aid to the underdeveloped nations, however well intentioned, is a part of the development process of the advanced nations, the other side of the coin of domination.

Development requires an inversion of the economy by structural reform (the name given to many of the new economic thinkers—structuralist school —comes from this central statement).

4. It becomes clearer and clearer that the problem of development does not concern economy alone, but all aspects of social life. The obstacles to development are not only economic. There are also political and cultural impediments. The politics of the dominating nations and the repressive underdeveloped states prevent the necessary structural reforms and extend the dominion of the privileged classes without dealing with the problems of marginalized peoples. The culture (or lack of culture) that results from the invasion of traditional peoples by Western powers—the pseudo-culture of the elites and the subculture of the traditional masses—is an impediment to an increased awareness of the problems of development; moreover, it legitimizes the establishment. Consequently, true development implies both political and cultural liberation at the same time as economic liberation.

If one accepts Pierre Bigo's definition of revolution as "conscious and intentional change of one society into another society,"[3] the conclusion is that development is possible only by means of revolution.

Development and the Church. Such a change in ideas about development has had repercussions within the church. Accepting the truth of these new concepts means that forwarding development is not only a question of giving or receiving aid, but also of forwarding revolution. This is especially important in those countries where the Christian church is already a national and traditional institution. Where Christian men and women hold important positions in social life and Christianity has deeply entered the national culture, no revolution can possibly remain outside the church. Conversely, the church cannot remain outside the revolution.

Inevitably the questions are, What responsibility does the church have for maintaining and nourishing underdeveloped cultures? Must it foster their traditional manner of thinking by teaching submission and resignation? What action is incumbent on the church when it is shown to be helping the dominating nations and classes in their utterly selfish behavior? What degree of responsibility should be attached to the church when political power remains in the hands of a domineering oligarchy, which does not hesitate to use many religious symbols to its profits and to take advantage of the position of ecclesiastics? What responsibility must the church accept when it keeps obsolete economic structures within its own economic system (for instance, the cherished private property of clerical institutions)? A revolution would imply deep changes in the church, as much in its material structure as in its methods of working in the world. Is the church ready to promote such a change, and not merely accept it?

Such questions and others have opened an extensive process of reflection. Out of this process of reflection the theology of liberation—the Latin American chapter of a theology of revolution—was born.

That reflection was not made in the abstract world of universal ideas. It was, rather, the work of the ecclesiastical institution itself, in several areas. It was part of, and inside, a process of change of the church itself. There are many examples of this change. Recall, for instance, the Chilean bishops' land reform of rural properties belonging to the church; the conscientization and popular-education movements in several countries; the many exhortations and actions promoting peasant leagues and workers' associations or unions; the frequent condemnation of police repression and the defense of human rights. These are just a few of the more spectacular phenomena of a vast program. The theology of liberation is intended to build up theory in support of the program of the church as it practices Christianity in this way in Latin America.

The Growth of Liberation Theology. There have been several notable milestones in the development of liberation theology. The origins of the movement were, on the one hand, the Christian Democratic movement, which spread throughout major parts of the Catholic countries in the 1950s; its intellectual leader was Jacques Maritain. On the other hand was the Economie et Humanisme group, whose leader was the French Dominican, L. J. Lebret. At least the influence of both movements was extensive in most Latin American countries. Both had centers in Brazil; the former was especially strong in Chile, and the latter in Uruguay. These movements prepared a whole generation of Christian laity for a new way of theological thinking. Then, in 1961, came *Mater et Magistra,* the first official Catholic document to make reference to the Third World and the problems of development. Until that time, most Catholic churches of the Third World had remained passively awaiting warnings from above. After the encyclical appeared, the more advanced groups in the Catholic Church began a process of reflection about development that inevitably led them to the theology of liberation. (European theology accompanied Latin American theology in this process of evolution, especially through the mediation of a few French Dominicans living in Brazil and Uruguay.)

After 1961, the process snowballed. History—formerly slow, almost sluggish in Latin America—accelerated. The more moderate were pushed by the more advanced.

From this point, the growth of liberation theology can largely be traced by noting the increasing use of revolution or liberation language. (There is some distinction between the two, a distinction that many Catholic theologians of Latin America insist upon, or it is thus that they distinguish their work from that of the European theologians of revolution. Liberation language has a greater scope than revolution language; it is also less defined and its social consequences are less obvious. It is therefore more acceptable in some circles. Nevertheless "liberation" includes "revolution" and every revolution intends to promote liberation. Thus it would seem that the differences between the two are not of great importance.)

In the beginning of this period, the language of revolution was used primarily in Brazil (by university movements and young Christian followers of the Dominicans) and in Chile (by the Christian Democrats; "Revolution in Freedom" was the central slogan of Eduardo Frei in his 1964 campaign for the presidency).

Around the middle of the decade, revolutionary language became the norm of the Protestant movement in Latin America. At that time, a most brilliant theological reflection was made by an American Presbyterian scholar, Dr. Richard Shaull, now a professor at Princeton University. At the Geneva Conference on Church and Society (1966), Shaull led a group of young Latin American theologians and experts; they became the center of ardent debates at the meeting and divided the assembly by putting the question of revolution to the churches. It was the first time that Christians speaking from the developed and underdeveloped nations manifested a radical opposition in their points of view. The Latin American Protestant movement continued the reflections and tone of Geneva. Supported by the Ecumenical Council and the Iglesia y Sociedad para América Latina group (ISAL), and in spite of the opposition of almost all the established churches and their institutions, this Protestant movement always supported the most advanced or radical statements legitimating various Latin American revolutionary projects and groups. This movement always used revolutionary language.

Meanwhile, advanced Catholic groups had also been using revolutionary language, and some of them were modifying it to the language of liberation.

In 1968, the language of liberation appeared openly and very publicly at the second Latin American Episcopal Conference at Medellín, Colombia. Documents prepared for and accepted in the Medellín debates proceeded from the theology of liberation and used liberation language. The language (almost more than the content) was a great shock to most Christians; the Medellín documents and other works that soon followed met almost immediate opposition in many areas of the Catholic world. Nevertheless, the Latin American church held firm. After its bishops signaled official acceptance at Medellín, the theology of liberation could be extended throughout most Latin American countries and ecclesiastical institutions. It influenced social and popular movements and spread into teaching, education, preaching, and worship.

Meanwhile the theology of liberation continued to develop in almost all the Latin American churches. Among Catholics, liberation language reached its height between 1968 and 1973. In that period, many works were published by the leaders and principal spokesmen of the movement: Gustavo Gutiérrez (Peru), Lucio Gera and Juan Luis Scannone (Argentina), Juan Luis Segundo (Uruguay), Hugo Assmann (Brazil, but now living in Costa Rica).

In 1971, a movement was born in Chile which is sometimes grouped with the theology of liberation but is actually completely independent of it. Known as Christians for Socialism, it is now found throughout the world (except in the Chile of today, of course). Its original purpose in Chile was to take part in a political movement that was simultaneously socialist, Marxist, and democratic. Such a problem was encountered only in Chile, where two small Christian political parties broke from the Christian Democrats during the government of President Salvador Allende and attempted to form a genuine amalgamation with the Marxists. (In other countries, collaboration with the Marxists was solely a defensive action against the common enemy.) Whether the Christians for Socialism movement is wise or well based in Christian thinking is not properly a subject for the theology of liberation, since the problem of connections between Marxism and Christianity is formally an independent one. Some theologians of liberation believe connections can be established; others, for instance the Argentinian authors, are openly anti-Marxist.

The year 1973 marked another radical change in the Latin American situation and consequently in liberation theology. With President Allende's death and the military pronunciamento in Chile, on the one hand, and the self-destruction of Peronism in Argentina, on the other, the possibility of liberation and revolution disappeared for Latin America, at least for a long time. That presented a new problem for the Christian churches. What should they do when revolution is simultaneously necessary and impossible? Should they retreat to their own quarters, worship, cultivating their inner life, wait for better times? Or should they preach nonacceptance of injustice, as the prophets did, lonely and facing a closed society? Dare the churches affront power and repression to claim the rights of humankind?

The theology of liberation has now entered into a crisis because its subject matter has disappeared from the historical perspective, at least for the moment. The dilemma is giving birth to a new action that has not yet received a suitable name. Some authors suggest the "theology of captivity"; they are not without reason.

Whatever the future holds, it is clear that Latin American development problems, as one of the sources of the theology of liberation, have exerted some influence upon the evolution of European theology since 1970 and have been one of the strongest challenges to a universal theology of revolution.[4]

Latin America is not, of course, the only area of the Third World in which the move to development has raised the problem of revolution for Christians. The churches are encountering a revolutionary ideology and practice in Tanzania and Zambia, where the pioneers and leaders of the revolution— Julius Nyerere and Kenneth Kaunda—are staunch and consistent Christians. The same problem also exists in other African countries, although under less favorable conditions (sometimes very unfavorable conditions, as in Guinea). However, the Africans have not yet elaborated a new indigenous theological line that would correspond to the theology of liberation in Latin America.

Some people do see a correspondence between the theology of liberation and recent black theology. But I believe that black theology is something entirely different. Racial liberation is new for the churches—for all Western culture. It goes deeper than other new movements and its differences from former movements are much more radical.

The Political Theology of Metz

Although the political theology of Johannes Metz was a vital element in the confluence that became liberation theology, we shall not detail his ideas here. It would take too long. Moreover, the meaning of Metz's theological thought has received several different interpretations and can lead to endless debates. It is sufficient to mention two of his themes: the deprivatization of Christianity and the reappraisal of modern Western civilization. Although many writers and thinkers have not been able to understand Metz (indeed, there is a possibility that he was irresolute and unable to follow his insights to their conclusion), the introduction of these themes in the few articles he published during the late 1960s decisively influenced Catholic theology. After his work, and the parallel work of Jürgen Moltmann and Wolfhart Pannenberg, the thinking about the relationship between faith and the world could not remain unaltered. In the Catholic Church, the social doctrine that had endured for a century collapsed. By 1971, Pope Paul VI completely renewed the perspective of social teaching by his letter to Maurice Cardinal Roy,

Octogesima Adveniens, written for the tenth anniversary of *Pacem in Terris.*

Metz himself stayed at some midway point concerning the relationship between faith and the world, but Moltmann took over and followed the direction of Metz's theology of hope until he arrived at its natural conclusion. He is now the principal and perhaps the first author of the theology of revolution.[5]

To what is the influence of this political theology due? Probably to its very simple themes. These themes have succeeded because they are so obvious that they have convinced and gained the acceptance of many authors, even many who do not wish to follow Metz's thought in every respect.

The Deprivatization of Christianity. The idea of the deprivatization of Christianity, for example, is extremely simple and self-evident. It expresses an obvious fact and an evident necessity. Current Christianity, born from the Reformation and the Counter-Reformation, is a privatized Christianity. It reads the Bible as a testimony for individual faith; it expects only an individual response, individual faith. The perspective is Newman's: "God and myself," "God and my soul."

But, the true biblical perspective is different; its testimony includes not two terms but three: "God, people, and myself." The Bible speaks constantly of a people; before being the history of my salvation, it is the history of the people of God. The biblical figures never forget their place within their people's destiny. The most basic words in the Bible have a collective meaning: "people," "kingdom," "liberty," "charity," "covenant," and so on.

Historically, Christianity has always been a public institution related to the state and public life, even during periods when the Christian churches were privatized—retired within their own private lives, problems, and values—for privatized Christianity also legitimates and supports the establishment. Christian testimony can only be lived by communities and refers to the people who live in communities. All human beings and institutions participate in public life, if only by their silence. Churches and Christian persons do participate in politics, even when they deny the fact. The only question is whether they participate consciously or unconsciously.

This is so obvious that it is amazing that theologians ignored it for so long and that some still refuse to accept it. Perhaps the reason for the latter is that political theology does become confused when it begins to speak about politics in historical and concrete terms. The problem is that it fails to distinguish between "politics" in the wide sense of the word—that is, public or social life generally—and "politics" in the strict sense of the word—that is, state and power. The political theologies of Metz and others deal mainly with politics in the wide sense of the word: they speak about politics without considering the main political realities, namely, state and power. Such theologians should be transcended. The real future of a political theology is in the renewed but traditional, constant problem of the relationship between church and state. The problem has not been solved or removed, only hindered by the modern liberal constitutions with their idea of separation of the two. Actually, there is never separation between church and state. There can be support or struggle but never separation.

Reappraisal of Modern Civilization. The second main idea from political theology that has strongly influenced the theology of revolution is its radical reappraisal of modern Western civilization and European history since the eighteenth century. Until ten years ago, the basic appraisal of modern civilization by the Catholic Church and the other established European churches denied the entire inheritance of the Enlightenment: liberalism, rationalism, socialism, and, in general, all the ideologies and movements that were developed during the past century. Consequently, it can be said that Metz continued the Catholic renewal of the eighteenth century. Such radical change in appraisal was tolerated, and even sympathetically received, thanks to the liberal circumstances of Vatican Council II.

Here, too, one has to be very careful because political theology left some dangerous doors ajar. Certainly, over the last two centuries secular culture had developed many valuable ideas. There is no question that it was time for the church to recognize and accept them. (Actually, one should say "recover" them, because their remote origin was Christian.) By so doing, political theology exhibited an "anti-*Syllabus*" aspect that was as necessary as it was sympathetic.

However, this new political theology was unable to give us sufficient criteria to distinguish the positive aspects of modern civilization from the negative ones. Consequently, it could not help but open the door to secularization.

Secularization means invasion by all the devils of capitalism, nationalism, the state, absolute power, elitism, fascism, and so on. Pius IX had tried to contain these devils with the *Syllabus*; his goal was wise although his means were obsolete medieval barriers. Now, with secularization introduced into Christian ideology, the theoretical obstacles to these devils disappeared. Amid the blissful peacefulness of Christian Democratic Europe of 1955 to 1965, it was easy to believe that the devils were dead. The unshakable self-confidence of the United States in that period made it easier still. A decade later it became quite clear that they were not dead at all. This failure of political theology has not made the acceptance of liberation theology any easier.

But in spite of the dangers and failures of Metz's political theology, there is no question that, by affirming the modern world and the cultural process, it led the church to a new view of the world-church problematic and liberated it from various archaic patterns. More especially, the Christian church became more able to consider the world itself, outside its own particular ecclesiastical interests or noninterests. This change was a prerequisite for posing the question of the role of Christianity in history, for rightly judging the meaning of past, present, and future revolutions.

The New Theology of Freedom

In some sense, all the sources of the theology of liberation or freedom are biblical. On going back to the traditional theological synthesis, I am always struck by the modest importance attributed to freedom. It is even more amazing when contrasted with the prominence of freedom in the Bible. How can such a long silence be explained, a silence that lasted for many centuries, almost since the second Christian generation? Probably the domination of Greek philosophy restricted Christianity from spreading the freedom proclaimed by the gospel. (In spite of the fact that Greek philosophy was the most liberal philosophy before biblical Christianity, it gave little value to freedom. And such a restriction would be cumulative.) But whatever the reason for the long silence, the rediscovery of freedom by theology is a return to the Bible transcending Hellenism.

Christian Anthropocentrism. Freedom is at the center of Christian anthropocentrism, as Karl Rahner and Johannes Metz showed at the beginning of Vatican Council II. Christianity is a testimony to human salvation. And salvation is the restoration of the human person to the fullness of God's image. God is freedom much more than he is power. A favorite formula of the last ten years is the quotation from Irenaeus: "The glory of God is the person fully alive." This means that human beings do not grasp the salvation message because of their intellect, their power, their sensibility, or their ability to work or to play. They have all that, but reaching salvation depends on another principal quality. Men and women are God's image, God's interlocutors; they receive God's word, and their ability to achieve it is called freedom. At the present moment, Christian theology is searching for a Christian anthropology, and it becomes more and more clear that this search essentially implies an endless search for liberty.[6]

Biblical freedom is not merely concerned with a human being's relationship to God, or to his or her own body, or to the material world. More important is the relationship of person to person, of individuals to one another. Freedom means a way of living with the other, a way of life defined by reciprocity and community. For that reason the proclamation of freedom is an event that can give rise to revolutions. The scope of freedom has to do not only with personal acts, but with the whole of society, as well as with the possibility of choosing new societal patterns. It is true that revolutions carry the weight of collective determinism and of individuals with all sorts of human passions, but they also form the most extensive act of human freedom.

The New Christology. Freedom is also at the center of a new Christology. Think of the Christologies of Moltmann, Pannenberg, Duquoc, Schillebeeckx, and Kasper, to cite only the greatest. They have one important quality in common: they all start in Jesus' human life and human history amid the people of Israel. That is the way they all show Jesus' freedom and discover freedom at the center of his personality and behavior.

It is true that a few imaginative authors have used this new emphasis on Jesus' humanity to depict a figure that turns out to be a revolutionary Zealot, or Sicar, like the contemporary Jewish sect well known to historians. (Oscar Cullmann and others have bothered to respond to this characterization, although it was not necessary.) Such nonsense aside, the new Christologies are important because they underline the scope of Jesus' freedom concerning social life. His freedom included a new way of understanding relationships among persons as well as those between individuals and authority, a way that opposed the law and experience of all the peoples and civilizations in existence before Christianity. Jesus did not change any government for the simple reason that he did not come in order to supersede his disciples' action. But since his way of acting was to be imitated, not merely contemplated, unavoidably it gave rise to conflicts between his disciples and the Roman god-emperors and their successors, the totalitarian states, and the various kinds of slavery or exploitation of the working class. Jesus did not specify these conflicts or how his disciples should act in them; it was not his mission to predict the whole of history. He simply created a tremendous problem for it without providing any clear solution.

The Pauline Message. Another introduction to the Christian statement on freedom is Paul's explanation of the law and freedom. This Pauline message not only concerns a few obsolete rules of the old Jewish law, which needed to be removed; it has a universal scope. It shows the new meaning of ethics, authority, and social structures. Unfortunately, much of this teaching was lost for many centuries. Medieval theology was inspired by Roman law, so its ideology saw Christian revelation as divine law. But it failed to see that this concept of divine law, when not counterbalanced by a concept of freedom, could—and did—lead to a new version of Old Testament legalism. The Reformation returned to the freedom theme, but it understood freedom as a message of liberation for the interior life of an individual human being. Its field was the individual's relationship to God, a message of liberation for life in society and for relationships in political life, including relationships with authorities. (Think, for example, of the opposition between Martin Luther and Thomas Münzer.)

The Rediscovery of the Spirit. Another important strand in the new theology is the rediscovery of the Holy Spirit. "Where the Spirit of the Lord is, there is freedom" (2 Corinthians 3:17). In the past, Western theology generally dealt with the Spirit as a supplement without decisive importance because it brought nothing that was not already present in Christology. The Holy Spirit and freedom were forgotten together and the common fate of both is significant.

New Historical Circumstances. As we examine all these new emphases, it becomes clear that the rediscovery of freedom stems from a new reading of the Bible. But simultaneously it arises from the most recent of circumstances: the evolution of social teaching in the churches. In the past, the Catholic Church in particular was indifferent to the value of freedom; indeed, it generally warned the people against the dangers of freedom. But at the present time, it realizes that the chief danger to the people of God and the institutional church is not freedom, but widespread totalitarianism. In facing this new danger, the church has changed its former perspective. Now it views the defense of freedom as its most urgent task, a consideration that can be noted in all the latest official documents.[7] What will result from these new historical conditions in which Christian freedom is confronted with modern totalitarianism? We shall see that there are several pathways leading freedom to revolution and revolution to freedom.

New Trends in Church History and the Sociology of Religion

In the Catholic Church and other established churches, church historiography used to relate the events and processes of world history, not according to their inner value, but according to their consequences on Christian institutions. In searching for the connections between church and society, traditional historiography emphasized learning the advantages and disadvantages of ecclesiastical institutions in any given time.

Later a few scholars introduced another point of view; they began to search history for Christianity as a way of life, as a human life pattern, as a new system of values entering into and affecting peoples' cultures and civilizations. They considered the influence of Christian faith and action on society and, reciprocally, the influence of culture and society on Christianity.

Study from this point of view showed that, especially during the last millennium, Christianity has had two opposing functions. In almost all times and places, the church has been divided on all its levels—bishops, priests, orders, laity. On the one hand, church and churchmen supported establishments. They helped legitimate emperors, kings, princes, bourgeoisie, modern states, feudalism, capitalism—whoever held power. They were not without justification for these actions. Their goal, which was often conscious, was to try to teach the powers faith and charity and to educate them according to the principles of social justice. (Whether they succeeded in doing so or not can be debated endlessly.)

On the other hand, the new historians show that at least some trends of a popular Christianity have always been present. There has always been a democratic, spiritualist, reformist tradition existing alongside the church of the establishment, like a lower level, a low church alongside a high church. Within this low church were to be found a few popes, a few bishops, some priests and other ministers, the orders at the moment of their foundation, and especially various lay associations. This democratic tradition within Christianity was present in the origins of the Gregorian Reformation of the eleventh century, in the democratic movement of the Italian, Flemish, and Hanseatic free cities, in the Franciscan movement of the thirteenth century, in the democratic popular movement in Switzerland and Bohemia in the fifteenth and sixteenth centuries, in the German Revolution of 1525, in the Netherlands in the sixteenth and seventeenth centuries, in the English Revolution of 1640, in the American Revolution, and so on. During those times, these popular Christian movements demanded both church reformation and social revolution. Both elements have always seemed inseparable —or more accurately, the Christian populists of many different historical situations have always come to believe that some degree of reformation within the church can occur without revolution, but that revolution cannot occur without reformation in the church.

It is true that most popular Christian movements were judged very harshly by the contemporary church of the establishment. Often they were rejected outright by the church as heresies; therefore they now appear in the history books as false Christian movements and condemned heresies. But the more modern historical schools are showing that it was the strong connections with the populist social movements that caused many "heretical" doctrines to be rejected. Logically this implies a historical denial of social change on the part of the established church. Any change of both church and society was refused in the name of the true religion, which meant a sacralization of the establishment in both religious and civil power. Many of those judged heretics were never heretics in any way. (Some of these maligned witnesses to the social and political meaning of Christianity have since been reinstated entirely or in part, such as Joachim of Floris, the Franciscan spirituals J. P. Olivi and his companions, John Hus, and Savonarola.) Others of those named heretics felt impelled to deny some elements of the ecclesiastical system (for example, the hierarchy or the sacraments) just because these elements were functioning as barriers to social change. The reform of social structures that they sought implied the denial of some privileges of clergy or church, and consequently, a denial of the sacral definitions of clergy and church that legitimated such privileges. These heretics, according to the famous saying of the Catholic saint Clement Hofbauer, became heretics because they wanted to live as Christians.

There is not space here to do anything like a complete analysis of this new vision of church history. However, we should note that for at least one thousand years portions of Christianity have been a ferment of social change appealing to evangelical principles and that generally the most evangelical persons have been the initiators of these processes of social change. Two examples should be emphasized because their effects still ripple to affect the present moment. In the Catholic Church the two great orders—the Franciscans and the Dominicans—are extraordinarily important for originating a democratic way of life. They started with the inspiration for a democratic common life within their own communities, but their founders intended to transfer such a social relationship to the life of the larger society. Many members and communities of those orders have never stopped searching for ways of accomplishing this.

Likewise, historiography is now showing the Christian inspiration behind more recent revolutionary movements—the liberal revolutions of the nineteenth century and the socialist revolutions of the twentieth. Former interpretations of these revolutions, especially Catholic interpretations, perceived them from the mythical view provided by Romanticism and the Counter-Revolution. From that perspective they appeared to be the advent of the kingdom of Satan. But the latest historiography shows how these movements were in some way new manifestations of the ancient division of Christianity. It demonstrates that the church has always been (and is still) simultaneously for and against revolution. Its institutions and persons intimately connected with the establishment stand against revolution; its evangelical message of poverty, community, and liberty can only stand for it.

The new religious sociology is continuing the work of the new historians. For almost a century, the sociology of religion considered that the connections between society and church could be expressed by two simple equations: traditional society=mythical irrationality=Christian church; modern society=scientific rationality=secularization. The church and Christianity were considered to belong to the old, prerational age. (Marxist sociology said it with more aggressiveness; Western sociology, more tactfully and not without some pity. But both ways of thinking implied the same kind of rejection.)

Now the new sociology of religion is beginning to accept the idea that traditional societies were also rational, and that modern society—industrial, technical, and urban—has irrational aspects. It sees that the latter is as irrational as the former, perhaps more. And thus it realizes that the Christian church is also simultaneously rational and irrational. Church and Christianity have connections with the irrational aspects of both traditional and modern society, but they also have connections with the rational aspects of both. The new sociology shows how modern society needs religious expression as much as traditional society did, although with other kinds of expressions.

The new historiography and sociology of religion lead to only one conclusion: Christianity cannot be a stranger to the revolutions of the future, no more than it was foreign to the revolutions of the past.

The Dialogue Between Christianity and Marxism

Changing Attitudes. During the 1950s, most Christian theologians considered any relationship between theology and Marxism to be impossible. In the Catholic Church the predominant note was struck by the classic apologetic works of French and German Jesuits—Calvez, Chambre, Bigo, Wetter. These authors accepted a monolithic Marxism, the Stalinist version, a rigid unity that is entirely dependent on atheism. This was the ideology referred to in the encyclical *Divini Redemptoris* of Pope Pius XI and in many other church documents through the time of the cold war.

Much the same view prevailed among Protestant theologians, although a few, less bound by ecclesiastical discipline, did seek a kind of dialogue with Marxism, for example, through the peace movement created by the communist international movement during the cold war. (Thus J. L. Hromadka, contemporary leader of Czech theology, was well acquainted with the spring movement of Prague and, like this movement, is presently the victim of Soviet repression.) But such instances were not frequent. Protestants, like Catholics, tended to stay on the safe side of the wall.

Then came the end of the cold war, marked by the Kennedy-Khrushchev encounter in Vienna in 1961. This political change had repercussions for relations between the churches and the whole Marxist movement. Both sides allowed some lukewarm encounters to temper the absolute coldness that had existed.

Actually, those communist parties who were in power changed very few of their antireligious politics. But they sought (or admitted to) a sort of *modus vivendi* and recognized that some connections exist between the Catholic Church and the peoples of Eastern Europe, of Cuba, and of other countries where there is a Catholic majority. This was the meaning of Monsignor Casaroli's journeys. The Communist parties not in power took more interest in coming in touch with Christianity, especially in France, Italy, Spain, and Latin America. Was this simple opportunism or sincere conversion to religious tolerance? The theory and practice of Communist parties inclines one to the opportunist interpretation. But it is entirely possible that the policies of the parties in different countries have not been entirely the same. For example, probably there is more opportunism in France and more self-criticism in Italy.

Whatever the motivation, Communist parties and individuals did begin to explore connections with the church at this time. Some even went too far. Several communist authors, such as Roger Garaudy and Ernst Bloch, ended by being expelled from the party after beginning to be interested in Christianity. But a warming up was evident and even officially sanctioned in some countries.

Simultaneously many persons within the church—even at high levels of the establishment—began to search for possible relationships with Marxism. Again, motivation is very difficult to judge, but some were certainly influenced by a growing realization that there are different sorts of Marxism and that it is important to recognize them in order to judge them according to their relative connection with atheism or totalitarianism. From *Mater et Magistra* (1961) to *Gaudium et Spes* (1965) to *Octogesima Adveniens* (1971), official Catholic doctrine accepted an ever more open realization of the Marxist heterogeneity.

This insight is, of course, correct. Indeed, there are not only different sorts of Marxism but outright schisms in both the movement and the ideology. Several Communist parties have their own politics and are moving apart from each other. Today there is a Russian orthodox branch, a Chinese Maoist branch, a Yugoslav branch, a Trotsky branch, and several leftist branches (*gauchistes*). (It can be shown that this political separation is based on the diverse possible interpretations of Marx.) There are also several ideological movements, independent of the practice of the various parties, which are trying to rediscover the authentic Marxian inspiration—for instance the Frankfurt School (Horkheimer, Habermas and, in a way, Marcuse). Finally, in France, Italy, Portugal, and Latin America, there are several Social Democratic parties that regard themselves as Marxists.

Christians and Marxism. Vatican II opened the way to dialogue with any of the different Marxisms willing to participate. The first important and public result of the new openness was the Salzburg Encounter in 1965, which included about 240 professors from European universities. Since then, dialogues and encounters have become normal events.

Although these dialogues have had limited reach, it would be false to conclude that they have been ineffective in changing Marxist ideology or practice. Garaudy's evolution during the last ten years is an astonishing symptom, and there is no doubt that such cases are numerous. The influence on the parties themselves is less visible. But how could the strength of the gospel not be felt in the long run?

On the other side, several Catholic and Protestant theologians have also changed their way of interpreting the chief Marxist categories, such as class struggle. These theologians reject the elements of Marxist theory and practice that are incompatible with faith and charity, but accept the other elements that they find compatible. They reject atheism or totalitarianism, but accept the criticism of capitalism, the class struggle as a way to revolution, the criticisms of alienation and other aspects.

Is it truly possible to make such separations within the Marxist ideology? Certainly a number of Catholic priests, Protestant ministers, and laypersons from several churches accept some kind of Marxism. They have found supporting arguments in Althusser's philosophy. Is Althusser's interpretation of Marx solid enough to justify a change in the ideology and practice of the church? The debate does not seem to be over yet.

It is interesting to note, however, that most Christian Marxists do not accept the orthodox parties and prefer Maoism and leftism. Practically speaking, Christian Marxism is a kind of leftism. Most Christian youths who join Marxist movements end by forming their own leftist parties (as in Chile) or working with existing leftist parties. It seems that something in leftism appeals to the young as well as to Christians. Leftism is a kind of utopian Marxism (if the expression is not contradictory). It is hard to see how it would ever be able to seize power and keep it. It has not succeeded in any country.

(Even in Cuba a leftist Marxism had to yield to Soviet orthodoxy after a long resistance.) Leftism thus remains on the level of utopia; in other words, it does not enter into political reality. It is possible that this utopian feature is the special interest for the young Christians who have joined Marxist movements.

Far more numerous than Marxist Christians are the Catholics who are members of socialist movements. In practically all the Latin and German countries, in Great Britain and its former dominions, and in several African countries, their number is constantly increasing. Most of them remain hesitant about establishing connections with Marxism, although they are at least as determined as the communists in their search for economic and social revolution.

The Challenge of Marxism. The Marxist problem cannot be solved by denying it or passing over it in silence. Freedom from Marxism can be achieved only by solving the problems that Marx pointed out. He did not create these problems and no one can say they are solved. Any Christian scholars or activists who discover their existence (which means any who meet social reality) will meet Marx and Marxism.

For theologians the encounter with Marxism led immediately to the necessity of defining Christianity with regard to revolution. Marx's work, according to all possible interpretations, is above all a theory and a practice of revolution. Given present historical reality, such theory is an unavoidable challenge to the new theology.

Change in Theological Method: Theology and Ministry

Theological method has undergone great changes in recent years, but only one aspect of this change is essential to this study. The classical idea of theology was that it was a system of ideas, propositions, and statements, which was a true representation of God's revelation, a good translation of God's word. It supposed that in God there are a collection of logically connected ideas, that God communicated this system to human beings by means of the Bible, in which Divine Providence adapted the extremely abstract thought of God to the weak understanding of primitive peoples, and that theology comes back to the abstract divine ideas. Understood this way, theology is a system of ideas, universal and equally valuable in all times and places.

The new theology has a new understanding of itself and, therefore, a new subject. Its aim is no longer to discover a system of ideas, but to enlighten and judge the action of Christians. It seeks to connect God's word to the present circumstance in order to express what God's word is saying to human beings who are engaged in concrete processes. The rationale for this change is the new understanding that Christ did not come to teach a system of ideas but only to help humankind to be saved. Christ's word means concrete actions in the present time. Knowing abstractly that we must love our brothers and sisters helps us very little. It is more important to know what love means in our concrete society and how we can love amid our actual conditions of social life. The subject of theology is not Jesus' words in their universal sense, but their meaning historically revealed by the Spirit at this moment.

The world is in a revolutionary period. The Spirit has to tell human beings what Jesus' words mean for those who have to act in this revolutionary world. That is theology now.

THE FUTURE OF THE THEOLOGY OF REVOLUTION

The theology of revolution is the result of the convergence of the six movements just discussed. Actually nobody is working exclusively on this theology of revolution. It is simply an abstract reference of many authors, the common perspective of the theologians who have been led by these six factors. But these authors do not intend to dedicate their lives to a theology of revolution. They met each other around the theology of revolution and continued their journey.

What are the possible directions of such a journey? Probably the easiest way to suggest these is to examine the present situation of the world and society, in itself and in relation to the church. After all, since any theology must be considered within the actual circumstances of its development and the real life of those it is intended to serve, it is necessary to examine in some detail the political, social, and religious realities of the present day—particularly those of Latin America, the area that this author knows best.

This analysis may be sufficient to suggest to the reader the probable directions of the revolutionary theologians, at least in the near future. (My own brief general conclusions will form the conclusion of this book.)

3

Understanding the Present Condition of the Catholic Church in Latin America

In considering the theology of revolution, there are two reasons for examining the history of the Catholic Church in Latin America. First, no one can understand the goals and methods of the theology of liberation (or any theology) without knowing the social and political context in which it was developed, and no one can grasp this context without knowing something of the antecedents that created it.

Second, although every situation is different, and the experience of one place and time is never duplicated exactly in another, many of the factors already noted as leading to the theology of revolution generally are very specifically present in Latin America. Some have been present for centuries. These factors include such phenomena as the perennial dualism in the church—being simultaneously for the establishment of power and for the revolution; the ravages of colonialism and the resultant problems of development; the influences of many of the ideologies developed in Western Europe in the nineteenth and twentieth centuries—liberalism, Marxism, Christian Democracy, and the newest: the national security state.

Once we have an overview of the Latin American situation, we will progress, in the following chapters, to more specific analysis of the political situation, society, and the church as both an institution and the people of God.

HISTORICAL ANTECEDENTS

The Colonial Period

One key to understanding the Catholic Church in Latin America is the realization that it has had a basic ideological split from the earliest days of

50

Western colonization. This split was an example of the eternal division in the church—legitimatizing the establishment or supporting justice for the people—but it was particularly specific and important in Latin America.

In the beginning the problem was expressed as what attitude to adopt toward the Indians. All Spanish and Portuguese society was divided on this issue, and the church followed suit. The division marked the whole history of the colonial empires; it was the main issue from the time of the discovery to the time of independence. Two parties represented two opposed ideologies—the "mystical" theory and the "realistic" theory.

According to the mystical theory, the Indians were persons and had human rights like the Spaniards or the Portuguese. They were also citizens of the kingdom and had the same rights as all its citizens. Consequently, they could not be obliged to compulsory labor, have their land conquered by arms, or be converted to Christianity through violence. This theory was adopted by the Crown, some of the royal officials, some of the bishops, a few clerics (both secular and in religious orders), and, above all, by the Jesuits and the Dominicans. (The Jesuits have been especially indefatigable supporters of the Indians and defenders of their rights.)

On the other hand, according to the realistic theory, the Indians were persons of a lower rank; their mental condition made them unable to achieve a civilized life. Unaided, they could not learn how to work, to reach civilization, or to lead a real social life. Moreover, the only effective way of teaching them how to work, to lead a civilized life, or to transmit culture was by means of coercion and violence. Neither would they ever accept the Christian religion willingly; conversion by arms was the single method they could understand. Thus, by submitting them to compulsory work, the conquerors were giving them the best possible education; they were also introducing them into Christian civilization. This theory was supported by almost all the civilian white population, by some royal officials, and by most clergy and members of religious orders (except the Jesuits and Dominicans).

It is noteworthy that the opposition between the two theories has continued until now. Even today, the traditional aristocracy still thinks that the lower classes are persons of a lower rank, unable to lead a normal human life unaided, and are to be led by the social elites. Thus, the majority of Indians, Negroes, and Cholos (half-breeds) are practically without the common rights of citizenship and are defended or supported only by a few intellectuals and clergy, who still represent the mystical theory or party. The division of the first colonial era has never been overcome; until now this division has been the underlying structure of society and culture in Latin America. And the consequent split of Christianity into two parties—the "realistic" supporters of the elites and the "mystical" supporters of the masses—has been the primary factor of division inside the Catholic Church. It has carried through all the years of theoretical independence, influencing society under the second (British) empire and the third (American) empire of today.

The present church is also a divided church. The roots of each of its divisions have never changed: the action of those who are fighting for social change is based on the same reasons as were used in the past; the agreement of others with the aristocratic elites is also based on the same theory as in the past. The latter firmly believe that the Latin American people are not yet prepared to receive a democratic way of life.

In considering various influences on the Latin American society and church, it is important not to forget this basic division.

The Liberal Period

In Latin America, the triumph of liberalism began with the suppression of the Jesuits (1759 in Brazil, 1767 in Spain, and 1773 in Rome by Pope Clemens XIV). It continued with the theoretical independence of the colonial countries in the first half of the nineteenth century, reached its climax with the liberal revolutions around 1850, and dominated state and society up to the world crisis of 1929.

The definition of liberalism in Latin America is important here, for it is quite different from that used in either the United States or Europe and it represents the challenge of church and state. In Latin America, liberalism does not mean separation of religion from politics, as in the United States; neither is it the European concept of autonomy and mutual tolerance, as Montalembert expressed it. Liberalism in Latin America means control of the church by the state and its reduction to a mere religious function for the poor people of the haciendas. Free-thinking is reserved to the upper classes, but religion is regarded as necessary for women and the poor. The liberals intend to limit and control religion, but they do not give up its social influence. Therefore they attempted to form clergy submissive and linked to the urban dominating classes, and they succeeded almost completely.

In Latin America, liberalism also means connection with foreign imperialism (England and the United States), defense of the privileges of the urban classes, total oppression of the peasants (especially the Indians), and robbery of their lands by the aristocracy. Liberals and landlords have a strong agreement and are often the same people; the victories of the liberals have been victories of the landlords. In short, the liberals have continued the tradition of the "realistic" party.

Within the church, control by liberals means unity and often suppression of the mystical party, the supporter of the Indians. So liberation or autonomy of the church means a resurrection of the mystical party and renewed internal division.

It is important to understand that the separation or differentiation of church and state, such as exists in the United States, has never been the aim or goal of the Catholic Church in Latin America. The struggle for autonomy or separation has sometimes been a tactical way of liberating the church from the control of the oligarchy—nothing more. The Catholic Church in Latin America was a political church from the outset, and it has never stopped acting in this role. Its permanent alternatives are: submission of the church to the state and use of the church for the "realistic" objectives of the state; or submission of the state to the church and use of the instruments and power of the state by the church to achieve its "mystical" aims. Autonomy is no more than a step toward the transformation of the state to serve the mystical-social ideas of one party of the church.

So the real division within the church is between the party searching for the integration of the state within the Christian liberation of the people and the party searching for integration of the church within the political project of the aristocratic elites.

In the present condition of Latin American society, the situation cannot be other. The radical dualism of the whole society is the chief challenge the church cannot avoid. For the church, the chief issue concerning the connection of Christianity and the world is how to relate to the state. Problems of economic or social or cultural transformation are secondary.

Until very recently, there has been a kind of agreement between the church and the poor masses of Latin America, no matter which party—realistic or mystical—was dominant. During both colonial and liberal periods, the rural masses relied on the church as their sole protector. True, the clergy often betrayed the confidence of the peasants, but with or without the clergy, Christianity has been the ultimate refuge of the oppressed. Any free church of the future should not remain indifferent to such a heritage. ⋅

To the liberals, the alliance between the masses (the Indians) and the church is the best proof of the "barbarian" nature of Christianity. For the church, such an alliance is the starting point of any pastoral strategy. The present history of Latin America cannot be explained outside this perspective.

LATIN AMERICA IN THE TWENTIETH CENTURY

Foreign Political Factors

Several new political systems have appeared in the world during the twentieth century. As we shall see in the following oversimplified sketch, such systems have entered into the political history of Latin America and their presence has confronted the aims of the church. Foreign political systems have conditioned history in Latin America, but they have not made it. The specific condition of the continent has led to a specific Latin American evolution unlike that of any other area of the world. The problem of church and state has been influenced by the new political systems, but it has not been replaced by any new basic problem.

Marxism. In all the Latin American countries after World War II, a Communist party was created, either by transformation of a previous Socialist party or by formation of a new political unit. But the Marxist parties have exerted a role of importance in only two special cases: in Cuba, after Fidel Castro came to power, because of the mistakes of American politics which obliged him to rely on Soviet support; and in Chile, under Allende's minority government of the Popular Unity coalition from 1970 to 1973. Generally, political evolution in Latin America has been and remains until now independent from the Communist parties, although political Marxism (and more specifically, the fight against it) has had some temporary influence in certain cases.

In Latin America, as in other countries all over the world, the strategy of the church is totally anticommunist. After World War II, especially during the cold war, the warnings of Pius XII against communism had deep repercussions in Latin America. Before the International Eucharistic Congress in Rio de Janeiro (1955), the pope called for a general movement of the Catholic churches of the rich nations to send manpower and money to manage a strong counteroffensive against communism in Latin America. But the lack of a serious and imminent communist danger has made these warnings relatively secondary in the whole political management of the Latin American churches. Anticommunism has sometimes limited the church's action of protecting the poor; when there is some danger of collaboration between the social protest of the church and Marxist agitation or propaganda, the whole institutional system of the church limits such protest. In other words, Marxism fosters the unity of the church against the left and paralyzes any leftist trends within it. But as soon as the Marxist danger is removed, the chief division—between the supporters of mysticism and of realism—reappears.

The National Security System. Fascist movements, based on the Italian, German, or Spanish model, were created quite early in some Latin American countries, especially in Brazil and Chile. But for many years their role was neither relevant nor important; they were mere imitations of European models, mostly supported by German or Italian immigrants.

Then, after World War II, a new but similar political system and ideology came out of the United States and spread all over the continent, chiefly under the armed forces. This is the national security system, proselytized primarily by the Pentagon, the Central Intelligence Agency (CIA), and other American organizations. Its principles are: integration of the whole nation into the national security system and the policy of the United States; total war against communism; collaboration with American or American-controlled business corporations; establishment of dictatorship; and placing of absolute power in the hands of the military. Supported by the United States, especially after the Rockefeller report was issued in 1967, the national security system has come to dominate most Latin American nations and is likely to conquer the rest very soon.

Such a system tends to align the church against the totalitarian state. The movement toward unity varies according to the strength of the local rightist dictatorship, but unquestionably it is getting stronger and stronger throughout the Latin American church. The reason for this phenomenon is simple: the need to defend and protect the oppressed peoples tends to unify the various trends in the Catholic Church.

Christian Democracy. Christian Democracy has had a little influence in Latin America, chiefly after World War II, when it was playing such a large part in shaping the new Europe of the Common Market and the management of most West European countries. Christian Democratic parties were formed in some Latin American countries, though not in Brazil, Mexico, Argentina, or Colombia. They were not very successful, reaching power only one time each in Chile and Venezuela (under Eduardo Frei and Rafael Caldera). There was also an unsuccessful attempt to create a Christian Democratic international movement. But generally the proper conditions for such a movement did not exist; the political structure of most nations did not allow a Christian Democracy relevant to the Latin American problem or parallel to more properly Latin American movements.

The main problem was that Christian Democracy presupposes the unity of Catholics; such a unity is not possible in Latin America. This unity presupposes that the chief social problems have already been solved, which has certainly not happened in Latin America. In Chile, Christian Democracy was possible in 1964 when almost all Catholics united around Eduardo Frei because of the imminent Marxist danger of an electoral victory by Allende and the absence of a conservative candidate. After Frei's election, the unity vanished.

Specific Religious Factors from Outside

The Social Encyclicals. The social encyclicals *Mater et Magistra* (1961), *Pacem in Terris* (1963), and *Populorum Progressio* (1967) had a deep impact on Latin America. They helped the Catholic protest movement against social domination, increased the church's inner division, and strengthened the leftist trends. The encyclicals did not create the social movement, but they provided it with many strong arguments. They offered the mystical party authority and defense against the conservatives. After these encyclicals the mystical movement seemed to represent the Catholic orthodoxy—at least as long as it remained distant from any Marxist inflection.

The social encyclicals also lent orthodoxy to "aiding" the development of underdeveloped nations. By implication they also supported aid from the European and North American churches to the Latin American church as a kind of aid to development. The results, mostly negative, are well known: bureaucratic staffs within the Latin American church, conflicts between line and staff, disagreements over aid distribution, and so on.

Vatican Council II. Most social movements in Latin America (those in Brazil, Chile, Colombia, and so on) were born before Vatican II, but were confirmed by it. During the Council all the Latin American bishops learned from their colleagues that a change was necessary, that the developed world did not accept the idea of the Latin American church remaining passive in the face of such circumstances. This gave rise to a general disposition to some change. What had once been regarded as a conservative but proper position soon became intolerable. The Council provided the most advanced bishops (Manuel Larraín, Helder Camara, Marcos McGrath, and so on) with international support. Vatican II, however, did not have enough strength to lead the Latin American evolution; it was able to supply some help, but it could not manage a strategy for the national churches. After the Council, the Latin American bishops returned to their own problems and history.

The Influence of Some Social Factors

Latin America, like all areas of the world, has been influenced by the scientific, technical, and economic development of Western society. The challenges of industrialization, demographics, and urbanization have claimed the attention of church and society in Latin America since the beginning of this century. But the Latin American way of entering the modern industrial age is very different from the way of other areas. No one can understand the influence of modernization on the church and Christianity in Latin America without seeing the particular way and particular challenges of the continent. Some of the same social factors that have been active all over the world have operated in Latin America, but they have produced results related specifically to the Latin American situation. It is necessary to look at these specific expressions of modernization because the Latin American church has been influenced much less by universal factors than by their specific local influence.

The Economic Crisis of 1929. For Latin America, the great economic crisis of 1929 meant a breakdown of the "second colonial pact" that had been established in the second half of the nineteenth century, first with England and then with the other capitalist powers. This breakdown opened the road to the beginning of economic, social, cultural, and political autonomy, as well as the beginning of industrialization; consequently a whole series of social changes was put in motion. Politically, the breakdown of the colonial pact meant the end of the silent control of societies by the traditional oligarchies and the traditional agreements between the liberal and conservative parties. The end of the colonial pact began a period of political instability and a search for a new political equilibrium. For the church it meant an awakening after the long sleep of the liberal period, the end of a long period of powerlessness. The end of the second colonial pact was the time for the church to return to political life as a specific unit, independent from the state.

The Decolonization Movement, 1947–1960. World War II influenced Latin America much less than the decolonization that followed the war. The breakdown of the colonial empires (English, French, Dutch, and Belgian) and the access of more than fifty new nations to independence had two results. The first, which was worldwide, was the disappearance of the concept of civilization as primarily Western European civilization (which had been the basis of the colonial system), and the appearance of the idea of development (with its corresponding concepts of underdevelopment and the development process). Thus began a new idea of international relations. Second, Latin America learned to consider itself as part of the underdeveloped world. Once it did so, the decolonization movement supported Latin American nationalism, criticism of the colonial situation, and aspirations for a second and real independence. Latin America awoke to the idea of a new independence process and tried to express its own personality with the help of the development theory.

At the same time, the church became aware of its own identity: it began to feel itself different from the European or North American churches. The development concept was used by the Catholic Church to foster its own self-consciousness. The mystical party of the church used this new identity as a support for its own program. Many connections were formed between the nationalist movement and the mystical part of the church; inside the nationalist movement, the church found a way of situating the defense of the poor.

The Third Colonial Pact. In the mid-1960s a new agreement arose between the traditional Latin American oligarchies and a new colonial power—the multinational corporations, especially the American-based ones. The United States ceased promoting democracy; the oligarchy reconquered the power in its own nations with the help of the multinational corporations. The agreement between oligarchy and international corporations promoted and continues to maintain the military dictatorships all over Latin America. The myth of total war against communism hides the awareness of an opposition between developed and underdeveloped countries. The ideology of the new colonial pact uses the vocabulary of development, while avoiding any contagion of nationalism or independence.

For the church, the new colonial pact has meant a violent eviction from political action and a new attempt to integrate itself within the project of the oligarchy. But the church is now stronger than in the past. The struggles of the new oligarchical systems, even though based on the violent power of sophisticated armies, are not as easy to win as they once were. Sometimes the violence of the state has to give way before a total opposition by the church.

Crisis of Violence in the West. The crisis of violence by Western youth reached Latin America in 1967–1968, a time that corresponded to the end of the nationalist, democratic, and development period, and to the beginning of the new colonial power. In some ways the "violence movement" precipitated the advent of the new military dictatorships. Violence (as exemplified in the guerrilla movement) showed the irrelevance of democratic liberal institutions and prepared the way for authoritarian governments of the armed forces.

A few members of the church were connected with revolutionary movements that got involved with the prevalent violence. As a result of the crisis of violence these individuals left the church. Nevertheless the oligarchy still invokes their example as a powerful argument for control of any social action of the church; any social action is suspect of being used by violent revolutionaries. Indeed, the chief excuse of the oligarchy is simply Marxist infiltration into the churches. (The fact, of course, is that the Catholic Church has never stopped being primarily anticommunist.)

THE RECENT EVOLUTION OF THE CHURCH
IN THE LATIN AMERICAN STATES, 1955-1975

The States

The main issue of the twentieth century in Latin America is the awakening of movements of independence and of liberation of the people from both oligarchy and colonialism. Such an awakening has, of course, led to a long conflict between the traditional powers and the liberation movement. A precursory event was the Mexican revolution in 1910, after which Mexico became the refuge of many popular leaders from all the Latin American countries. But the liberation movement spread only after the second colonial pact was broken by the world crisis of 1929.

In Latin America, liberation movements are usually called populist movements. All of them have followed the main lines of the program of the first, the APRA (Alianza Popular Revolucionaria Americana) of Peru, which was founded in 1924 in Mexico by the exiled Peruvian leader Víctor Haya de la Torre.

Haya de la Torre's program consisted of five points: (1) action against American imperialism; (2) the political unity of Latin America; (3) progressive nationalization of the land and industries; (4) internationalization of the Panama Canal; and (5) solidarity with all the oppressed peoples.

Other populist programs express or order their goals slightly differently, but they are all an attempt to join the oppressed classes with the new progressive and modern classes; to form a coalition of peasants, workers, intellectuals, and "national bourgeoisie" against the traditional oligarchy and its foreign allies. The method proposed is threefold: nationalization of foreign manufactures, mining, public services, the land (agrarian reform); modernization of life and industrialization by creation of national industry; and social reform and collective social conventions.

The first phase of populism occurred in the late 1930s (Irigoyen in Argentina, Vargas in Brazil, Pedro Aguirre Cerda and the Frente Popular in Chile, and so on). However, the true expansion of populism came after World War II (Vargas, Kubitschek, and Goulart in Brazil, 1955–1964; Perón in Argentina, 1943–1955; Ibáñez in Chile, 1952–1958; Frei in Chile, 1964–1970; Rojas Pinilla in Colombia; Paz Estenssoro in Bolivia; the list could go on and on).

During the 1960s the inner tensions of the populist coalitions, the contradictions of the whole Western system, and the natural radicalization of a more permissive society led to a more radical trend in the populist movement. Its adherents attempted to apply their programs more radically and there was instant reaction, nationally and internationally. For example, Allende's campaign and government in Chile, Goulart's government in Brazil, and General Torres's government in Bolivia provoked agitation urged on by the traditional oligarchy and the traditional imperialist interest. Each country knew a short period of social troubles and then began a new imperialist period. In spite of the growth of the populist movements, neither the oligarchy nor the foreign corporations had ever lost their power: they could rely on military force. Now with the help of the third colonial pact, the traditional elites have returned to their former leadership. Coups in Brazil in 1964, Argentina in 1966, Uruguay in 1970, Bolivia in 1970, and Chile in 1973 have rendered the populist movement almost completely powerless.

The Catholic Church During This Evolution of the States

The first authors who made an attempt at understanding the church in the present time were European or American. Unfortunately, when they considered the Latin American church, they projected their own problems and categories onto it. They wondered whether what occurred in Latin America was a development process or a revolution; they wondered whether the church was promoting development or sharing a revolutionary process. Such questions are, in reality, alien to Latin American history.

The current behavior of the church and Christians in any particular area can be understood only in the context of their own past and the way in which various processes are unfolding in those particular countries. There are many social and cultural factors at work all over the world, and they produce some unexpected or unusual results in the particular conditions of a given area. This is especially true in Latin America.

Anticommunism is and has long been present within the Catholic Church of Latin America—except in some insignificant factions. But the present evolution of the Latin American church cannot be explained only by considering its anticommunism.

On the other hand, there are some Catholic groups in Latin America that are interested in modernization and development (in the American sense of the words). But generally the Catholic Church there does not deal with development and modernization. Its aspirations are totally different.

The church in Latin America is not opposed to a revolution (provided this revolution is not communist), but it does not propose to prepare it or lead it. The last twenty years have proved this reality. The church is ready to follow a revolutionary process, but is not going to promote it.

Nevertheless, the church has changed during these years. It has taken a relevant place within the social change of the Latin American society. How can we understand such a change?

Certainly we cannot understand the present process of the church from any one of its components. It is necessary to look at their development historically. There have been four stages since 1955.

Development Concern, the First Stage. At first, the church entered into the whole concern about development as development was determined and defined by European and American authors. Sharing the process of development appeared to be a new task for the church; nevertheless, as the Latin American church conceived it, development was a form of promotion of the oppressed classes, and hence very much within its tradition.

At first, following the ideas suggested by international ideology, the Latin American church asked for foreign aid in order to create social works for development. But after a few years it came to understand that any real "popular promotion" must be based on the active participation of the oppressed themselves. Consequently, it undertook the task of "popular education." Conscientization became the focus of the educational work promoted by the church, and it usually collaborated with populist governments. Indeed, collaboration sometimes reached the point of strong mutual support (for example, in Brazil, 1960–1964; in Chile, 1964–1970). (In such situations, the cooperation between church and state did not mean integration or instrumentalization or contamination of the church by secular goals. Both church and government were liberating the oppressed people; they had no problem with their coalition.)

Radicalization, the Second Stage. Although this collaboration for development appeared to be proceeding well, within a few years it ran into problems. It looked as if it were leading to widespread radicalization. In fact, only a few priests and laypeople entered the radical movements (including the guerrilla movement with Camilo Torres). But the excessive declarations and actions of a few extremists brought about a broad reaction of the majority, led by the representatives of the traditional oligarchy. The church suffered an inner contradiction, or split, and its mystical sector was soon almost defeated. It was attacked by both the reactionary majority and the radical minority. To the reactionaries it had to justify its sharing in the development process, which now looked suspicious. In this it was often unsuccessful, and the anticommunist campaign succeeded in paralyzing many development works and liberation enterprises.

The radicals, on the other hand, wanted to go much further than development and even liberation. For them, Cuba was the only model. But for the Catholic majority, the condition of the Cuban church became the strongest argument against revolution, increasing fear and revulsion of any radicalization. For the early radicals of this stage, Cuba had been the chief sign and model. But for the Latin American church, as indeed for all the populist governments, Cuba became the cause of the worst troubles, the source of strength for both reactionaries and revolutionaries. The populist governments were not prepared to resist this radical pressure; they could not prevent military coups that were aided by national and international anticommunism.

In short, during this period, the church (and society) was no longer separated into two but into three: radicals, reactionaries, and what, for want of a better term, can be called mild reformers.

Socialist Experiments, the Third Stage. As radical pressure grew for new political systems, the church agreed to collaborate with certain experiments, like Chile's Allende government and that of Argentina after Peron's return, as long as it remained independent from specifically Marxist systems. In other words, the national church accepted the status quo but did not itself undertake the task that the new political and social system had set for itself, nor support it explicitly. The most advanced sector of Catholics, clerics as well as laity, did support the experiments, and they were tolerated by the official church as long as they avoided communism. But some programs— such as Christians for Socialism—were condemned, at least for clergy, because of their close connections with Marxist ideology. In this way, Christian radicals were isolated from the whole church, and only the breakdown of Allende's experiment prevented them from being expelled from the church. The church did express a general approval of the populist program of the socialist governments' experiments—nationalization of foreign corporations, land reform, nationalization of the trusts, and so on. But this was not enough for the radicals—and too much for the conservatives.

Military dictatorships, the fourth stage. The number of real radicals was never large enough to support socialist governments, and soon the fears of the conservatives toppled them, replacing them with governments of the right, run by the military. In the beginning, the church was seduced by the new systems' program seeming so favorable to it. Even today the military governments offer the church a more important place in society than it has had or imagined since Independence. But most clerics and lay people quickly discovered that this offer is mere illusion, that social status and privileges were to be paid for by total submission to the purposes of the totalitarian state. The upper classes have accepted this "golden slavery," but as a whole the church has preferred to seek a real autonomy. In Brazil, for example, after seven years of military dictatorship, the majority of the episcopal conference arrived at a clear statement of opposition to such policy.

Analysis. In short, the church has conveyed its message in four quite different ways, to four different societal contexts in Latin America since 1955. But, although they are different, there is certainly a deep inner continuity among these four insights as well as a continuity with the Latin American church in preceding centuries.

This continuity underlying different insights is important. It shows the Latin American church has simply resumed its traditional mission. As in the past, it is divided. And since the basic problems remain the same as in the past, the divisions are the same. The realistic part of the church is still allied with the aristocratic elites. The mystical part of it has resumed its mission of defending the oppressed against the oligarchy. The divisions are the same although their expression is somewhat different—that is simply a sign that the church is adapting itself to the conditions and stages of the present century.

Indeed, it is interesting to note that during two of the stages—the second and third—the church became divided into three factions, rather than its traditional two. In both cases this led to a lessening or defeat of the mystical movement. On the other hand, the first stage (and today's fourth stage) promoted the old dualism and allowed the mystics to be victorious within the church. During both of these periods the faithfulness of the church to its historical mission in Latin America gave rise to a double role of defending and proclaiming human rights and of supporting the economic rights of the poor masses against the elitists (even today, when elitism sometimes masquerades as "development").

Such a mission is much simpler than a modernization process or a revolution; it is more limited, but more permanent. The church understands that some modernization and industrialization are necessary in today's world, but in itself it has not touched this area by either its mission or its action. It has dealt with some of what Oscar Lewis calls the areas of the "culture of poverty"—first with the peasants (through promoting land reform), and second with the urban masses, the unemployed *favelados*.

It is important to understand, however, that the Latin American church does not conceive such work to be "development" in the European sense but a continuation of its mission to the masses. Development programs in Latin America are a process of assimilation of the upper classes into the developed nations' way of life so that the whole economy is dependent on the metropolis and directed to the interests and progress of the upper classes (who continue the historical role of the oligarchy). In Latin America there is no social context for, and consequently no possible program of, modernization, as there is in developed nations. Consequently, the problem does not exist for the Latin American church.

This is understood by almost all sectors and groups in the Latin American church today; there is a convergence of the episcopal documents, the priests' movements, the social welfare works, the lay movements, the main currents in the church, and even the radical minorities. They all are dealing with the underdeveloped sectors; however, their problem is not modernization but justice and bettering of the condition of the oppressed. In the sixteenth century, the church claimed justice for the Indians. Today the circumstances are different, but it continues to work to protect the "Indians."

4

The National Security System
in Latin America

THE CREATION OF THE NATIONAL SECURITY SYSTEM

No theology and no institutional church can be examined in a vacuum; they must be considered in the context of the political and social reality in which they exist and act. In Latin America today political and social reality means being part of the postwar American Empire and living under its farthest-reaching export—the national security state.

In 1947, the United States created two new political institutions which established a new pattern for the state and, in the long run, a new pattern for society. The National Security Council (NSC) and the Central Intelligence Agency (CIA), both established by the National Security Act, were organs invented to fulfill and further the new imperial role the United States had undertaken.

The NSC caused a radical change in the state's balance of power. More and more the Executive Branch, through this new agency, reserved for itself the initiative, direction, supervision, and responsibility for defense and foreign policy. The Congress—and even other departments of the Executive Branch —witnessed or rubber-stamped accomplished facts. Meanwhile, the CIA became a secret service that assumed (often illegally) the right to supervise the lives of citizens and officials and the right of intervention in foreign countries according to the secret interests of the United States—or more precisely, those of the National Security Council.

In recent years, Congress has indeed tried to recover its constitutional power against both institutions. Given the strong democratic traditions of the United States, one may hope it will be successful. But what is germane to this discussion is not the United States situation but the repercussions of these new institutions in Latin America.[1]

This is not simply a question of what the CIA has done (or not done) in the countries of Latin America or how the NSC has coerced or seduced them into following its policies. More important is the fact that the Latin American nations have copied the United States in creating similar institutions and have followed their ideology to its logical conclusions with devastating results. In most of these countries today there exists a National Security Council and a secret service like the CIA. For example, in Brazil in 1964, the National Security Council became the supreme and absolute power of the state. Since then, it has had the power to make or change the constitution—and to appoint or reduce to nothing the president of the republic; in short, all political policy now depends upon this council. The same thing happened in Argentina in 1966, and not long after in Uruguay, Bolivia, Chile, and other nations. And as these councils, which are basically military dictatorships, came to power, they organized duplicates of the CIA—the SNI (National Information Service) in Brazil, the DINA (National Intelligence Division) in Chile, and so on.

These new organizations had a more immediate and profound effect on the social lives of Latin America because these nations are quite different from the United States. Neither the national security councils nor the secret services in Latin America have to cope with the limits of constitutions or the reaction of a congress. There is no longer either a constitution or a functioning congress in most Latin American countries. Sometimes appearances are maintained, but they are only appearances. In Brazil, for example, there is a puppet congress that meets but has no power. The National Security Council and the SNI are able to determine events without any restrictions. This is true in most of the countries where the new institutions have replaced the former organs of the state. They are building a new pattern for the state wherein the traditional legislative, executive, and judicial powers are nothing but administrative services functioning under the real power—the new institutions.

Any institutions that have so changed society need an ideology, and the new institutions of the state have one. Although their ideology looks relatively modest in comparison with traditional philosophical systems (indeed, it is almost worthless from the philosophical point of view), its persuasive power is great, and we may not ignore it.

This ideology has no official name, but I call it the national security ideology because it is the ideology of the national security system, the new political system of today. This ideology has not yet been philosophically elaborated by its disciples, but since it covers virtually all individual and social activities of the nation and gives a new meaning to all human existence, it is universal and totalitarian enough to exclude any interference by another philosophy.

Since the national security ideology is behind that great United States export, the national security institutions, it is perhaps fitting that its main source and propagator is Washington's National War College, founded in 1948. The college's stated task is the political preparation of future members of the U.S. Joint Chiefs of Staff. But it also teaches the new ideology to civilians through the courses of the Industrial College of the Armed Forces, which are organized annually for a group of 100 to 125 important persons from various professions, and through its two-week "Seminars of National Security," which are organized in cities throughout the United States.[2]

Many Latin American countries have created their own educational institutions in imitating the American ones. Brazil founded, in 1949, its Escola Superior de Guerra, which prepares its armed-forces officers for the most important political missions in the state and also offers courses and short-term seminars to select civilians, all drawn from important social categories. In Chile, an Academia Superior de Seguridad Nacional was founded in 1975 for the same purposes.[3]

And thus the national security ideology is spread to those who are—or soon will be—putting it into practice.

EXPOSITION OF THE NATIONAL SECURITY IDEOLOGY

Like any ideology, the national security ideology must first be investigated apart from the institutional system that has its legitimization in it before we can attempt to consider it, theoretically or practically, from the point of view of Christianity.

The national security theory, like all ideologies, claims to be supported by evidence provided by several sciences. Actually, all ideologies do contain some elements of scientific knowledge. If they did not speak to some essentials of social reality, they would not be able to manipulate real persons or control real social situations. But ideologies contain that scientific knowledge within a mixture of irrational elements. Moreover, they choose their facts selectively and build a whole intellectual structure from partial truths.

It is this very partiality that allows ideologies to give their respective structures the appearance of universal value. Ideologies always seem more scientific than the sciences themselves because many persons mistake a logical structure made up of conceptual patterns for science; when a conclusion is rigorously logical, they believe that it is scientific knowledge. The truth is, of course, that if the human sciences remain faithful to the observation of facts, they have very few opportunities to offer any logical structures.

Moreover, the base sciences used by many ideologies are social sciences. And the social sciences, much more than the natural sciences, are to some degree ideological in themselves. In other words, they all assume an understanding of people and society from which they can never completely free themselves. This implicit assumption acts constantly on the ideology that makes it by influencing the selection of the subject matter to be investigated, by directing or twisting the perception of facts, and mainly by suggesting a methodology that always includes a value judgment as well as some plan for the future of humankind.

The national security ideology has chosen geopolitics and strategy as its privileged, or base, sciences. These are social sciences raised to the level of universal and comprehensive sciences, to which the national security ideology appeals for truth. This is particularly interesting because geopolitics and strategy are ideological to a considerably greater degree than any other social sciences, a fact that is immediately apparent upon adequate analysis. Consequently, these sciences merit a particularly thorough investigation of their underlying assumptions and options.

Geopolitics

Definitions. All authors point out how difficult it is to define geopolitics, and agree only that it lies somewhere between geography and political science. The definitions, therefore, are countless.[4] Most authors try to provide a definition conveying the idea that scientific objectivity and a complete lack of prejudice are inherent in geopolitics (as suit a true science). They try to hide its real nature, which is that of a political program. Historically, geopolitics has never been anything other than the legitimization of certain political programs by useful geographical data. In other words, geopolitics is the use of geography to rationalize a political program.

Which political programs it has been used for is important. These are suggestive of the subject of geopolitics, and, of course, the whole system depends on the selection of the subject.

The subject of geopolitics is the "states" as centers of power, geographically situated, conditioned by their situations, and permanently concerned about their continual rivalries. According to geopolitics, every state is a power dynamic that strives to defend itself against all other states and to expand to the outermost limits imposed by its geographical situation. Thus it may be said that geopolitics means the most thorough pursuit for maximum power for the state at any given time.

According to General Augusto Pinochet Ugarte, a former professor of geopolitics, geopolitics

is the science that studies the influence of geographical and historical factors on the life and evolution of the states, in order to arrive at political conclusions. It serves as a guide for statesmen in managing both internal and external politics and directs the military in preparing the National Defense and in working out strategy; for geopolitics makes it easier to forecast future events, provides a way to attain objectives, and consequently offers a means for the most suitable political or strategical policies.[5]

Another classical definition is that of the Geopolitics Institute of Munich, which played a relevant role in preparing the rise of nazism between 1923 and 1932:

Geopolitics is the science of the relations between earth and political processes. It is based on the fundamentals of geography, especially political geography, that is, the science of the political organism in space and at the same time of its pattern. Moreover geopolitics furnishes political action with the necessary weapons as well as with the orientation for political life as a whole. In this way geopolitics becomes an art, the art of conducting practical politics. Geopolitics is the geographical consciousness of the State.

Geopolitics is the theory of the state as a geographical organism.[6]

However, one must note that the last sentence is not a complete definition. It is necessary to add, "as a space-dominating organism," because the state is not present in space just in order to stay inside it, but in order to control it.

Basic Concepts. The definitions of geopolitics lead to its basic tenets. Obviously, the first concept of geopolitics is the state. To geopolitics the state is an "organism," a kind of superbeing with its own life; accordingly, it is born, grows, and can die like any organism. Most writers on geopolitics agree with the basic notion of Rudolf Kjellén, the Swedish founder of this science, who wrote that the state is a person with its own life, its own features, its own behavior, its own world of feelings and wishes, always competing and fighting with other states.[7] (In assigning all the human characteristics to the state, the theorist's first step is to identify the people with the nation, then the nation with the state, and finally the state with power.)

In this organism, according to General Golbery do Couto e Silva, chief spokesman of the Brazilian School, we have a synthesis "of Herder's organism, Hegel's idealism, Fichte's statism, and List's economic nationalism" (in short, all the devils of German idealism are indicated).[8]

Such a theory of the state means a political project: a plan of promoting the state as a purpose in itself. Theory and practical plan cannot be separated. Geopolitics takes both theory and plan as the starting point of its investigation; the subject to be studied is the possibility of achieving the plan of the state. (Of course, by speaking thus about the state, the authors are not referring to an abstract, fictitious state. There are several places in the world where such states were very well established in the past or can certainly be achieved at present. Consequently, a science that takes such states as the subject to be investigated makes a direct and important contribution to their propaganda and strategy.)

Which are the essential elements of the state? They are three: "a territory, a population, and the sovereignty."[9] Territory and population are, of course, static elements; the dynamic one is sovereignty. Territory and population are mere means serving sovereignty. Sovereignty is the absolute power that enables the state to use and take full, exclusive advantage of the means of territory and population. In order to maintain its sovereignty, the state holds something that is equivalent to a definition: power.

"Power" is the magic word that discloses the fascinating reality of geopolitics. It is the key word because geopolitics is the science of national power, its various forms of struggle, its history, its possibilities.[10]

What is power? Power is the ability of the state to make its own will reality.

Domestically, it is the ability to rule the population in such a fashion as to make the people the executors or the agents of the will of the state. In foreign relations, power is the ability of the state to submit other states to its will in order to achieve its national purposes.[11]

The history of geopolitics has meant nothing other than the glorification of power. Here is a revealing quotation from Kjellén:

All civilized life leans finally on power. Struggling is one of the basic aspects of life, and, consequently it is an element of any relationship between persons, groups, or states. In an international society, all coercive ways are allowed, including destructive wars. This means that the struggle for power may be identified with the struggle for survival and therefore the improvement of relative power conditions becomes the one task of prime importance for both the external and internal politics of the States. . . . In such a world, the states can survive only provided they practice power politics.[12]

If the state is an organism, no wonder it tends to grow. Growth is the law of all life. In the perspective of geopolitics, it is *Wille zur Macht*. "The interest, the feelings, the instincts, and especially the instinct for self-preservation, the will to grow up, the will to life and the will to power determine the life of the nation."[13]

Consequently, the state must try to conquer all the space it deems necessary for its security and for the development of its activities. From this imperative is deduced the basic concept of a *Lebensraum*. The conquest of *Lebensraum* is a law of geopolitics. Indeed, it can even be said that the actual subject matter of geopolitics is the laws of the conquest of *Lebensraum*, that it is the science related to the conquest of space in order to achieve the state's expansion. The authors study laws known as, for example, the laws of Ratzel, of Maull, Henning, Korholz, and so on. Two typical laws are:

All states want to extend their frontiers more and more: there is a necessity of expansion.

The impulse to extend its own space is one of the basic and most absolute laws of any state able to exist.[14]

Such a science makes use of the historical experience of the imperial states of the past. Indeed, such a science is actually the investigation and formulation of the means that such states used to conquer their empires. (In like manner, it might be possible to invent a "science" of the Mafia, a "science" of piracy, a "science" of smuggling, or a "science" of prostitution.)

As a matter of fact, geopolitics was born amidst Pan-Germanism. Its founder, Kjellén, was an ardent follower of the great German movement. Its theory was developed principally by the school of Munich, which was intimately bound with nazism in its ascendant period. The authors of geopolitics gathered and developed the dreams of the Pan-Germanist writers of the nineteenth century. Outside Germany, geopolitics became known in England through Sir Halford Mackinder, the theorist of the British Empire. In the United States, it was not widespread at first, although it was studied by authors such as Admiral Thayer Mahan, who established the theoretical bases for the American imperialism President Theodore Roosevelt was creating. Then, after World War II, geopolitics gained prestige and importance, as the United States developed its new military and security system and found it was badly in need of an ideology to back them. From the United States, geopolitics was transferred to the armed forces of Latin America (and to many other areas of the globe).

The inescapable question arises: What is the purpose of such a science in Latin America? The states able to respond to an imperial calling are few. It is true that Golbery's geopolitics devises a program of domination over not only all South America but the entire South Atlantic. But does the Brazilian government really intend to attempt to put that program into practice? Many factors point toward a permanent expansion of Brazilian power, at least throughout South America. However, one suspects that the other Latin American states—and even Brazil to a large extent—give geopolitical theories a purpose other than domination.

Remember that, thanks to its supposed imperative of national survival, geopolitics justifies and stimulates the foundation of absolute power. In actual practice, the absolute power of the new Latin American states is not intended to face other states, but rather, the people, the citizens who are to submit to and be involved in governmental programs.

Moreover, geopolitical writings teach that states are not able to remain isolated. For protection and growth, they must enter into partnership, into ever more powerful coalitions with other states. Geopolitics demonstrates and encourages rivalry and permanent struggle between the two world coalitions: the Eastern, or communist, world, and the Western, or "free," world. (This is today's expression of the opposition that Liddell Hart once showed between the continental Eurasian power and the world island. The tradition of total opposition can, in fact, be made to seem unbroken throughout history: Greece and Persia; England and Germany; now the United States and the Soviet Union.) Thus geopolitics justifies the integration of the Latin American states and their armed forces into the total strategy of the American armed forces.

And thus we arrive at the second most important geopolitical science: strategy.

Strategy

According to traditional concepts, strategy is the art of war, of preparing and conducting military operations. But the last few years have witnessed a major extension of this concept. Many persons are now making strategy the chief political science, a comprehensive science of the principles ruling all political knowledge. They have succeeded to the extent that strategy has acquired the rank of basic science from which other political and social sciences receive their principles, postulates, and criteria.

The Total Strategy Concept. General Golbery has shown that the stages of strategy change from a simple military science to a comprehensive one. He has also shown how this evolution corresponds to the evolution of political problems. The recent development of strategy is an attempt to follow and justify the metamorphosis of various societies into military dictatorships.[15]

The roots of the new strategy are to be found in the French Revolution and its idea of an "armed people." There began the decline of the old pattern of limited wars, "free plays for the princess," and the simultaneous creation of the new pattern of total war. The change, however, was not immediate and has gone through several stages of evolution.

The first true concept of total war was conceived by Erich Ludendorff, who based his opinion on the experience of World War I. Ludendorff's conception of total war seems mild to us today. To him it meant that war mobilized the whole material and human means of a nation, abolishing the traditional distinction between "civil" and "military." All citizens were soldiers and took part in the war. The entire wealth of a nation was meant for the war, so any distinction between state expenses and war expenses disappeared.

After Ludendorff, the idea of an even more total war appeared in theory and in practice. War extended to space. The World War II experience showed that the new warfare included the whole earth with all the peoples of the world. After World War II, the theorizers of the cold war abolished the idea of neutrality: there is and can be no neutral nation in modern warfare.

Finally, in the most recent stage of the evolution, war is perceived as continuing at all times. The idea of peace is abolished, and, in consequence, so is the traditional distinction between peace and war. All times are times of war. Peace is nothing more than the conventional name given to "the continuation of war by other means," according to a well-known parody of Clausewitz's famous sentence. All peoples are permanently in a state of war. This is a postulate fundamental to present-day Latin American politics, and fundamental to the politics of all the military governments based on the national security ideology and system.

According to this new idea of strategy, all politics is a politics of war. And today's peoples are indeed conditioned by the reality of war. Nothing in human existence is free from war. Consequently there is a superscience called "strategy." Planning military operations is only one part of this science; total war also demands an economic strategy, a political strategy, a psychosocial strategy, and so on.[16]

Basic Concepts of Total Strategy. The basic concept of a national strategy is the National Plan[17] (sometimes called the National Objectives[18]). The national plan is the synthesis of the national aims or aspirations plus the possibilities resulting from the actual conditions of world forces.[19] In general, the plan is "to be a Nation and to continue to be so." The survival of the nation is the absolute goal. National strategy intends to incorporate the whole nation into the national survival plan, to make it the total and unconditional object of each citizen's life. The idea of survival includes all that makes up the nation's essence. That which forms the essence of the nation is a national option, based on the corresponding national history, which is called national interest.

Nevertheless, when authors try to explicate the contents of this national interest, they cannot avoid repeating the platitudes and popular proverbs that refer to the "national soul." Actually, national interest is concentrated around the ability to survive against negative forces—in other words, to obtain national security. So, finally, the subject matter of the celebrated national plan is national security, which brings us full circle. The whole ideology becomes a theory of national security embodying a comprehensive set of purposes and ultimate meanings for political action, as well as for all personal action.

As Argentinian General Osiris Guillermo Villegas has said, the beginning and the end of politics is national security: "National politics is to be understood and determined from the point of view of National Interest and Security."[20] And the Argentinean National Defense Law decrees: "National Security is the condition in which the vital interests of the nation are shielded from any substantial interference or trouble."[21]

If the aim is national security, the means for achieving it is national power, another touchstone in the ideology.[22] Consequently, the immediate objective of any politics is the building up of national power. Without national power, national security cannot exist.

National power is the whole expression of all the means (political, psycho-social, economic, and military) available to the nation at any time to guarantee its national objectives.[23] All the means of a nation—including all the activities of all its citizens—are understood to be elements comprising one corporate national power. Thus, through national power, the national security state confers ultimate purpose on all the activities of the citizens and institutions of the country. National security is the final and unconditional point of reference for everything, the absolute necessity, the unqualified Good; national power is the radical characteristic or nature of all things.

Logically, then, the institutions that have been created to protect the national security, such as the National Security Council or the SNI, have jurisdiction not only over all persons and private associations or enterprises, but over all the services and offices of the state. The secret service becomes a superpower, almighty and omnipresent, which assures the strength and the primacy of national security at any time and place.

Of course, no nation can neglect economic development, but even this is always to be understood as a tool for national security.[24] Ultimately, in the national security ideology, economic development becomes the process by which the state may acquire more and better weapons to defend itself. This is perfectly logical within the ideology. In a technologically developed world, any handicap implies serious danger; some other nations might be able to accumulate more power. "We have to answer suitably the growing challenge of a changing world."[25] So, for the national security state, the image of development is one of competition among nations, all of which are trying to secure the most favorable conditions by means of technological progress and economic growth. In other words, development is the economic side of the war.

Development has also a second purpose within the national security ideology: providing social harmony. Without some degree of social harmony, internal order cannot exist. People who acquire more products will better appreciate the social order. Economic progress is a necessary condition for producing more and, consequently, for consuming and distributing more things. Thus economic development that leads to social harmony is a factor of internal security.[26]

Security and Persons. The secondary goal of development to promote social harmony suggests something of the relationship of security and persons within the national security ideology. The secret service should be able to prevent anything detrimental to national security, and this prerequisite sometimes produces actions against the behavior of some citizens. According to national security ideology, enemies are powerful and the consciousness of the masses is always receptive to infiltration. Therefore, all citizens are suspected of subversion, and it is appropriate to study them closely; this is the task of the secret service. But it should be a mistake to think the goal of security is always directed against the people. The secret service does not want to hamper all the activities of citizens. On the contrary, the national interest necessitates the satisfaction of some individual aspirations. The aspirations that the state will try to satisfy, however, are not to be chosen by the citizens themselves, because they might choose dangerous goods. All the private enterprises or aspirations of citizens are to be controlled by the intelligence service and submitted to the national security, which is everyone's supreme aspiration.

To "maximize National Power," according to General Golbery, is not possible without requiring sacrifices from citizens. "The primacy of National Security," he said, "imposes the dreadful weight of a radically destructive economy on the normal aspirations to development and welfare which are natural for all the people."[27] So within the ideology there is a kind of opposition between welfare and security. (Here Golbery was referring to Goering's saying, "Either butter or cannons.") On the other hand, security itself requires some minimum level of welfare, since when welfare is too low, the people are no longer interested in security and refuse to fight for it.[28] Consequently, the politics of national security has to recognize those limits.

The will of the state has to stop at the moment when the people are losing the will to live. Thus it would be a gross mistake to say that national security is absolutely contrary to the people's welfare.

The problem of individual freedom is solved the same way. There is a dilemma in choosing to provide the people with security or with freedom, and generally the national security ideology answers it by requiring the sacrifice of individual liberties. But antagonism has practical limits. The state can destroy itself by abolishing individual liberties completely; "slaves are bad soldiers."[29] Consequently, the state has to know the limits of citizen resistance; it has to search for the exact point to which its citizens will suffer loss of freedom without losing courage for working and struggling. It is not advisable to reduce individual liberties beyond this point.

Agents: The Elites

Given these basic concepts of the ideology at work in the national security state, who can be responsible for carrying out its total strategy? Who is able to conceive its national plan or objectives? Who can see to national security and create national power? Obviously, not the masses. The masses are sluggish, stupid, and passive. They are always liable to be "conned" by demagogues or fall victim to infiltration by subversives.[30]

Since the running of a national security state clearly requires "the capacity to make decisions energetically and reliably and to foresee with certainty and responsibility,"[31] only some elites are able to assume it. The elites have two parts to play: expressing the permanent objectives of the nation and educating the people.[32] First, they have to decide, and after that they have to convince the masses. They must have the "imagination and the will to convince the nation concerning the alternatives on evolution and development, their part in America, and their contribution in the space of the present and future world."[33]

Who are the elites in Latin America? They are the military. This is a necessity in Latin America based on two reasons not yet touched on here: the betrayal by civilians and the demands of the present war itself.

The Betrayal by Civilians. The management of the state by the military is not a necessary consequence of the nature of politics or the state as defined by the national security ideology. Rather, it results from special Latin American conditions. (To be more exact, in each Latin American nation it is thought necessary on account of some special characteristics of that nation, although actually these characteristics are the same in all nations.) In all the Latin American countries, the condition that has justified the military assuming power is the betrayal of the state by all the civilian elites. The civilians are seen to have sinned in two ways: by their demagoguery they have lost their credibility completely; by their inefficiency and inability they have led the country to the "brink of the abyss."

Concerning demagoguery, take, for example, the Chilean military junta's Declaration of Principles: "Owing to the long erosion, brought about in our country by many years of demagoguery, and the systematic destruction that since 1970 Marxism increased in all the aspects of national life, Chile's Armed Forces and other Forces, faithful to their classical doctrine and their duties toward the survival of the nation, had to take to themselves all political Power."[34] (Notice the inclusion of the two basic principles of the national security ideology: the fear of the destruction of the country and the question of survival.)

The second argument, "the brink of the abyss," was spelled out specifically in a letter sent out in 1975 by a director of the propaganda service of the Chilean government to all ecclesiastical houses in the nation: "The soldiers were pushed to take on a great responsibility to save the country and to rectify the vices which had led it to the abyss."[35]

The Argentinian Revolution's Act of 1966 said the same thing: "The worst management of public affairs by the present government, as the highest point of the manifold mistakes of the movements that preceded it during the latest decades, . . . brought the breakdown of the national spiritual unity. . . . "[36]

In Brazil, Marshal Poppe de Figueiredo, a highly respected figure in the armed forces, wrote: "Normally the Armed Forces have no recourse to this decisive argument . . . except in a time of national crisis, when the civilian elites fail or betray the country. Thus the military fill the vacuum left by politicians. By so doing they try to avoid the eventual political troubles that would divert the nation from its true way."[37]

The nature of the danger to the nation—as well as its importance—in the eyes of the military can be determined by the mode of intervention. The military do not wish to remedy a provisional sickness of the country by, for example, restoring the national constitution and allowing it to administer correctly the diverse powers of the state. They really think that the nation has been in serious danger from a very old sickness. Several generations of corrupt politicians tried to destroy the country. Now the task of the armed forces is to create the nation again. A true rebirth will take place by military salvation. The military are able to act metaphysically—they touch the national substance; they can regenerate the nation; they are the new founders of the national life. Therefore, they often call on the nation's founders as their witnesses. They place themselves on the same level as the founding fathers; they are the second founders of nation and state.

What gives them this ability to regenerate the nation? Nothing other than force and power. Their entire doctrine is based on their ability to create force and violence. The essence of the state is force and power. The military are in possession of power. Consequently, the military alone are able to give power to the state again. Within such a system, military force reaches the level of a metaphysical attribute: life is power, military power; the essence of being is violence. It is the old argument of Pan-Germanism, linked with some

Hegelian concepts, some intuitions proceeding from Nietszche, and, at bottom, Hobbes's political philosophy with its sublimation of violence.

Let me quote some expressions of this metaphysical aspect of force in the national security state. In Chile, the military junta announced:

The Armed and Order Forces will not set any term to their government control, because the task of morally, institutionally, and materially rebuilding the country calls for a profound and continuous action. Finally, it is important to change Chileans' mentality, . . . opening the road for the future Chilean generations, formed in the school of healthy civic customs.[38]

The Argentinean junta's Declaration of 1966 said:

The Armed Forces, interpreting the highest common interest, assumes the responsibility, not to be relinquished, of guaranteeing national unity and making general welfare possible, incorporating into the country the modern elements of culture, science, and technology. By so doing, they make a substantial change that raises the country to the place that it deserves, given the intelligence and human value of its inhabitants and the wealth with which Providence has endowed its territory.

Necessity of War. The other reason used by the national security ideology to justify military takeover of the entire control of the state is the seriousness of the present war. At this point geopolitics, total strategy, and military government meet. The present condition, according to the national security ideology, makes evident what geopolitics and strategy have been studying and perceiving all over the world: military government is necessary because the nation is involved in a total war.

Geopolitics shows how the present world is divided into two worldwide blocs or coalitions. All the Latin American nations, except Cuba, belong to the Western coalition, the "free world," and their survival as independent and free nations depends upon the victory of the "free world." Consequently, Latin American national security is identical with Western security, and especially with the national security of the United States. And it is the armed forces that integrate the whole nation into the security plan of the United States.

This radical subordination to American strategy is not being seen as a threat to the national security of the Latin American nations but, rather, as a guarantee of it. The doctrine of all the nations of the Southern Cone, from Brazil to Chile, is in agreement here. They have all taken up the Brazilian doctrine that the war against communism is the fundamental opposition in the present condition of the world. The survival of the nations is identical with their fight against communism.[39] They all ratify the thought included in the Declaration of Principles of the Chilean junta: "When facing Marxism, Chile is not neutral. . . . Consequently the present government does not fear or hesitate to declare itself anti-Marxist."[40]

The war against Marxism is an all-out war within the present definition of total war. The communist world is making (total) war against the West. The survival of the West compels the Latin American peoples to make war using all their resources. Their own survival can be achieved only by their total integration into the war against communism as led by the United States. (It is assumed that the United States, by its very ideology, is the leader of the West's total war, just as the Soviet Union is seen to be leading the war of the communist world.)

Only a military government is able to lead such a war. Experience shows that civilian governments are dangerous because they open the nation to its worst enemies: Marxist infiltration and extremist subversion. The enemy is not only—not even principally—outside the nation's frontiers. The enemy is inside the country; every citizen is potentially a Marxist, and thus an enemy. Consequently the war against Marxism is first a war against internal enemies. The chief task of the Latin American armed forces is the repression of communism inside the frontiers of their own nations. Such a task necessitates the seizure of all power and the control of all the services of the state.

Conclusion. What is this "West" that we have to protect by means of a war and a total national security dictatorship? Why does the defense of the Western world need to control the entire life of the state and its citizens? What is the meaning of this "West" that is so often invoked?

The ideology of national security sets three bases for Western civilization: science, democracy, and Christianity.[41] In setting priorities, the Argentinean military prefer the first of these elements; the Brazilian and Chilean, the second and third. But they all yearn for all three. They all praise democracy and Christianity with the most lyrical enthusiasm. According to their own declarations, the only purpose of their entire politics is the salvation of democracy and Christianity. They all want to create a new society based on Christian principles. Reading the Declaration of Principles of the Chilean junta, one has to weep tears of joy and wonder—surely no government in the modern world has ever had such a Christian purpose.

The tragedy (or comedy) is that this scientific, democratic, and Christian purpose is only imagination (or hypocrisy) and does not lead in any way to real political management. To protect democracy and achieve a Christian society, the most far-reaching dictatorship is established, a dictatorship that may be called the image of Hobbes's Leviathan, a dictatorship that has nothing to do with democracy or Christianity. A basic postulate of the ideology is that war and dictatorship are the means with which to establish democracy and Christianity. In actual practice, war and dictatorship never end; the promised utopia never does reach the level of concrete beings. The Declaration of Principles and all the similar statements will remain "future utopia" forever; dictatorship and war will remain the "present reality" forever. The armed forces will never want to relinquish the power that they have monopolized. They will never believe that the country is now sufficiently protected against its enemies, sufficiently regenerated, sufficiently free from corruption. Their ideology of national security contains nothing that is able to justify the end of the war; it does not even encompass a need to clear the way for a peaceful government.

The ideology of national security is generally called nationalism by its authors. But it is a radical, absolute nationalism. As General Golbery described it in his master book:

To be nationalist is to be always ready to give up any doctrine, any theory, any ideology, feelings, passions, ideals, and values, as soon as they appear as incompatible with the supreme loyalty which is due to the Nation above everything else. Nationalism is, must be, and cannot possibly be other than an Absolute One in itself, and its purpose is as well an Absolute End—at least as long as the Nation continues as such. There is no place, nor should there be, nor could there be place for nationalism as a simple instrument to another purpose that transcends it.[42]

Consequently, the nation takes the place of God. What happens then to the God whom the military elite claim they want to worship by establishing a "Christian society"? This Christian God is only a cultural symbol. In actual practice the action is commanded by no god other than the nation and national security, the unconditional goals of all citizens.

5

National Security and Christianity

The national security ideology contains a certain conception of the church and Christianity, and the political system based on it offers the churches collaboration of a sort based on this concept and other ideological tenets. In this chapter we will first examine what role the ideology offers to the church. After that we shall examine the reasons why the church cannot accept such a role. Finally, we shall analyze the ideology of national security in relation to the New Testament. (Note that this study is limited to the ideology, setting aside religious practice under the national security system.[1])

THE ROLE OF CHRISTIANITY
ACCORDING TO THE NATIONAL SECURITY IDEOLOGY

The authors of the national security ideology are not aware of any contradiction between their theories and Christianity. On the contrary, they generally believe that their ideology gives the church an important part in society, that in their state the church will have more leverage than in any other political system. And because they believe this, they are often scandalized by the lack of enthusiasm of some bishops, priests, and laypeople.

They think a general agreement between church and armed forces would be a firm support for the whole society, as well as the most favorable solution for both "powers." Specifically, they desire the collaboration of church and armed forces, the integration of both into one united national power, for two reasons: to fight communism and to build a new society.

The War Against Communism. According to the national security ideology, communism is the primary enemy of the church, since it intends to destroy Christianity and the church completely. Given the premises of the total-war concept, the primary opposition of the church should then be against communism. But in the eyes of these observers the church is unable to check its primary enemy by itself; it needs help. Consequently, the church should

79

agree to a collaboration with the national power, which has the same primary enemy. Only national power, represented by the armed forces and the military state, can offer the church sufficient protection. The church wants security, and power gives security. Moreover, national security and total strategy seek nothing other than saving Western Christian civilization. Since the aims of Christianity and national power are identical, since both want to protect the "West" against communism, why should they not collaborate?

This collaboration would not even involve a silent partnership for the church. According to national security ideology, the church could take a relevant part in the struggle; in fact, it can be said that its part is irreplaceable. The struggle against communism is, to a great extent, an ideological war. And clearly the collaboration of the church in such an ideological struggle would be a relevant contribution because the masses still listen to the church, and its influence is powerful enough to destroy the arguments of communist propaganda.

A New Society. According to the national security theory, the armed forces and the church agree in rejecting the traditional underdeveloped anarchical, corrupt, sinful society. The armed forces want a regenerated society, free from corruption and based on national values, traditions, and principles, which, in fact, are Christian. The church wants a society based on Christian ethical principles, according to the Gospels and papal encyclicals. Neither the armed forces nor the Catholic Church is bound by liberal principles. Who cannot understand the identity of purposes of the two groups?

Moreover, the military ideology likes to use clerical language. The military governments have ecclesiastical councilors who have taught them the art of quoting papal encyclicals.[2] Their official documents are written so that the clergy may believe they are Christian documents. Never since the independence of the Latin American nations has Christian language been used as it is presently by the military governments. When reading such documents, even a bishop has no feeling of danger: they are in his own language. It is so familiar that church people may become a little absent-minded; if they do so, they may very well fail to compare the means (the language) with the end (the objectives of the documents).

Of course, if one does compare end and means, it is easy to see that there is nothing in common between Christianity and national security except language. The "new Christian society" of the national security system is a mere idea, simple imagination, with no connection to actual politics. Present politics is based on principles that have nothing to do with the utopian language of the new society of the documents. The principles of national security policy as they are presently applied are exactly coincident with what the church has fought against throughout its entire history, from the Roman emperors through the German emperors, from Macchiavelli through the modern political ideologies.

What the Church Is Offered. It is true that the national security system offers the Catholic Church a privileged social condition that it lost at least as long ago as the end of the colonial era. The church will never recover such privileges by a free agreement of the citizens alone; the violent system of the armed forces could hope to restore them.

Such privileges include, for instance, the development of religious teaching in public schools; various guarantees and help for Christian private schools; censorship of all publications contrary to the interests of the church or its official ethics; the presence of civil authorities at some religious acts and the requested presence of clergy at certain public events; use of ecclesiastical language in some public documents; state defense of certain laws of the church, especially those concerning family or public morality; use of Christian symbols on public buildings; celebration of Christian worship (Mass, confirmations, first Communion, Easter, pilgrimages, etc.) in the armed forces; institution of the military chaplaincy.

The letter of a Chilean colonel to his country's various ecclesiastical institutions summarizes this collaboration theory well:

The Church and the Armed Forces are the two great and only defenses that can oppose the growth of atheism, and, at this historical moment, can develop a society of brothers, a society in which the general social conditions enable all Chileans and each one to reach their complete personal achievement.[3]

Such an offer cannot help but be tempting to many church people, individually and as representatives of their institutions. It cannot be said that the Catholic Church—or the evangelical churches in places such as Chile—has never yielded.

This does not even count the fringe groups, those who needed little temptation. Integrist movements outside the established church do exist. One is Tradition-Family-Property, which began in Brazil and presently has branches in various Latin American countries. Tradition-Family-Property is based on the military system's program, purposes, and means. It is a pathological phenomenon; its members are almost neurotics, and many of them directly help the secret services. For them the secret service is a kind of evangelization, a new inquisition in which they can worship God by delivering the church from heresy and corruption. Ideologically they are living in the Middle Ages. The government often grants them an importance they do not have; the mass media, controlled by censorship, publicize the "fact" that they are the only faithful Christian persons, that the present pope and bishops have betrayed the faith, that the only true popes were Pius V and Pius X. In reality this movement (and others like it) has no importance within the church. Although it was born within the church, it now exists outside, having been denounced by the Brazilian bishops (although it can still rely on the support of two of them).

THE CHURCH'S RESPONSE TO THE ROLE
PROPOSED BY THE NATIONAL SECURITY SYSTEM

The position of the true Catholic Church is more interesting than that of fringe groups. With regard to proposals of the armed forces, there has been and still is much ambiguity. Two trends are pulling the church in opposite directions.

The Reasons for Acceptance of Coalition

In Latin America today, there are several degrees of acceptance of the coalition, and some groups and individuals have changed their attitude over time.

Some Catholic movements, especially those of the Catholic bourgeoisie, actually took part in several of the military revolutions and in the creation of the new total power;[4] some important women's groups directly prepared and promoted the military coups in the name of their religion and their children's souls.

Several bishops, many priests, and many laypeople, especially from the upper classes, were and still are enjoying the advantages of the privileged condition of the church. They appreciate Argentinean General Onganía's devotion to Our Lady of Luján, the religious enthusiasm of the Brazilian armed forces toward Our Lady of Fatima (who was invited to go for a walk along the avenues of São Paulo), the fervor of the Chilean armed and order forces toward Our Lady of Carmen, General Stroessner's moving sorrow when the Paraguayan bishops did not allow him to carry Our Lady of Kaakupo in her annual procession.

On many occasions, Catholics have been seduced by the argument of the struggle against communism. In many documents laypersons, priests, bishops—sometimes even episcopal conferences as a whole—have admitted, in a way, to guilt regarding national security; they have confessed weakness in fighting communist infiltration within the church, have humbly asked to be forgiven by the state and the power, and have promised to be more vigilant in their task. So strong is the ideological propaganda that they have fallen into the trap of believing what national security propaganda suggests to them: their chief task is struggling against communism, and this task is the measure of all pastoral care.

National security's other argument, the one of the new Christian society, has also seduced some naive church people.

But although many have been trapped by these ingenious arguments, not so many have failed to see through them eventually when reality has not lived up to the promised utopia. The most successful seduction of the national security ideology has been that offered a segment of the Catholic bourgeoisie. This segment is quite aware of political realities, and the temptation offered them did not need to be at all ingenious to convince them of the concurrence between their own interests and their religious faith. After a few years, some of this group do remain faithful to the coalition with the national security system. This minority is moved by a geopolitical concept of the church and, consequently, a geopolitical understanding of evangelization. For them, evangelization consists of increasing (or at least maintaining) the prestige and power of the church in society. In short, they believe that the number of Catholics depends on such prestige and power and that evangelization succeeds by using all the opportunities offered the church by the dominating historical forces. At the present time the national state is the center and source of numerous historical forces; therefore, in order to reach the masses, the church ought to come to some agreement with the favorable national powers. These persons think that because the first evangelization of America took place in such a way, its new evangelization must follow suit. They believe that agreement with the armed forces might be like a new *patronazgo,* a new expression of Constantinianism with a view to a new Christendom.[5]

Such, for instance, is the geopolitical conception assigned the Vatican by General Pinochet:

The Vatican, like every well organized State with definite direction, moves according to some geopolitical doctrines. The Catholic church, by losing temporal power, lost a good deal of its spiritual power too, and now is trying to recover some power by means of the worldwide Christian social renewal that offers it some promising expectations. But there is a marked similarity between the Society and the Vatican schools.[6]

On the other hand, the majority in the Catholic Church have not fallen into the trap, have not succumbed to the very real temptation. There is a virtual break between church and state that is apparent in a good many circumstances. At the same time, there is a split within the church itself between those who accept and those who do not accept the new Constantinian agreement (although each party has given up any hope of converting the other party).

The Rejection of Coalition

As we have seen, only a minority of the church in Latin America have accepted the role proposed by the national security system, and these persons and groups have done so for a variety of reasons, some very naive, some quite shrewd. But the majority have adopted a critical position toward the proposals of the military system, although as normally happens, only a small number openly and actively manifest this criticism. It is through this open criticism, however, that we can come to understand why so many individuals and organizations have rejected the very real temptations of the proposals.

(This same criticism is also interesting from a more theoretical viewpoint because this is what has given the church a new awareness of true evangelization, a new concept of the special presence of the church in the world.)

It is easiest to study this criticism by looking first at the discussion of the arguments presented by the military and then at the analysis of the national security ideology itself.

The Military Argument for a New Society. The first argument to be criticized is the military government's proposal to build a future Christian society. This argument is countered by posing the next logical questions: What kind of Christianity does the military power want to establish in the new society? What does it mean by "Christians" and "Christianity"?

The ideological documents of the national security system show that the Christianity it seeks is essentially a cultural phenomenon. Probably its proponents do not even know that Christianity can be anything other than a cultural phenomenon. What they call Christianity is the cultural inheritance of the past—a collection of beliefs and ritual patterns, laws and traditions—that is able to lend identity to a nation, a collection of symbols that can pull a whole people together in the same mindset and make them feel kinship. They never appeal to the gospel as a force that can criticize an establishment, bring about new realities, change social patterns. Their religion is a fixed religion to be used by the authorities according to their political needs. Within the ideology of national security, this is logical. To national security, nationalism is the sole principle driving social dynamics. If religion were a force, it would be in tension with nationalism. Therefore the system and its proponents cannot suppose the existence of a Christianity that could be a rival.

Neither does the religion of the national security system include faith. Faith is necessarily the last law or it is nothing; either faith is absolute or it does not exist. We have seen that the nationalism of national security does not obey any absolute law above itself. Since such a nationalism cannot accept the existence of a higher absolute law, it must destroy Christian faith. Unavoidably, the religion of the national security system becomes a simple instrument guided by a political system. In dealing with the radical distinction between religion and faith, national security must oppose Karl Barth: it chooses religion and refuses faith.

Golbery clearly says that Christian faith has no relevance to Christian civilization. (Relevance, to him, means the defense of the cultural inheritance of Western civilization.) To show the place of Christianity in present geopolitics, General Golbery quotes the poet-critic T. S. Eliot:

The dominating force in creating a common culture is religion. . . . I am speaking of the common tradition of Christianity that made of Europe what it is now really, and the common cultural elements that the common Christianity brought. If tomorrow Asia were brought over to Christianity, it would not be brought over at the same time to a part of Europe. In Christianity were developed our arts; in Christianity the laws of

Europe remained rooted till a little while ago. All our thinking becomes meaningful against a Christian background. A European may have doubts about the truth of the Christian faith, and nevertheless, what he says, what he makes, what he does, comes from this Christian culture and depends on this culture to mean something. Only a Christian culture could have brought about a Voltaire or a Nietzsche.[7]

Such Christianity is only a cultural background, the only relevant Christianity for General Golbery and his fellows.

It is true that Golbery also refers to Crane Brinton, quoting him on the elements of Christian culture:

high degree of strain between ideal and real . . . untiring searching . . . scientific knowledge . . . consciousness of the dignity of man . . . hope of a better life on earth judged as a possibility . . . above all an inalienable feeling of individual freedom that guarantees a fruitful variety, a creating undiscipline, an exciting heterogeneity based on a climate of comprehensive and fraternal tolerance.[8]

Unfortunately, the national security system reduces Brinton's themes to platitudes for speeches. They are quoted to be applauded and reverenced, not to be practiced. They are topics for the mythical future, but have nothing to do with present politics. One is reminded of the Marxist idea of the vanishing of the state that is "prepared" for by intensifying the dictatorship of the state itself.

This is not the first time that the Catholic Church has had to deal with the problem of a Christianity reduced to no more than culture and submitted to an absolute nationalism. In this century the problem first arose in the Action Française affair, which was censured in 1926 by Pope Pius XI, who forbade Catholics to belong to the movement. In that case, the French rightist movement wanted to restore the social ideals of medieval Christianity without its faith. Action Française started explicitly from the distinction between faith and religion and proposed a Christian civilization without faith. Charles Maurras, the founder and leader of the movement, accepted the Christian social pattern, the Christian integration of Roman law and order, without the dangerous virulence of the gospel.[9] Although errors of Action Française were clearer than those of fascism and nazism, we think it is a good precedent for reflection on the present problem of the church and the ideology of national security.

The Military's Argument of Anticommunism. The second proposal to be criticized is the national security system's anticommunist crusade. The appeal here is for a coalition of church and state to fight the atheistic tenets of Marxism. Since the church is and must remain anticommunist, there is a great temptation to join forces against the common enemy.

There are two reasons for opposing such common cause. First, atheism is not the exclusive property of a coalition of nations or of the Marxist ideology. Atheism also exists within much of Western civilization. All faithful persons living today experience atheism at least as a temptation. Atheism is present in all the omnipresent forms of modern idolatry—for instance, in the idolatry of nationalism and national security.

Second, the roots of atheism are in the hearts of men and women, not in social patterns. The church struggles against this atheism by means of God's word. It is not possible to struggle against it by violent means that destroy social patterns and persons simultaneously. In fact, such a way of fighting atheism is likely to generate more atheism. Arms can expel the outward signs of atheism from social life, but they cannot expel atheism from the hearts of human beings.

This argument is supported by common sense and experiences as well as by remembering the true nature of the knowledge of God. God is known only by love. The true knowledge of God cannot be found by the possession of God's names or in any discursive or notional activity concerning God's names. The knowledge of God is the invisible term of the visible experience of love. "Anyone who says 'I know him,' and does not keep his commandments, is a liar" (1 John 2:4). Consequently, atheism cannot be identified with particular social or political systems, not even with the official ideology of the socialist nations.

Many persons—some of them quite well intentioned—do not think of these arguments. Consequently, many forces exerted considerable pressure against the church, trying to oblige it to enter into an anticommunist crusade, a total war against its enemy. The extreme rightists' movements inform the secret services about communist infiltration in the clergy, even in some Vatican departments; they accuse the bishops of cowardice and blindness, pointing to their lack of enthusiasm as the best proof of communist influence in the church. Not so long ago, Hitler tried (unsuccessfully) to throw the churches into an anticommunist crusade. The present phenomenon is very much the same.

Awareness of True Evangelization. The difference between Christian and national security views of a new society and their opposition as to the total war against communism has encouraged the Latin American church to study the difference between the official Manichaeism and the task of the church, which is evangelization. Consequently, the concept of evangelization has become clearer, indeed the new understanding of it is the most solid result of the present discussion. Evangelization is the radical expression of the nature of church and Christianity and is exactly what national security excludes. By studying the concept of evangelization, it is possible to see more clearly why Christianity and the national security system are incompatible.

To do this, one must first understand what the term "evangelization" means in present-day Latin America. The concept—and the term used to name it—was first used to show the opposition of the Catholic Church to any agreement with the revolutionary movements of *foquismo* (Che Guevara's ideology, which dominated almost all leftist movements in Latin America between 1959 and 1973, except those of orthodox communism and the

Peronists). The problem of this leftism was debated in several countries, but nowhere with more intensity than in Chile, where there existed the practical problem that many Christians were collaborating with Allende's government.[10]

At the time the church was afraid that *foquismo* would use the entire contents of Christianity simply as an instrument for political action. Many Christians realized that the content of Christianity could remain without any specific meaning; it could be used as an ideological tool of a Leninist party that was hoping to avoid conflict with the church. The leftist parties called such action "instrumentalization of Christianity," so the church adopted the word "evangelization" to convey the specific meaning of its true task. In other words, evangelization is the reverse of politicization, or the use of Christian content for political aims.

The concept of evangelization allows us to step beyond the old conciliar distinction between "spiritual," or "religious," and "temporal." This is important because it has become increasingly clear that all the "temporal" realities cannot be left outside the reach of Christianity. Evangelization does not accept the absolute distinction and, indeed, makes it irrelevant. Evangelization is a specific way of dealing with temporal as well as spiritual realities.

From such a viewpoint, political realities do not—cannot—remain outside the action of the church. But there is a specific way for the church to deal with the political world; the word "evangelization" denotes it.

Clearly, the danger of instrumentalization—the use of Christianity by a political party for its own purposes—can be found in the present national security system. Facing the possible instrumentalization of Christianity by the national security system, the concept of evangelization can well fulfill the same task it undertook against *foquismo:* protecting the true mission of the church.

What then is the meaning of the concept of evangelization? That is a difficult question, and cannot be answered fully here. Evangelization was the subject of the Roman Episcopal Synod of 1974, and it did not even succeed in establishing a definition. Here we shall deal with only two features of evangelization, each of which directly concerns the problem at hand.

First, evangelization is a method of action opposed to the use of violence. In former times, this feature was not as clear as now. Evangelization is more than an appeal to freedom: it is an act of awakening freedom. Evangelization cannot be achieved in a climate of force, by the use of violence, or by means of pressure. Consequently, if the purpose of the church is evangelization, it cannot join with violent movements or submit to them. The church can evangelize only if it remains completely independent of violence.

Such a concept raises many questions for theologians: for instance, what should the connection between state and church be if any state is based on violence? In the context of this book we are dealing primarily with particular movements that clearly manifest their violent nature, so when facing such movements and their ideologies, there is no longer any doubt for the church: any solidarity with a system like national security is impossible, definitely incompatible with the task of evangelization. It is possible to spread a Christian culture by collaboration with such a movement, but it is not possible to evangelize by such means.

The concept of independence from violence raises other questions concerning the church and political systems which use pressures or coercive methods that are not obviously violent, means such as pressure on the family and the environment, propaganda, pressure through public education or control of culture and social life. The Catholic Church itself has used—and still does use—many such methods in many ways and places. (Agreements with the state usually tend to ensure the possibility of continuing the use of such pressure methods.) Is evangelization compatible with them? Discussion of those problems would be somewhat off the point here, but there is no doubt that they can be solved by applying the simple principle of freedom. Their degree of compatibility with evangelization depends on their corresponding degree of granted freedom.

From this principle arises a corollary that is relevent to our topic. The church should consider not only the purpose or the result of an action, but also the means used. Evangelization lies not only, not even primarily, in the results, but in the method. Evangelization consists of choosing and selecting the available means. Among the available means, evangelization selects some as compatible with freedom and rejects others. The means that are offered by national security may be able to shape a traditional culture and traditional Christian behavior, but they are not able to awaken faith and freedom.

The second feature of evangelization to be discussed here concerns the task of the church in relation to the rise of any political party toward power. The church should not collaborate with such groups. If it does, Christianity appears as a legitimization of a party or a group, the very thing evangelization is opposed to. Such an objection was raised against the Group of Eighty and Christians for Socialism in Chile; it was said that they identified the liberation of Chile with the rise of certain minority groups, salvation with power, and Christianity with the legitimization of a particular political party.

The same objection can be raised against the present national security system, which identifies people with nation, nation with state, state with power, power with armed forces, and armed forces with groups of officers who control the national security system. In this situation, any collaboration with the political system gives direct support to a small group of persons and legitimates its total power.

CRITICISM OF NATIONAL SECURITY IDEOLOGY

In addition to mistrusting and criticizing military government proposals of collaboration for various reasons, the church also criticizes the national security ideology itself. These critical arguments are directed specifically against the ideology, not against the whole system in its patterns or in its practice.

The Latin American church has not produced a Christian doctrine for facing this dominant ideology. The elements for preparing such a set of statements exist, not only in the Bible, but also in some recent ecclesiastical documents. Nevertheless, an explicit statement is lacking. Moreover, the official doctrines of the church cannot appear by miracle; they grow out of countless theological works. This is the task of today's Latin American theologians.

Christian Anthropology and the National Security Ideology

Implicit in the national security ideology is an anthropology that is radically opposed to a Christian one. There is opposition on two points: the antagonism of friend vs. enemy, and the idea of freedom. On both points, the national security ideology is drawn from the philosophy of Hobbes. (It is interesting to observe how fascinated General Golbery was by Hobbes. Actually, Hobbes alone has stated the ideas that so influence Latin American military authors.[11])

Friend vs. Enemy. According to Hobbesian anthropology, the human is, above all, a weak and limited being, existing in permanent danger, always afraid and living in a feeling of permanent insecurity. Between human beings there is no spontaneous agreement. By themselves human beings are not able to put peace or order or reason into the world. Human beings are wolves to other human beings. Any human is a danger to any other. Human life is fight, competition, struggle, survival of the stronger individuals—of the fittest.

Consequently, all individuals have to seek friends for protection against their enemies. The whole of existence is marked by the distinction friend vs. enemy. Every individual sees the world through this criterion: Where are my friends? Where are my enemies? Every person belongs to one of these two categories. And with our friends we must always agree, even if that involves the most absolute hypocrisy; between us there must be absolute harmony. Alternatively, we can never agree with our enemies; we must always fight them to the point of absolute security. This is true because the situation and dilemma of each human being is to dominate or to be dominated.

Given this human condition, says Hobbes, only the state is able to create peace and order. (Justice is the name given to the order and peace settled by the state.) To establish justice, human beings have to give up their natural freedom; freedom is the price they must pay for security. Only the state is able to control the war condition of human life and to create some islands of peace. Moreover, the only peace is security. The state creates security. Security is its reason for being—its object, its essence.

The state organizes its human relations along some pattern of friend vs.

enemy, but on a larger scale. The state makes friends of all citizens by submitting them to the same pattern, and makes virtual enemies of all citizens of other states, except eventually those of allied nations.

Merely recalling these themes suggests the fascination that they have for the military elites of our times, a fascination as great as they had for the founders of geopolitics and total strategy. In the present condition both groups see the perfect actualization of Hobbes's anthropology. For example, General Golbery says:

Actually the general and growing insecurity in which distressed mankind is struggling today is the venomous opium that gives rise to and feeds these awful visions, able meanwhile to become a monstrous reality. The insecurity of citizens within the nation and the insecurity of the State facing the other States, the omnipresent vision of war—civil war or subversive war or international war—dominate the world of our times and explain the neurotic distress with which panic-stricken crowds and the helpless persons, the disillusioned and afflicted peoples, and finally humankind rises up and complains and struggles, ready for slavery if some lords or tyrants offer them on a dish of lentils a little security and peace.[12]

In this text there are three statements that directly contradict the Christian message. The first is the concept of war and distress as the normal human condition, the radical meaning of existence for both the people and the state. Contrary to this statement, Christianity poses the announcement of peace and the kingdom of God through Jesus Christ. Of course, the biblical concepts of peace and war do not concur exactly with Hobbes's concepts of peace and war. But the fact of the salvation of humankind by Jesus Christ makes it impossible to consider war and struggle of the essence of human nature.

The second statement in the Golbery quotation claims that the only stance of a human being in a world of virtual enemies is one of fear, and the only rational reaction is to take flight and search for shelter, thereby renouncing one's freedom to lords and tyrants. But the gospel commands love of enemy, and this command means that the evangelical message must exclude any doctrine that gives an absolute value to security. In Christian ethics, love is the absolute value, even in the face of the overwhelming danger of losing security. In opposition to the absolute of security without love, Jesus Christ taught love without security. Love of the enemy comprises a relativization of the criterion of security.

The third statement to be criticized is that human beings alone are not able to create peace and justice, so that all justice and peace must proceed from power. The gospel is an appeal to all people to practice peace and order and justice. Moreover, the gospel not only published the new command of love and peace; it also announced the coming of the Holy Spirit so that the practice of this command became possible. Consequently, defense against enemies cannot possibly be the first purpose of humankind. Human beings *are* able to create peace and justice. They must not give up such a task to the state or the power. They must make peace and justice themselves, and state and power must remain subordinated to their personal responsibility.

In the name of national security, modern authors object that the Christian message lacks political realism. The geopolitical and strategic vision of the world, they say, is a cruel but correct image of empirical experience. What can the gospel say to that concrete reality?

Here we reach the main problem for present-day theology: the relationship between the biblical words and the concrete circumstances of today. If reality is in agreement with the image given by Golbery and others, the Christian message becomes empty and meaningless, except as a utopian document of the past. And even if Golbery is wrong about reality, may a Christian theology discuss the political analysis of a particular political school? Has it enough criteria to make such an analysis? Is Christian theology also a method of political analysis or anthropolitical observation?

To these questions I would answer that if we believe in the truth of the gospel and its ability to be actually lived in this world, its contents cannot possibly be emptied of political meaning. Faith in the gospel gives us the certainty that historical situations cannot be such that any application of it is impossible. Accepting this concept of Christian faith necessitates a new review of the analysis of present-day reality. With what criteria? Not with theological criteria, but with the criteria of the universal consciousness of humankind.

Once we stop using the consciousness of some group as the criterion for reality and use the consciousness of all humankind, especially the new humanity proceeding from Jesus Christ, the vision of what is happening today changes. The present condition of humankind is not universal war and struggle. This tragic vision is only a projection of a previous system. There are wars, but war is not the whole of the present condition. The Manichaeism of the national security ideology turns out to be a useful justification of a neurotic practice of absolute power. This power feels the presence of many enemies because it has made enemies of all citizens. The idea of universal war can be seen as a useful excuse for the neurotic behavior of the secret service. Even the famous basic antagonism between East and West does not constitute the true image of reality. In our world there are a great number of powers and struggles between powers, various kinds of antagonisms, but there are also various kinds of coalitions and associations that are not necessarily defensive. People need not live in a permanently distressing fear of their enemies.

Nevertheless, although the biblical criteria can so easily show these aspects of Hobbes's philosophy to be false, their spectacular revival does serve to remind us of an element of human nature that had been forgotten by the majority of the Western philosophies, especially the Enlightenment philosophy with its inheritance in the democratic liberal political system of the West. Human beings are not as ready for freedom as was assumed in these philosophies. There is a dark side in all human nature, including its political nature. That dark side is manifested by fear, distress, and a deep yearning for order, security, and even slavery. Not unlike European fascism of a few decades ago, the national security system works on the irrational side of human beings; it enhances and develops this dark side in order to promote itself.

The dark side of human nature exists; it cannot be denied. But it is monstrous to build up a society based on its systematic development. The task of humankind is simply to fight against the dark forces in human nature. The national security ideology bases a whole way of life on the illness of human nature and society and then develops that illness to justify its intervention. Such an ideology is not only a mistake, but a perversity.

Freedom. In Christian anthropology, freedom is the chief attribute of a person. The nationalist ideologies are not able to give any human meaning to the concept of freedom. They cannot remove either the word or the concept, but neither can they give them any serious meaning. Consequently, most authors of these ideologies simply do not deal with the problem of freedom; they work as though it were not a political problem. The more advanced authors know this is impossible. They admit the words "freedom" and "liberty" and try to give them some meaning within their work. But in so doing they simply show the incompatibility of freedom with their system.

For example, the most brilliant representative of nationalist philosophy, Charles Maurras, the founder of Action Française mentioned earlier, looks at social life in such a manner that he sees no place for freedom in it. According to Maurras the common good has objective norms which can be known by the social sciences. Order results from the objective pattern of being. Neither the people nor their subjective feelings can change the laws of society. Persons do not deal with social patterns. Rather, social order comes from above; it is never the result of discussion or an agreement between opposite opinions. Order gives rise to society, not society to order. "A right law is not a law that is regularly voted, but a law that agrees with its subject and suits the circumstances. It is not created, but extracted and discovered out of the secret of nature, places, times, and states. The purpose of politics is to command all people to accept the objective order that the social sciences show to be evident. This is a task for some elites; therefore, politics is a movement from the upper classes to the lower levels of society. Freedom as a participation of the citizens in government is absolutely meaningless, contrary to the nature of human beings, the victory of subjectivity over objectivity.

What has been said by Maurras is the practice of today's Latin American military governments and deeply imbedded in their ideology. Like fascism, like Leninist centralism, like all nationalisms, the national security ideology radically criticizes liberal democracy's concept of freedom. In it all these

ideologies see nothing but decadence, licentiousness, demagogy, inefficiency, anarchy, and corruption. That such a judgment is historically a glaring
untruth is no matter to them.

From their viewpoint, what is left for freedom? Maurras said: "Freedom is
power." To be free is to have the power to do one's will. Human persons are
free in proportion to their power. Without power, freedom is nothing.
Consequently, every freedom is a gift of the state, in which all power resides.
Every freedom is a concession or delegation of some power by the state.
Therefore, liberties are necessarily unequal and distributed in proportion to
the efficiency of the citizens.

It is certainly true that this concept of freedom has been put into practice
by Latin American geopoliticians and strategists who have not dealt with
philosophical roots of their thoughts. But these roots are present in their
system, acting as an underlying background, and if they had any ability to
study philosophy, they would have to acknowledge Maurras's spiritual
fatherhood.

And what must Christianity do in the face of such an abolition of the true
meaning of freedom? Christianity must oppose it loudly with the proclamation of liberty, which is the whole Bible.

Let us consider here a few aspects of Christian freedom that contradict the
national security ideology, and which the church has proclaimed in opposition to that false concept.

First, freedom is not the power to impose one's will or to submit other
persons and society to one's will. The wayward person is a slave of his or her
own way and own determinism. Each person's own will and own way are
expressions of slavery and dependence rather than freedom.

True freedom is a process, a continuous liberation. It does not exist as a
static condition. It is a process by which persons struggle against their own
alienated will in order to recover their own authentic will. The will of human
beings is by nature an alienated will, submitted to the drive of other entities
(their own biological or psychological forces, social pressures, another person's conscious will). Liberation, as has been illustrated by Paulo Freire, is
people liberating their own humaneness—that is, their human responsibility,
the will to deal with their own condition and historical vocation. For such a
task, state and power are useless. On the contrary, power is often a factor of
corruption: unshared wealth or economic power corrupts; political power
without opposition corrupts; esoteric or secret knowledge is a cultural power
that corrupts.

Freedom means, first, to get rid of the slave who dwells within oneself. This
is the most evident biblical concept. One of the various kinds of personal
slavery is the slavery of fear, the slavery of the need for security. A person
entirely committed to security loses all freedom. There is, to some degree, a
contradiction between liberty and security. People become free upon becoming independent of their own security.

Second, to be free is to claim the right to be regarded as a person in social life, not as an inanimate object. The free person is the one who claims the right to be an individual among others and in facing the state and power. Therefore, liberation is a process of recovering individual rights. If these rights are not the basis of the whole social structure and all social relations, there is no freedom. Even with all the wealth available in the world, with all political power in hand, with the highest personal culture, people can be nothing but slaves if they may not rely on their individual rights. Such persons are submitted to a process of permanently seeking to increase personal power, becoming slaves of the necessity of increasing power in order to defend their security. Such persons can do many things but are not free. Freedom results not from power but from a state of mutual confidence that guarantees the rights of persons. It is false to consider freedom as a power to do something. On the contrary, there is no relationship between the degree of economic, political, or cultural development of a society and its degree of freedom.

All nationalists and fascists appeal to the famous sentence pronounced by Professor A. Carrel: "Man has no rights, he has needs." It is true that biologically a person is born weak, without freedom, and with many needs. So a biologist may see a person as a need rather than as freedom. And it is also true that during all of our existence, we continue to be weak and full of needs. But this weakness is not the essence of the human condition, just its limitation. A person is not born with freedom but with a calling for freedom. The ideologies that want to answer the needs of a person by trusting in state and power are based on an idea of human persons that is the image of their weakness or limitation, rather than of their force and dignity. They deny any spirituality, although they celebrate the word "spiritual" as a cultural datum.

Third, freedom exists only by means of free associations, free agreements, and free covenants. Individuals who are unable to make associations, agreements, and covenants with each other are not free. Persons who seek to accomplish their own will as individuals are not free; rather, free persons are the ones who can and do make agreements with other persons and cooperate with them. Persons create their own being with others, not in the sense of helping each other to accomplish their own purposes, but in the sense of creating a common store of common goods.

In this way, freedom is a dynamic process that creates a free society. A free society is a product of personal liberty, not of the state or power. A society entirely organized by the state by means of the absolute will of some elites can only be a society of slaves; it does not allow any possibility for freedom, so freedom cannot arise. If the human person is not called to collaborate in the definition of the rights of human persons, there is no liberty. Liberty cannot subsist outside the activity of conquering or building it.

By virtue of these three elements—independence from security, individual rights, and free common efforts—there are three contradictions between the idea of freedom of the national security system and the Christian idea.

The Christian Idea of State

The ideology of national security clashes with Christianity not only in its view of humanity (anthropology), but in its view of the state.

Unfortunately, this is hard to prove because modern Catholic theology deals with the concept of state or nation discretely. It does deal with the concept of political society, but it forgets the realities of state and nation. There is a Christian idea of the state, but it is not explicit enough or applicable to much of the present condition. We are better off looking for it in the Bible or the documents of Christian history, but there we find it in a form not quite suitable to the present political situation. (Here is another task for the Latin American theologians of today.)

One of the reasons for this gap in modern theology is that the Catholic idea of politics and state is ruled by the condition of the Western way of life in general and the liberal democratic states of Western Europe and their Anglo-Saxon political society in particular. In these countries there is a feeling that the state is less a power than a service—the management of the services necessary to the common life in the nation. The citizens of these countries judge by their own recent experience and think that the state as a power has been tamed, that it has lost its irrationalism, that it has been put in its proper place in a rational system of ethical norms. For them the state is not yet the Beast of the Apocalypse. Consequently, there is some indifference toward the problem of the state. When it is considered at all it is thought of as a series of technical problems, with power as the guarantee of individual liberties, according to liberal theory, or the "management of things," according to the positivists. Nevertheless, most countries in the world are not living within the Western way of life and the problem of the state is very real. Indeed, the West is naive—and forgetful—not to realize this. The state is now, as always, a monster in which all the irrational forces of the human being meet. People may think the monster has been defeated, but it is always able to reappear. Rationality in political life is a kind of miracle not very frequent in the history of humankind. Even the Western world of the twentieth century has very clear experiences of what the state can be, if it would only look. Unfortunately, it has almost forgotten the fascist experience; because of trading relations, many people try not to look at soviet centralism. It is impossible not to see that the Third World is falling into the hands of new monstrous powers, of new kinds of dictatorship, but it is easy to explain the phenomenon by underdevelopment, just as the communists explain Stalinism by Russian underdevelopment in 1917. (It would, of course, be more advisable to suppose that the political problem is always underneath, that the monster survives, remembered or not.)

In any case, the state as power is appearing once again; all over the world power is victorious in present-day history. For instance, national security ideologies are based on a simple if radical idea of the state. The state is the nation and the nation is the people. The state is its own power, and that political power is entirely in the hands of its most representative bearer, the armed forces. All the barriers built—during more than one thousand years of European history—to contain this beast, power, have fallen; the distinction between civilian and military, judiciary and police, judiciary and executive, legislative and executive, law and necessity, and so on have simply disappeared.

In some countries the authorities try to hide these disappearances by means of legal formalities. To settle the formal legitimacy of the dictatorship, the different states have used different legal tools: "state of siege," "institutional act," etc. It does not matter. These are irrelevant formalities that some governments want to keep because they happen to care about appearances. But the only thing of importance is the absolute power of the state.

As mentioned earlier, it is possible to criticize this idea of the state by using the documents of Christianity. This criticism has not been thoroughly developed and there is little space here to do so, but a few aspects of the topic vis-à-vis Christian political thought can be touched on.

First, the state is not the origin of the human political society. It is called to serve, not to rule. The idea of service is a fundamental tenet of liberal democracy but it is also applied by the Bible to political power (Romans 13:4). The makers of a political society are the peoples. The security and survival of a state, a government, a political program may not be the main purpose of the peoples. All the states, governments, and other political apparatus are relative realities. They may remain in proportion to the social service they fulfill; they may be replaced by other political systems more suitable to new circumstances. The states pass; the peoples remain.

The purpose of the state has to be useful to the political society. The reverse is not true (in other words, the political society does not have to be useful to the security or survival of the state). Indeed, in several modern circumstances one might think that the most important purpose of the present national state is to prepare its own destruction and the rise of new continental units. Think, for example, of Western Europe, Latin America, the Arab world, black Africa.

Second, the state plays a positive role in one of St. Paul's teachings (Galatians 3:24): preparing the conditions of freedom. The state has no power over persons of good behavior, but only over the citizens who are doing wrong (Romans 13:4). After having punished the evildoer, the state may disappear. It is not the author of good, nor the leader of persons of good behavior; to create good is not its task.

In the same sense, the state is not the author of law and justice, but their servant. Consequently, if law and justice are not embodied by some institutions above the power of the state, there is always either the reality or the danger of totalitarianism. The only good power is a limited power; there must be laws and principles above it and stronger than it. These institutions above the power of the state are the embodiment of the Spirit in history. A political society without such organs to limit the power of the state cannot possibly be a Christian society. Only the presence of Christianity in history gives rise to such institutions.

Of course, such institutions do not belong to the same category of power as the state does. They are spiritual powers (such as the spiritual power of a constitution, a supreme court, a congress, and so on). In the Middle Ages, after the struggles against the absolutism of the German emperors, many people thought that the pope's authority might be this spiritual power, able to limit the power of the prince. Unfortunately, the pope's power quickly became another material power, and the whole of Christendom protested.

How can law, as embodied in "spiritual" institutions, be powerful above the material power? Of course, the strength of the law first proceeds from the mutual agreement of the citizens. But this agreement has to be embodied in some external forms. In the United States, the primacy of law is embodied in the Constitution and the Supreme Court. The old Christian states had guarantees in the systems of customs and traditions and covenants. These led to constitutions. Indeed, one can say that constitutions are a concrete actualization of the Christian idea of a limited power.

This consideration leads directly to another chief theme of Christian political thought: the distinction between the people and the state. It can be said that Christianity founded the reality of the people (starting from the Bible and the Jewish community, of course). And it can also be said that Christianity made people confront the state and the power and, to a degree, struggle against them. Jesus Christ gathered a new people, which has its origin in the people of Israel and now includes all the masses and crowds of the world. Christian history is the worldwide movement of turning crowds into a people, actually giving birth to a people, a universal people of which the various peoples are only parts (in proportion to their awakening to the condition of being a people). The social result of Christianity is precisely the liberation of crowds and the raising up of peoples from among them; history itself is the story of peoples achieving independence from the power states who have tried to submerge and vanquish them.

By virtue of its nature, power always tries to destroy the distinction between the state and the people, tries to identify itself with the people. When the state succeeds in abolishing the independence of the people (or the institutional guarantees of this independence), it can be said that Christianity as a dynamic principle is dead and that the church is surviving simply as an inheritance of the past. In such a situation the church is definitely misled; it is no longer a people led by the Spirit and ruled by Jesus Christ. All the church can do in this condition is manage the leftovers of what was once a people.

That is the current danger in the Latin American churches. Consequently, the most enlightened and conscious sectors of the church have accepted the challenge of remaking a people from the masses produced by the new power of the national security system. The struggle may be open or silent. The visibility of the battle makes no difference to its importance. The church knows that its future depends on the struggle: either Christianity will be able to save the peoples from the powers, or it will become nothing but a mere cultural symbol in an essentially pagan society.

6

The Church's Pastoral Practice
vis-à-vis the National Security System

The new military governments of Latin America are by no means interludes or accidents interrupting an otherwise continuous historical process. They are creating a new societal model that carries with it a new value system and a new conception of person. Confronted with this situation, the church cannot respond with mere temporary measures to update its pastoral plans. In the course of the last ten years, the urgency of the new situation has moved the Latin American church to elaborate a new pastoral practice. And more recently this practice has given birth to the elaboration of a new theory.

When the military juntas started taking power, most church people and the general public thought that what they would have to deal with were brief military interventions appearing under certain special circumstances. These are not uncommon in Latin American history, and it was thought that their transitory, occasional nature made them meaningless to church or theology in the broad scheme of things. Besides, as we have seen, the church was very much caught up in the problems of development, radicalization, and socialism. Then it became increasingly obvious that the "certain special circumstances" leading to military intervention had become (as they remain today) the normal state of affairs. The church, as protector of the oppressed, had to respond. At the outset, these responses were improvised, but little by little it became clear they were following a consistent pattern, which soon became the rule. Today there is no longer a need to improvise. The church now knows what lies ahead and what should be done to respond to such situations.

This did not, of course, happen overnight. Initially only a handful of people perceived the significance of the military governments or the fact that they were constructing a new type of society which would radically alter the church's position in the world, i.e., the meaning of the world and thus the relation of the church to it. (The promises held out to the church by the military juntas did not, as we have seen, make this perception any easier.) So the earliest manifestations of the new ecclesial practice were nothing less than prophetic expressions by persons who stood practically alone. Dom Helder Camara, for example, during the years 1964 to 1968, found himself isolated, as the "voice of one crying in the wilderness." Then, as the new political system became more firmly and obviously entrenched, the courageous opposition—once the domain of small prophetic groups or individuals— became a more commom response and was incorporated (or, more precisely, is striving to be incorporated) into the very structure of the church. Of course, there have been many individual deficiencies, inevitable weaknesses, and those innumerable betrayals which are all part and parcel of the human condition. Nonetheless, the pattern of opposition in response to an unjust system now constitutes the new model of pastoral action.

AN OVERVIEW OF THE NEW PASTORAL APPROACH

The two basic theoretical premises of this new pastoral approach are the doctrine of human rights and the criticism of the model of development (which necessarily includes a critique of the societal model). We will examine both at some length in this chapter, but an introductory overview of why these have become the two main points of pastoral opposition may be helpful.

In coming to the defense of human rights or in criticizing the societal model, the church is doing nothing more than applying its mission to preach the gospel to concrete circumstances. In facing these social questions, the church proclaims the Christian message and its implications for the relation of the people to the state, the message that is God's answer to and judgment on humankind today. The word is an expression of God's judgment, which, in a concrete situation, rouses people and places before them an option: believe and be saved or do not believe and be condemned.

Human rights and development are not scientific problems but the subject matter of God's judgment. Therefore, when the church turns to either the defense of human rights or a critique of the societal model, it is not in any way attempting to use them as political arms with which to overthrow the established government, to take the place of the government, or to push groups of its political friends into power. Neither is it acting from the geopolitical motives ascribed to it by Pinochet in *Geopolítica*. The church is not angling to have the government handed over to the Christian Democrat movement, which would then act as the instrument of Vatican power. Obviously, some individual Catholics may have such intentions but this is not the goal of the church in general.

The church knows that its evangelization process is subject to manipulation by various movements, but it rejects the accusation made by the government agencies of intelligence and repression that the clergy have become "mindless instruments" or puppets of communism. The danger of manipulation exists in every situation, but it is especially present when the church believes that it can remain entirely outside the scope of politics. In the past, government or social elites in Latin America have manipulated the church's activity at almost every turn or without the clergy even realizing it. Now the church is very conscious of the danger of manipulation and recognizes it for what it is, so that the possibilities of manipulation by political groups and power seekers are minimal.

The new practice and theory of the church naturally include the concepts of both the intention to transform and the action of transforming established society. In this sense, theory and practice herald and work toward such complete change that denying that the process is revolutionary would be impossible. It would also be untrue, for, as we have seen, the church's mission of evangelization is, in some senses, a call to revolution. But by no means does the church want to aid, support, call attention to, or otherwise help any persons, groups, or political movements who seek to become the next leaders of the established order. Any such persons or groups or movements act alone in assuming that responsibility.

In one sense the work of the church is always mixed in with the work of other movements, including questionable movements. Because the church works through human agents it is inevitable that there is interaction between what the church does to fulfill its mission of proclaiming the gospel in a given situation and the action of various movements, especially opposition movements, in the same situation. This is part of the historical process; it occurs in every country, in every time, though not always with the same intensity. And only many years afterward can history tell which movements were actually helped by the fortuitous encounter with the whole evangelical process, which groups reaped the fruits of the transforming and conscience-raising efforts of the church.

This interface of the good with the bad (and the indifferent) reflects nothing more than the basic human condition. A perfectly good action is nonexistent. For example, in sixteenth-century Spain Bartolomé de Las Casas was vehemently accused of having provided material and arguments to his country's enemies, especially the English and Dutch Protestants. In a sense these accusations were perfectly true. The writings of Las Casas roundly denounced the actions of the conquistadores against the Indians, and Spain's enemies used this to make up the famous *Leyenda Negra* (Black Legend), which they used to fight for the destruction of the Spanish Empire. Thus the actions of Las Casas were, in one way, political actions which were supportive of his country's enemies. But the fault did not lie with Las Casas for denouncing the crimes of the conquest. The conquistadores were at fault for committing the crimes. What Las Casas did was to denounce them. The use of his just denunciation by his country's enemies was inevitable but had nothing to do with his purpose or with the mission of the contemporary church.

Much the same thing will probably happen in the present situation. It is possible—even likely—that the process of proclaiming the gospel and all that that implies will make vital information available to certain opposition movements and even to the nation's enemies. It doesn't matter!

For the purposes of this exposition, a Christian's personal options are not to the point. For the individual they are, of course, of the greatest importance, but they do not have much importance for the institutional church in a concrete situation. In the future these options could afford the church a new option or could be denounced by it. Here we will deal only with the institutional church of Latin America at this particular time in history.

HUMAN RIGHTS

A Historical Account

The concept of human rights in the modern sense dates from the eighteenth century and has been a source of conflict in the church ever since. The very phrase "the rights of man" comes from the Declaration of the French National Assembly of August 26, 1789. This, the first of a series of such declarations, was approved by an assembly in which sat a good number of bishops and priests, many of whom voted for it without hesitancy or reservation. Nevertheless, the declaration was not received well in Rome. Later on, with the simultaneous appearance of the French Revolution's anticlericalism and the faithful church's radical opposition to Rome, the Declaration of the Rights of Man came to be used as a sign of contradiction by both parties in question.

During the nineteenth century, the Declaration of the Rights of Man was a symbol of revolution. To liberals it stood for the republic, liberty, reason, and progress. To conservatives and the Catholic world in general (especially after 1850 when Catholics almost unanimously flocked to conservative parties and movements), it signified an insult to God, to the church, and to morality; it meant rebellion, satanic pride, lack of realism, utopian thinking, political anarchy, and social disorder. An object of worship for some, the Declaration of the Rights of Man was an object of sarcasm and criticism for others. Against "human rights" the conservatives counterbalanced human duties, social order, tradition, custom, experience, and the age-old wisdom of institutions.

For Catholics, the problem of religious liberty was a veritable stumbling block: How can you proclaim the rights of the individual in civil society and not accept them within the church society? Only a vertically structured society could correspond to a vertically structured church. So only a change within the church could enable it to change its attitude on human rights.

That change came in the twentieth century. In the ecclesial realm the century witnessed the laity's gradual rise to prominence, which began with the Catholic Action movement of Pope Pius XI's time and reached a high point with Vatican Council II. Meanwhile, in civil society, liberalism ceased to be the dominant movement as totalitarianism rose. Faced with this new danger of totalitarianism, liberalism ceased being the church's principal adversary and eventually began to be allied with it. The alliance continues to grow today. More and more the church is becoming aware that the principal threat is that of totalitarianism. *Octagesima Adveniens* is a clear testimony to this awareness.

This understanding has not been easy to achieve. Many believed that totalitarianism's worst excesses would burn themselves out or that it was merely a phase that would pass. Even as late as Vatican II some thought that totalitarianism was nothing more than the horrible memory of a buried past. Now we see that the "dead man" has risen (if he ever really was dead), more alive now than ever before.

As the church has come to recognize totalitarianism as its principal enemy, it has had to change its attitude with regard to human rights, for these are what totalitarianism directly attacks. Again, not all Christians have agreed. As far as Maurras and Action Française are concerned, the Declaration of the Rights of Man is nothing but the most obvious manifestation of mental degeneration, of moral anarchy, and of a total lack of political good sense. Fascism's judgment is the same. To Mussolini, human rights did not exist, because fascism teaches that the state makes laws and creates rights. Persons have no more rights than those given them by the state; the individual is born with duties to be performed but not with rights to be respected. As for communism or "democratic centralism," its vision of human rights is very simple: human rights are the mere imaginings of the bourgeois liberals' sick minds. No matter what lip service is paid "human rights," Marxism as set up in the Soviet Union and elsewhere was not the socialism that had been promised but the most antidemocratic system possible.

To counteract fascism and Marxism, Pope Pius XI invoked the theme of a human being's rights. He made no explicit mention of the historic 1789 declaration, but his concept of the human being's rights contained the substance of the French Revolution's message. In the encyclical *Mit Brennender Sorge* of 1937, aimed against nazism, he declared: "Man, as a human person, possesses God-given rights that are inalienable." This is a condemnation of the doctrine of Hobbes, from whence come, ultimately, all the present-day ideologies of national security.

After World War II, the United Nations proclaimed a new thirty-article Declaration on Human Rights. This document was designed to be a definitive rejection of fascist governments, which at that time appeared to be condemned by their own military ruin. The church was not called upon to join in this declaration, and Pope Pius XII remained silent. The United Nations document, however, was the natural and faithful successor of Pope Pius XI's own document of the rights of the human person. But the church was not quite ready for the two terms—the "rights of the human person" and "human rights"—to become equated. That equating had to wait for Pope John XXIII, who spoke out on the occasion of the fifteenth anniversary of the United Nations declaration. Moreover, in the same year (1963), Pope John included in his encyclical *Pacem in Terris* an extensive catalogue of the human person's rights—the first that the Catholic Church had published in its history.

Nevertheless, at the time, this section of *Pacem in Terris* went largely unnoticed. Catholic public opinion was much more concerned with social problems than with political ones, and next to the list of political rights or individual guarantees, the encyclical published a list of social rights. The latter drew much more attention as Christians attempted to see, for example, where the right of social participation fitted into human rights. The social problems seemed much more interesting because contemporary opinion, Catholic and non-Catholic alike, generally held that guarantees of personal security were no longer problematic in the Western world.

That assumption was quickly proved false when Latin America had the dubious privilege of opening a new era in the political history of Western civilization. In 1964, Brazil set up a new government prototype, a state whose announced goal was to create a new society based on the national security system. From that time on, as we have seen, the traditional governments of Latin America were abolished one after the other. Each nation adapted the new model to its own particular situation. The particular judicial formation of each new system is irrelevant. Some have suppressed the constitution, others have adapted it, still others have closed down the congress or turned it into a theatrical production.

The legal games that were played are of little consequence. What matters is that a new political system has become entrenched. In the name of a permanent (and false) "state emergency," individual guarantees and rights have been suspended and are rapidly disappearing. The state has become the source of all rights, and it does not recognize any right that it has not explicitly defined or established by decree. The National Security Council, regardless of any traditional figureheads that remain, holds total and absolute power. The secret police, likened only to the National Security Council, has become totally independent of other power groups and receives orders only from the president (perhaps it would be more accurate to say that they actually control him). The judicial system has been relegated to deal with trivia. The state has abolished the right of free association and the right to hold public meetings. The result is that the individual is alone and helpless before an all-powerful state.

When the national security states came into being, what first attracted the most public attention was the acts of repression—arbitrary imprisonments, disappearances, death squadrons, tortures conducted with impunity. The first of these crimes appeared in 1964. They were spectacular, well known, and much deplored at home and abroad. But few people saw them as part of the new system of government. Most attributed them to a specific set of circumstances, possibly those surrounding the civil disorders prevalent at the time. For a time it was possible to believe that there had been a turnover of government, and certain factions had committed regrettable but understandable abuses during the period of adjustment. But after a while, it became clear that the only possible explanation for these crimes is that they are intrinsic to the system. By December 13, 1968, with the Institutional Act #5, this system took on its definitive form in Brazil.

The new pastoral defense of human rights began in these circumstances. Initially it manifested itself through Dom Helder Camara's speeches and campaigns in the years 1967 and 1968. Until then, the dominant theme of the church at Medellín, and in most other institutional forms, had been development and liberation. Then Dom Helder Camara began to speak out. In those years, he was a somewhat solitary figure in the Brazilian church; despite the support of a few colleagues in the northeast part of the country, the president of his episcopal conference and a majority of its members opposed him. Nevertheless, the government's reply was brutal. Dom Helder was treated by the authorities and media as no other churchman in the Western world in this century has been treated. He alone is familiar with the details of a persecution which endured for almost two years on an hour-by-hour basis. The tragic death of Padre Henrique Pereira Neto on May 26, 1969, was a small chapter of the brutal campaign against him.

But the case of Brazil and the opposition to Dom Helder Camara was only a beginning. Argentina, Bolivia, Uruguay, and then Chile soon came under political systems similar to the archetype in Brazil.

From that time on, repression and torture increased in these countries and in others in the southern part of the continent. The church's pastoral practice had to respond as the struggle for human rights became a daily part of life. Soon Dom Helder Camara was no longer a voice in the desert. First other bishops, then entire episcopal conferences in Brazil and Paraguay, raised their voices in order to defend human rights. Finally Chile joined in with its April 1974 document. To this day there has been no respite in the struggle.

With such a historical background to the recent declarations of human rights by the church in Brazil, Paraguay, Uruguay, Argentina, Bolivia, and Chile, it hardly seems necessary to stress that they are not theoretical studies of an ethical doctrine conducted in a vacuum. They are public acts of confrontation with a political system. They define how the church perceives its presence in the midst of a real world and its real position in relation to the state.

To speak of presence implies having a definite idea of what the church's mission in the world might be. That very definiteness is what is new about the Latin American church's new pastoral practice (so different from the passivity of the church in Spain and Portugal when the same sort of circumstances were present there). It is also what makes it so important for the universal church. This importance was clearly recognized in the last two Roman synods, whose discussions, it is widely admitted, were inspired by the Latin American episcopate. The second synod (1971), for example, affirmed that from the church's mission of "giving witness . . . [to] the Gospel message" flows not only its right but its duty to denounce unjust situations when "the fundamental rights of man and his very salvation demand it." The statement added specifically that that mission "involves defending and promoting the dignity and fundamental rights of the human person."

Now that this ministry is clear and explicit, the church stands up and directly confronts the absolute state and its ideology of national security. This confrontation is now a ministry of the church.

The Meaning of the New Ministry

Events in Latin America have thus led to the formation of a new interpretation of the church's mission, that of ministry as defense of human rights. This interpretation is not simply a new way of acting; it includes a reinterpretation of all the functions of the church. It is not merely a new technique added to former emphases and actions but a new pastoral thrust that changes all the others. We must therefore analyze the impact of this change for all Christianity, how this new practice of the church alters the entire pattern of its pastorate.

The Center of the Gospel. The proclamation of human rights is not a new phase of Christian ethics, nor is it a peripheral function of preaching the gospel in the present time. It is actually the proclamation of the very substance of Jesus' message to our world today. It is the announcing of the kingdom of God to real persons living within the political structures of today's world. Indeed, the political circumstances of that world have provided a good means of distinguishing between the central and the peripheral ideas of the gospel. In making this distinction we find that the rights of the human person are the very nucleus, the center of the Christian message.

Before this point—and its importance—can be fully grasped, it is necessary to understand the distinction between center and periphery. In attempting to do so, the distinction between culture and faith, which is an element of the present political ideology, is very useful. As we have seen, national security ideology and its political system do not reject either religion or worship. On the contrary, their adherents view themselves as the supporters of Christian civilization, as the saviors of Christianity from communism and atheism, as the artisans of a new society built on the Christian principles that are essential to national tradition. As tokens of the sincerity of these ideals, national security systems offer the ecclesiastical institutions privileges, favors, prestige, and power.

But what is the Christianity that the national security system intends to support? It is simply a Christian culture—traditions, rites, customs, symbols. These elements are the cultural patterns of Christianity, its outer shell, its social and psychological periphery. As living patterns they can be used by the church to embody its life and faith. But such patterns can also survive without life and faith if social groups have any interest in continuing them. And dead patterns can be used by faithless persons as a mask; still worse, they can be used as social and ideological tools and even weapons. In short, for the church a cultural pattern alone is at best meaningless, at worst dangerous. Culture is the periphery of Christianity. And a peripheral pattern has value only if it is driven by a nucleus, a living nucleus that is faith, hope, and love.

The reason the national security system so actively promotes the cultural patterns of Christianity is that it finds in them symbols which can be used to mobilize national feeling without disturbing public order. Dead religious symbols are highly antisubversive. So the national security system seeks a fixed, passive, archaic Christianity—a Christianity consisting only of symbols, of culture, of the periphery. For the church, on the other hand, the most important part of Christianity is the nucleus that gives life to the periphery. The church may not simply follow geopolitics, seeking a position of power within state and society. The church is always to be judged by its mission of preaching and evangelizing. Accordingly, the function of the church must go far beyond using words, symbols, and even actions in order to manipulate the religious and social behavior of the masses. It has more important tasks than making sure that people know the "true" words of God, Christ, the Spirit or making ritual gestures in the sacraments and community life. It is much more important that the church help its members experience the life behind the exterior patterns of Christianity.

What is life for a Christian? The difference between spiritual or Christian life and spiritual or Christian death is liberty. Liberty is the origin of all faith and love, the direct effect of the Spirit. Where there is no freedom, there is no Christianity. Consequently, the whole activity of evangelization must deal with calling forth freedom in the hearts of human beings. Freedom is both the purpose and the effect of evangelization. The gospel does more than tell us about freedom. It produces freedom; it is the call from which freedom proceeds. Unless church people awaken freedom, all their work is nothing more than giving in to the power system of the state, manipulating the periphery without entering into the salvation process.

Critics may counter this analysis by saying that the nucleus of the gospel is "living in God." This statement is perfectly true. But when "living in God" is translated into the language of human realities, it means the growth of freedom. Preaching God's word is opening a space of freedom in the heart of a human person. The person who has been reborn after death and resurrection, who is a new creation in the Spirit, is free. Consequently, the church's defense of human rights is not to be understood as a call to the public authorities to change some laws or social patterns. It can be this, but only as a secondary effect. (Moreover, historical experience allows us very few illusions as to the ability of the church to change the methods and ways of governments.) Preaching human rights is primarily a message to the people. This message calls them to a new awareness of their real condition and their real relation to power and the state.

Another, similar criticism is that the freedom of Christian evangelization is not the same as the freedom of human rights, that the former is a religious freedom and the latter political. Since the time of Bartolomé de Las Casas, theologians have answered such a suggestion by replying that the human being is one and his or her freedom is also one. External conditions may fail; internal freedom is either universal or nonexistent. There are not two kinds of human freedom. Individuals live their faith in God and their Christian behavior vis-à-vis the state and power with the same personal freedom. We are not free and able to believe in Jesus Christ if we are not free from the pressure of power and its ideology. And we are not able to live a true life of faith without belonging to a true community, self-responsible and independent from state and power. For that reason, before human persons can live lives of faith, they must reach an awareness of self-worth and dignity, of personal rights and individual autonomy before the power and the state. Without such a consciousness, human beings can reach the level only of fulfilling their "religious needs," of making gestures or receiving the Christian sacraments. They will never be able to reach the level of Christian faith and true love of God. They will be bearers of a Christian culture but not Christian persons. Consequently, evangelization fails if it does not succeed in bringing human beings to freedom. The task of awakening human freedom is not "another" mission of the church besides that of evangelization; it is one and the same, a single process.

I think it is important here to make a point that is seldom treated by the pedagogical methods of liberation. The state is a power that tends to determine the entire behavior of all citizens. All persons are born into social patterns that begin to persuade them of the powers of the state before they even begin to think of their own reasons for existing. This trend has always existed but today it is stronger than ever before. While dreaming of freedom, we all grow up feeling ourselves to be dependent beings. More and more we appear to ourselves as insignificant beings facing a monstrous power machine. Consequently, all conscientization means some form of opposing power and the state, some process of becoming autonomous. (The problem is to solve the dilemma between unavoidable dependence and necessary autonomy.)

Any citizen who is not aware of the necessity of opposing power and the state has a reflex consciousness that is developed, dominated, and manipulated by the whole state system. The main purpose of all public education, for example, is to submit the students to the official dominant cultural patterns; it carefully creates a feeling of dependence on the source of power. There is no possible liberation from actual dependence without a fight against the deeply ingrained feelings of fear, insecurity, submission, and helplessness before the state. Consequently, the process of evangelization also means a process of liberation from feelings of powerlessness, from the passive submission to the pattern of domination.

Indeed, evangelization might be defined as the process by which a person, after hearing Christ's voice, liberates herself or himself from all forms of alien consciousness, especially from the false consciousness imposed by power, in order to begin a new life, to enjoy a freedom that allows one to join others in free associations.

The same thing can be said in Pauline language: evangelization is the process by which a person is "rid of the law, . . . free to serve in the new spiritual way" (Romans 7:6). We know, of course, that "the law" is not limited to the law of the Old Testament; rather, the term includes all the historical expressions of that same reality. The national security state is the most complete embodiment of a "law" domination. In it human existence receives its worth exclusively from the law; the cause of all value remains outside of human personality. A person is not able to do good by virtue of his or her own goodness. All goodness comes from outside, from an exterior law, from the integration of the individual into the system; any personal position is suspect. But in "the new spiritual way" of Christ, the principle of all value comes from the individual human personality.

With such definitions of evangelization, the new pastoral imperative of the church becomes clear. If preaching remains "otherwordly," if it does not touch the problem of person versus power, the faith that stems from it will probably belong to the cultural level of human consciousness. Such a faith remains on the periphery of mental and spiritual life, alongside the old consciousness of slavery and alienation. If faith does not succeed in destroying the old sense of submission to and dependence on the political system, it is not faith at all, but a mere psychological phenomenon.

We meet here the traditional objection to modern evangelism (either Protestant or Catholic), the objection Thomas Münzer spoke of to Luther. And we now understand Münzer's position better. A typical "spiritual" preacher says that the gospel is a call to faith in Christ, and that means faith in the biblical words, the literal evangelical words. Such an understanding of faith takes it out of any historical context; it decides that any reference to history belongs to ethics, that it is an application, a consequence, but by no means part of the essence of faith.

Such a faith is an ideal target for the anticlericalists of today, as it was for those of the nineteenth century (Marx, Freud, Nietzsche, and so on). Such a faith applies biblical words just to the experience of faith, and exhausts them in itself. It mistakes the psychological experience of salvation for the true salvation through Jesus Christ. Of course, it often does give the faithful a feeling of conversion and new life. But such a feeling can be given by any sect, any superstition. Indeed, the very strength of the religious feeling of faith is a suspicious phenomenon. Any faith that disengages a person from one's whole human condition is nothing but mystification. If a faith does not in actual fact liberate the person from ideological alienations, we can now see that it is nothing but a psychological phenomenon, an appeal to the periphery of culture and emotion. So we are not astonished that the most evangelical sects (and various similar movements within the Catholic Church) legitimate the national security systems of Latin America and provide them with ideological reasons for support. (One thinks, for instance, of Chile since 1965.)

The New Pastoral Christianity. The new pastoral ministry centered on the defense of human rights began in Latin America and is most developed there. But it has repercussions for all Christianity everywhere in all aspects. All the particular data of the Christian message gain strength and life from the awakening of freedom. We shall look at a few examples.

Everything in Christianity speaks of God. Who is the "God" who is the subject matter of the Bible? The documents of the Latin American church emphasize that human nature is made in God's image; in other words, God is known through his image—men and women. Such a concept is of special importance in our context because, for the totalitarians, God's images are the state, the nation, order, power, law. Their ideology emphasizes a "God" who appears in the manner of authority, law, obligation, commandment. It finds features of the divinity in every embodiment of order and law. It is the revival of the political theologies of antiquity in which God's images were kings, laws, and power symbols. Maurras's idea of God is very similar—authority, law, judgment. To him, God is the principle of social order; human beings will meet God by seeking the laws of society and obeying them.

True Christianity does not dare to say that even the pope is God's image, or the bishops, or the priests, let alone the civil or military authorities. On the contrary, God's image is the human being, the ordinary man or woman of the street, the person in simple human condition without any added prestige. God's image is the freedom of men and women, the simple little seed of freedom that has never disappeared.

If that image of divinity is accepted, God cannot possibly be thought of as a power, but only as an authority (in the strict sense of the word). "Authority" and "power" are quite different things. Power is the ability to impose something against the will of another; it comes from sin and does not belong to the essence of human nature. Authority, on the contrary, means being the author or the creator of someone. Etymologically, authority is the principle of being and life. This is the sense in which God has authority: he is the author of life, and his law is nothing other than the inner meaning of life. God's law and gift are, therefore, identical. God's will is in accord with the increase of the gift. God's law is free loyalty toward freedom itself. Such a law is neither dominating nor confiscating; rather, it is the very principle of giving rise to freedom.

Such a stance results in a Christian view on authority and social patterns. All moral authority should mean the ability and the tolerance to lead people from a lower degree of freedom toward a higher degree of freedom. Such a Christian concept of authority comes from the biblical idea of the relationship between God and freedom.

The principles of human rights also lead to a more Christian Christology, to a renewed meaning of Christology. After his resurrection, Jesus Christ did not remain alone. He should not be viewed as an isolated being. Rather, he is the head of a body, and no head can be alive without its body. The doctrine of the mystical body certainly means that the resurrection brought about some change in the human condition, but it also means there was change in Christ's condition. Jesus Christ may no longer be viewed separated from his body, which is humanity, those men and women who are the assembly of the church.

Jesus Christ has not yet accomplished the complete development of his own body. He is still seeking its scattered members, and he may not be viewed without taking into account all his dispersed members the world over. Christ's body is increased and developed by means of its scattered members becoming reconciled to him. That means promotion of and access to evangelical freedom for all the scattered members all over the world. Any other Christ would be a simple projection of idolatry, a type of psychological, religious, and cultural experiment. The only true Christ is Jesus Christ with his complete body.

Bartolomé de Las Casas's point was that the Indians were members of Christ's body. They were called to be incorporated in that body and belong to it in virtue of that calling. Las Casas frequently quoted Jesus' statement, "And there are other sheep I have that are not of this fold, and these I have to lead as well. They too will listen to my voice" (John 10:16). The Indians, said Las Casas, were such "sheep," they belonged to Jesus Christ. Now, obviously, people cannot say that they worship Jesus Christ and at the same time separate from Christ the members that belong to him. However, the landlords, the conquerors, the *encomenderos* did separate the Indians from Christ when they deprived them of their freedom. By depriving them of their primary liberty, the conquerors made it impossible for the Indians to believe in Christ. Faith is a free gesture. The landlords made it impossible for the Indians to approach Jesus Christ freely. The landlords could, of course, baptize them and even give them a Christian culture. But they were unable to enter into the hearts of the Indians which they had closed by taking the Indians' freedom. The baptism they gave could not incorporate the Indians into Christ's body. Consequently, the landlords destroyed Christ's body. They said that they loved God and Christ, but actually they destroyed his body. Their Christ was a docetic Christ, a phantom without body, a ghost reality, a mere projection of their own minds. He had no life because Jesus' life in that time and place consisted in being joined with the Indians.

Las Casas's argument is equally valid today. Simply replace the Indians of the past with their present-day descendants.

Another aspect of the Christian message that is illuminated by the pastoral emphasis on human freedom is the Spirit and pneumatology. (To some people the simple fact of taking the Spirit into account is already a revolutionary fact. The theology of a simple "cultural" Christianity does not mention the Spirit at all, except in the formal sentences of the traditional confessions of faith. In the daily life of the church, the Spirit is mentioned only to enhance the prestige of the ecclesiastical hierarchy or of powerful social patterns.)

It is said by Paul: "Where the Spirit of the Lord is, there is freedom" (2 Corinthians 3:17). The revolutionary nature of such a sentence is unmistakable: The Spirit is not present where power is, but where freedom is. In early times, the Spirit had been joined with power; now we have to view the Spirit joined with freedom. The authorities, the agents of power, may receive the Spirit only in order to serve freedom.

National security systems pretend to be the loyal upholders of the spiritual values of Christian civilization against communist materialism. They start with a distinction between spiritualism and materialism, between spirit and matter. But the spiritual values they support turn out to be no more than the ideological symbols of their national inheritance. Their "spirit" is a collection of ideological issues. For Christianity, on the other hand, the Holy Spirit is no more present in ideological data than it is in the economic or material ones. The Spirit is by all means a "form" that is able to give life to some "matter." The Spirit is not a "certain" form or a matter, neither is it the formal element of natural beings. The ideological superstructure is as different from the Spirit as the material infrastructure or the matter of society. The Spirit is the divine principle of all freedom, the source of human liberty. Consequently, it is the principle of the liberation of persons from patterns of material and cultural domination. The Spirit is the contrary of the flesh, and flesh is human nature without liberty, human nature able to be manipulated by the state and power, human nature reduced to the condition of object, fear, need of security. Indeed, "flesh" is the model citizen of a national security system. And the Spirit is actually the principle of destruction for such a system.

The message of human rights enlightens various other aspects of Christianity, but there is no space here to research the new interpretation of all the chapters of Christian theology. Let us , however, think about Christian love, or charity. According to the national security system, love cannot be anything other than a principle of adhesiveness among citizens, the psychological binding together of the soldiers of the same army. This very union of soldiers means fear and suspicion toward all the elements not completely integrated within the social system. "Love" means friendship with friends, hostility toward enemies. As soon as the secret service points to someone, all solidarity disappears. Everybody moves away; the "friend" has become a danger.

Christian love is, of course, very different. Charity is agape or mutual loyalty by which a people rises. (A "people" here designates collective accord among citizens, to which they commit themselves by means of a social covenant.) The biblical words for love mean fidelity to one's word and loyalty to others. Personal charity is the strength to win over different points of view and interests, the will to dialogue, and the disposition to accept a manner of mutual dependence. Within a vertical society no charity is possible. A political society is open to love and charity only when power is limited and there is room enough for citizens to make free commitments. Love is accepting, defending, supporting the human rights of the people and their exercise of them within the concrete life of a political society. Charity cannot have built-in limits. Consequently, the proclamation of human rights is a necessary condition for any exercise of love in social life.

A CRITICISM OF THE DEVELOPMENT MODEL

Negative Criticism

The History of the Critique. In a certain sense we can say that the criticism of the development model now being used in Latin America is nothing new. It has existed almost as long as the concept of development itself. But the coming of military regimes has given this critique a different form and, in consequence, a different scope and Christian meaning.

Before examining this thought, let us rapidly review how the critique of the development model began.

The concepts of development and underdevelopment were born in the 1950s, promoted by the dominant economy and its spokespersons, such as W. W. Rostow. Simultaneously, a critique of the theories and politics of development also appeared. In other words, from the moment of their appearance, the concept and theories of development encountered both theoretical criticism and practical opposition. This critique was promoted, to give one example, by the structuralist school of ECLA (United Nations Economic Commission for Latin America). In addition, prestigious Christian authors, such as L. J. Lebret, Father François Perroux, and Colin Clark, voiced fundamental criticisms that remain valid today.

The United Nations called the decade of the 1960s the "First Development Decade." Today few people would contest the failure of all the "development" initiatives taken in that epoch in the wake of the economic theory dominant in the developed nations. The Alliance for Progress, UNCTAD (United Nations Conference on Trade and Development), the international conferences held in Geneva in 1964, New Delhi in 1968, and Santiago in 1972, and many other schemes only served to show the fundamental disagreement between the developed and the underdeveloped countries and the contradictions of defining an international plan of development.

The encyclicals *Mater et Magistra* (1961) and *Populorum Progressio* (1967) manifested the Catholic Church's concern with development and pointed out the obvious contradictions between total human development and the applied models of development being promoted by international agencies working under theories from the developed world's universities. The encyclicals distinguished between a purely quantitative and material development and one that is clearly human, which touches the social, political, cultural, and moral aspects of life. The Protestant churches adopted similar positions. For example, the Ecumenical Conference on the Church and Society (Geneva, 1966), the World Council of Churches Assembly (Uppsala, 1968), and the Mission Conference (Bangkok, 1972) issued statements expressing the same concerns.

By 1966, development was so strongly criticized that the call for development was replaced to a large extent by one for liberation and for revolution. The program became, especially among leftist movements, revolution first and development afterward. To many people the problem was no longer one of looking for another model of development but, rather, one of substituting another priority for any sort of development. Their new priority was liberation. Development could be postponed until after the liberating revolution. This was the prevailing belief of Latin American leftists for several years beginning in 1966. But soon the perspective of an impending revolution disappeared—little by little at first, then definitively after the events in Chile and Argentina in 1973. In its place appeared the first effects of the politics of development, applied authoritarianly by military governments, under their program of national security.

Up to this point, Catholics had generally seen criticism of the development model as an ethical problem. It was important to the church, to be sure, but it was a secondary issue. The problem did not appear to affect the church's mission or the overall structure of its manner of functioning in the world. So the church simply proposed, to governments and to individuals, the principles of social ethics that ought to be respected in development projects and goals, and exhorted everyone to make the urgent decisions necessary for rapid development. This development was not considered the proper task of the church; neither was criticizing the type or model of development, except in regard to the proclamation of moral principles. The church, with many other private and corporate international organizations, did, however, participate in and contribute to development through AID projects. These projects followed the general pattern of aid to the underdeveloped world and strengthened the established development model.

But when the national security governments began to come to power and entrench their system, various sectors of the church thought that the time for preoccupation with development had passed. The states had chosen a type of development and were not accepting any debate on the question. They announced that their goals and methods were the very embodiment of the encyclicals and asked that they be given the people's trust in the application of these "principles."

There were many in the church at the time who welcomed this attitude for a variety of reasons. Some felt the government declarations gave the church prestige (even though the states clearly said that they wanted no ecclesiastical interference with their economic policies). Many prelates thought they had no choice but to give the governments the trust they asked for, to hand over the whole question of development to the civil authorities and, as they said, dedicate themselves solely to "church" activities. Some of the more "spiritual" ecclesiastics believed that the silence commanded by the state was the sign of the times through which God was revealing himself, and so they stopped speaking on the matter of development. They reasoned that the Medellín conference had got into questions that were outside the scope of the church's competence, and now they had an excellent reason for avoiding them in the future. For example, one Chilean bishop hailed the "values of rest" and congratulated the military junta for having suppressed political life in the country. "Now we can get down to pastoral work," said another.

The Antipeople Model of Development. Not all Christians—ecclesiastics or laity—accepted the new government view of development so calmly. Many had already begun to criticize the chosen model of development as "antipeople." To them, of course, the signs of the times looked quite different. Some of them believed that the new situation was actually proving the critique of this type of development and widening the scope of possible action against it to a degree not previously envisioned.

The most eminent spokesman for this view, the pioneer who opened the way, was again Dom Helder Camara. His famous speech in the Legislative Assembly of Pernambuco, on May 31, 1973, is perhaps the best statement of the new confrontation, although the documents published by the bishops of the Northeastern and Central Eastern regions of Brazil in the same year are also representative.

The importance of these and other similar statements lies not in their theory (although it is excellent) but in the very fact that they are not simple theoretical discussions of theoretical problems. They are not even criticisms of abstract programs for development. Rather, they are specific critiques of states that are systematically promoting specific programs. They are public acts, actual confrontations with the most powerful and absolute force that exists on the Latin American continent today.

According to the new critique, as represented in these and other statements, the problem of development is not a technical one. It cannot be reduced to economic issues. The question is no longer the selection of a way or model of development for the future. That way has been chosen and it is contrary to the chief postulates of the Christian message. Consequently, it must be opposed. Loyalty to Christianity does not consist in giving up but in facing the decision of the state even though it may not be possible to change its political program.

Such a critique has a prophetic function. It is a statement of the entire opposition of the people of God to a concrete process imposed on it by an absolute and unjust power. Here we should consider the profound meaning of the prophetic function. The prophetic office has always had a specific aim: to save God's people. The people of God are lost if they lose their own consciousness of being a people of God and of the possibilities of acting as a people of God. They cannot be a people if the system does not allow them to be a people. The function of prophecy is to renew this consciousness and to point the way to action.

The model of development adopted by the new military system is able to give the nation some degree of economic growth. More specifically, it is able to increase the national power so that it can gain its share in international economic and political competition. But at the same time this type of development destroys the people as a people. It destroys citizens' self-awareness of being responsible members of a social covenant; it destroys the associations and social agreements by which the citizens gain strength and self-confidence. What comes of such a model of development is an anti-people.

This can be shown by the most superficial analysis, as well as the most scientific. Both prove that the growing marginalization of the masses, even their very reduction to the level of "masses," is a consequence of this development model. The marginalized masses remain atomized under the almighty power of an absolute state.

Marginalization, therefore, creates an antipeople or a nonpeople. On the one hand, there is economic marginality. The development model sometimes greatly increases overall production and GNP, but this increase does not benefit the workers. It serves only the purposes of the national security state—the growth of national power. It is clearer and clearer that such economic growth seeks to create a power center able to vie with the other power centers, that all production is judged from the point of view of its strategic worth.

Within such a system, the government naturally favors the social groups with economic potential—engineers, technicians, economists, producers of materials strategically favorable for the world market. The economy is geared more and more to produce not for the people, but for foreign markets—for exports with which to accumulate stable reserves and build up armaments.

Such a system produces a growing marginalization because the masses are working not for their own growth but for the sake of a power that dominates them. The final goal of all activities is power. All citizens are asked to give more power to the state. Those who do not integrate themselves in the system that produces this power merit no respect or concern. There are two categories of citizens: the producers who give power to the state and receive prestige and material commodities in return; and the persons who do not produce and, consequently, do not exist for the established system.

Accompanying this economic-social marginalization of the masses is political marginalization. The national security state eventually abolishes all public organizations through which citizens could demand their rights. The national security state wants only isolated individuals, unarmed, submissive, and dedicated. Neither the masses nor the elites participate in making decrees or decisions. There is no public opinion, only public fear. Nothing is decided through deliberation, dialogue, or agreement; everything is decided from above. Political management is in the hands of the military elites who follow the school of military discipline and order. Economic management remains in the hands of a group of economists who appear to be purely scientific. They are generally young economists who have recently graduated from North American universities with high honors but with little real understanding of social life. They are the representatives of an abstract science; they merge science with power and apply the scientific principles of their books as the rules of a military law. A famous Brazilian minister has said that their economics is an "a-ethical" science.

The result of the whole system is a society without a people. There cannot possibly be a "church" if there is no people, if there is not even a possibility of creating a true people. Of course, nothing hinders the ecclesiastical organization from teaching the literal meaning of the Bible or from distributing sacraments or from having liturgical assemblies. But such elements alone do not make a church, only a culture to fill spiritual needs. A true church requires a true people at the center of its assemblies.

From such consideration, it becomes clear that the Latin American church is opposing this development model not only to announce some principles of social ethics but as an actual fight for its own survival as a people, as God's people. The church can never accept the condition of being a mere cultural organization which provides goods for "spiritual consumption." Its fate is bound up with the fate of a people of God. Faced with a system bent on destroying the people, it can make only one response—evangelization. And under such circumstances, evangelization must mean speaking out as the voice of a people confronting an antipeople system.

Positive Criticism

If such is the situation, the critique of it is more than a negative response and action. The critique is the starting point of a new and positive process. This process is the liberation of a people.

And that is the mission of the church—to be God's instrument for liberating his people, for making from humankind a people of God. We really cannot look to a government, a power, or a state to create a people by some spontaneous action. If they are obliged to contribute to liberation, they may do so, but only the citizens, through their own efforts, are able to give rise to a people. Nobody is able to liberate other persons; people must free themselves. The church, however, can and must awaken human beings from their condition of submission and unawareness to a condition of freedom and responsibility. The task of the church is to call both the masses and the elites to master the task of becoming a free people. The starting point is a mass of separated individuals, all seeking their individual needs. The task of the church is their conversion from the condition of being bearers of needs to the condition of being members of a people.

For the church the existence or nonexistence of a people is not an accidental occurrence. Only a people can make acts of faith, hope, and love. Only free members of a people can master their own way of life, can decide whether they will follow the gospel or not. Submissive masses can consume cultural ("spiritual") goods and repeat biblical sentences and even experience religious feelings. But they can never really have access to faith, hope, and love.

The relationship of the church with those called to assume their condition of being people is perhaps best expressed by the phrase Dom Helder Camara made famous and almost universal in the Christian church of today. The role of the church is "to be the voice of the voiceless," he said. In like manner, the 1971 Roman synod said: "Our action is to be directed above all at those people and nations which because of various forms of oppression and because of the present character of our society are silent, indeed voiceless, victims of injustice."

It is important to understand these statements precisely. It may not appear clear to some whether the task of the church is to speak for those who have no voice, or to speak as the voice of the voiceless. The concept of liberation puts the phrases into their proper context. To speak for the voiceless would be a task of intercession or mediation; such intercession would not lead to true liberation of a people, but only to satisfaction of particular needs. Without doubt, the Brazilian bishops and others who use the phrase intended much more than that. "To be the voice of the voiceless" meant to pronounce publicly the words that the people could not say or were not allowed to say. The objective was that the people hear the voice of the church and perceive it as their own voice, and by so doing become more able to utter their own words. The "voice of the voiceless" is the voice the people have forgotten or never learned; nonetheless, it is their own voice, the voice of a people that is rejecting slavery and seeking liberty.

Being the "voice of the voiceless" is, therefore, a task of education, an adult and collective education. (Paulo Freire's conscientization is a good example.)

Being the voice of the voiceless also, of course, means being a voice that confronts the power and the state. Such a voice is certain to provoke the resentment of the state and subsequently the repressive machinery controlled by the secret service. So such a voice gives rise to reprisals. And that is just the kind of contradiction that awakens a people. There is no people without an awareness of the contradiction existing with the power. Under a national security system, the norm is that all citizens live in a permanent state of fear. Being frightened becomes a metaphysical condition, a substantial way of life. By confronting the power and the state, by accepting the risk of speaking out, the church helps these isolated citizens to cross the barrier of fear. When bishops or priests or well-known laypersons take a stand for the people and confront power and national security, their gesture is the proclamation of God's kingdom. Their deed demystifies the power and announces the arrival of God's kingdom among God's people.

In the Christian tradition there are many examples of such proclaiming of the kingdom by confrontation. Today's prophets follow Daniel, in defiance of the paradigmatic King Nebuchadnezzar, a deed that strengthened the self-confidence of Israel. Today's bishops take on the role of former church leaders—Athanasius, Ambrose, John Chrysostom, Gregory VII, Thomas Becket, and many past bishops of the Latin American church. They have been the forerunners, they prepared the condition for free peoples within the nations and states of today.

There can be no separation between *libertas ecclesiae* and *libertas populi*. The freedom of the church is not only freedom to proclaim God's promises; it is also freedom for the people born in virtue of this proclamation. And the freedom of God's people is the radical reason for freedom for all persons and citizens. By virtue of God's people, all persons are called to share in the community of free people. By defending the freedom of the Christian people, the church provides all humankind with a permanent call to freedom.

Of course, the church cannot give freedom to the people. Nobody is able to give freedom to anybody. The people grow as people precisely through conquering their own liberty. The relationship of the church to freedom is one of a call to an answer. It is making the proclamation of the New Testament: "My brothers, you were called, as you know, to liberty" (Galatians 5:13).

Without a doubt, the people need the mediation of political parties and movements in order to embody their liberation. When judging the worth of such particular movements, the church has neither more knowledge nor more ability than any given human group. The church's prophetic mission does not allow it to know which movement or party is the one best able to assume responsibility. Prophetic knowledge gives no anticipation of the immediate future. Whenever the church "knows" immediate history, it is usually mistaken.

But this does not negate the church's task of prophecy. It does not remove the demand for it to be the "voice of the voiceless." It does not lessen the urgency of leading the people toward liberation. Rather, when the church represents the people by criticizing the present models of development, it is making a new but real application of the eternal gospel, it is giving this eternal gospel a true meaning for today's world.

7

Liberty and Liberation:
Principles from Biblical Sources

THESIS: THE DUALITY
OF PRESENT-DAY CONCEPTS OF LIBERTY

The theology of liberation and a pastoral practice emphasizing human rights are new in the modern history of the church. But liberty and freedom are certainly not new to secular thought and action. Indeed, for several centuries the idea of liberty has been at the center of Western life and culture. And never has the idea been defended so earnestly as in recent years. To today's culture, history is mainly the movement of peoples and individuals searching for and achieving liberty. At the present moment, the idea of liberty is applied to all areas of personal and social life: there are movements to liberate persons from society's laws, structures, and obligations; movements to liberate women from the masculine bias of society as a whole; movements to liberate youth from a society developed in terms of its adult citizens; movements to liberate sex from personal and social taboos; movements to liberate workers from a society established in terms of productivity as defined by the interests of the dominating class; movements to liberate colonized and dominated peoples from an international order founded in terms of the privileges of the more powerful nations. In short, the secular awareness of liberty has never been as intensive or as extensive as it is today.

The church has not held aloof from this trend. It is true that in times past it fought the concept; during the time of Pope Pius IX and the entire second part of the past century, the main trend within the Catholic Church was counter-revolutionary (in spite of several strong liberal currents). The historical reasons for such an anachronistic position are beyond the scope of this book. What is important here is that during the present century the church has moved closer and closer to the mainstream of Western thought. Finally Vatican II opened the doors to a real reconciliation with the idea of liberty and liberation. The Catholic Church as an institution at last gave up its

121

counter-revolutionary ideology, based on the writings of traditionalist phi-losophers and critics of the French Revolution, and accepted the main ideas of the political philosophy of the modern culture.

This was not achieved, of course, without overcoming many difficulties. One of the greatest was the problem of religious freedom. For a church that was still clinging to the last remnants of ancient Christendom and its concept of religious unanimity, religious freedom was a nearly insurmountable bar-rier. Nevertheless, after many debates, the Council accepted the principle of religious freedom and many other human rights.

After the Council opened the church to the ideology of liberation, a new theological movement appeared and continued the same inspiration (cer-tainly beyond the expectations of the Council). The leader of the new trend was the German theologian J. B. Metz, professor of fundamental theology at the University of Münster.[1] His short publications are generally considered most representative of the new trends and have become the center of the theological debate about modern culture and Christianity. Of course, Metz himself has been challenged by his own disciples, who sometimes pushed to more advanced positions, sometimes rejected him.[2] Within Protestant Chris-tianity, Jürgen Moltmann came to occupy the same position; he has been the leader of the movement to integrate the modern idea of political freedom with Protestant Christian theology.

In almost all Christian countries today (Protestant or Catholic), groups and movements based on these new theological trends have arisen to take part in the various liberation movements. In the underdeveloped world and in countries submitted to dictatorships, the main movements focus on social and political liberty, while in the countries or power centers of the metrop-olis, the liberation of sex or youth or women is of more importance. But such trends are not at all exclusive.

These liberation movements began with a base in the new theology, but they immediately provided it with new material, arguments, and problems. Thus was born "liberation theology," the second stage of the "political theology" of Metz and Moltmann. It arose as an answer to the expectations of liberation movements, appearing simultaneously in the Christianity of the metropolis and the Christendom of underdeveloped Latin America, though in two different ways, with two different vocabularies.

It should be noted that only in Latin America has a theology about lib-eration been formed as a homogeneous movement. Other situations, such as those in Europe, have produced many expressions of such a theology but only in the form of discontinuous articles, pamphlets, and lectures. In Latin America, however, liberation theology is being developed in a more systema-tic fashion. Its main ideas and patterns were present and active by the mid-1960s, its first written documents appeared in 1966–1967, and the Episcopal Conference of Medellín in 1968 was guided by the most represen-tative authors of the theology of liberation.

It would be an exaggeration to claim that the theology of liberation has been completely acknowledged or accepted by the church. On the contrary, it has often been considered as questionable and suspect, especially since 1972 in both Latin America and Rome. More recently, however, much of this opposition has subsided. More favorable winds seem to be blowing and the theology of liberation is no longer threatened.

If the Catholic Church has not acknowledged the theology of liberation as a whole system, it has at least assumed its language and consequently its problematics. The Medellín Conference expressed itself in liberation language, and since then few of the authorities of the Latin American Episcopal Council (CELAM) have missed opportunities to assert their faithful continuity with Medellín. In the larger church, the decisive step was taken by the second Synod of Bishops in Rome in 1971, which employed the language and problematics of liberation. This was an important step for two reasons. It showed the new importance being given to the churches of the Third World, the new churches to whom the language of liberation belongs. It also signaled that the scientific theology of established Western tradition is being replaced by the more aggressive theology of liberation.

The introduction of liberation language and problematics should not be understood as simple opportunism or an eclectic integration of some modern topics with the traditional language of the church. Christian theology has not added a few modern ideas to the ancient patterns. Rather, it has entered into a true dialogue with modern culture and been provoked to change its whole structure. Modern culture is a real challenge that has obliged the theologians to develop a new understanding of their whole position. Let us note the main shifts that have been provoked by the present dialogue with liberty and liberation.

First, the theologians have acknowledged that the modern liberation movements are not foreign to Christian thought, in spite of the church's counter-revolutionary trends during the last two centuries or so. Before that period, Christianity had always been present within or alongside struggles for freedom. It is no accident that only Christian civilization has given rise to liberation movements or that Christian inspiration has always been present in the beginning of any revolutionary movement for freedom. (Notice that I do not claim that such movements have been guided by the hierarchy or the institutional system of the church, which normally has not been the case.) So by entering into a dialogue with the liberation movements, theology and the church are only returning to their true tradition, reclaiming Christianity's place as a source of inspiration for the struggle for human freedom.

Second, the search for the sources of Christianity shows that there is a specifically Christian concept about liberty and liberation at the roots of the Western history of freedom. There are certainly several connections between the Christian concept of freedom and the older Greek idea of freedom. Undoubtedly, too, from the Septuagint (Greek translation of the Old

Testament) through Pauline theology, the Greek concept has been used in order to explicate the Christian one. But the Christian concept is both more extensive and more radical than the Greek or any other.

It is true that many writers on biblical theology have not given the idea of freedom the importance it deserves. (We do, of course, have the Pauline theology of freedom, which occupies a central place within the message of the New Testament, as we shall see.)

The new systematic theology has realized the importance of such a topic; unfortunately, it still lacks a sufficient pneumatology, so the normal context of a theological explanation about liberty is missing. (This must be developed soon because the Christian idea of liberty is tied to the revelation of the Spirit.)

Nevertheless, the new theology does have the latest works on Christology, and these have emphasized the human nature of the Savior and shown that Jesus is the clearest revelation of the liberty created by God, that in Jesus Christ liberty was made visible as the highest attribute of the human person and the fullest image of the Creator. Jesus was, above all, free man—freedom is the main feature and the reason of his nature and action. It seems that the ideas of liberty and liberation will be emphasized more and more in the future. It is no accident that even the veterans of conciliar theology, such as Yves Congar and Karl Rahner, are carefully developing these concepts today.

The Christian idea of liberty is not in complete accord with Western culture's current idea of it. Indeed, there are some radical differences. Consequently, Christian theology cannot simply take the current concept unto itself. This would go against the basic principles of theology, which cannot work from a concept that is not its own and is alienated from it in some very decisive aspects. On the contrary, according to its own tradition, theology has to submit to its own criteria all the concepts it receives from human civilizations, including those from civilizations like the Western one, which was born from Christian origins but has parted from them after a process of alienation. In short, developing its own modern concept of liberty is the present challenge to Christian theology. Modernity must neither be rejected nor assimilated as a whole. Rather, the task is to work out a new concept involving all previous aspects of biblical revelation.

We have to start with the following premise: there are, at present, two chief families of concepts about liberty and liberation. Of course, there are thousands of definitions of the words to be found in dictionaries and in treatises on ethics, anthropology, philosophical systems, and so forth. But there is no need to examine them all or to follow the process by which they evolved. With such a subject, details hide reality instead of disclosing it. It is better simply to accept the two broad concepts, whose main lines are clear and unmistakable. In brief, there are today two ways of understanding liberty and liberation: the traditional Christian understanding, and the typical modern interpretation. The latter is expressed in many different ways, but it has enough constant features to be seen as a clear and lasting system. We may call it the idealist system because it had its beginnings in the German idealist philosophies.

This idealist interpretation has given rise, for instance, to the modern totalitarianisms of the right and the left, as well as to the various academic Marxisms and intellectual leftisms. Indeed, it becomes clearer and clearer every day that the totalitarian ideologies of the right and the left are more similar than different. The radical difference is between the Christian idea of liberty and the idealist one. That opposition is the first challenge to a Christian theology about liberty.

In addition, most liberation movements are ambiguous because they use both concepts of liberty—the Christian and the idealist—in a very confused way. Inside many present-day liberation movements are some elements that proceed from the Christian tradition of Jesus Christ's liberation, some actualization of the traditional Christian influence on political life. On the other hand, most also contain an expression of the idealist understanding of God, the human person, and the world. It has never rejected them as its main inspiration, and even today it continues to be rooted in the thought of Fichte, Hegel, Feuerbach, Marx, Freud, Heidegger, Marcuse, Reich, and Sartre. (Of course, there are some important differences among these scholars, but they all have contributed to the formation and survival of a new idea about liberty.) The future of the liberation movements, the future of the Christian share in such movements, and especially the future of any liberation theology depends on the church's ability to make the distinction between Christian and idealist liberation and act on it.

Each way of understanding liberation depends on its own view or system or *weltanschauung* (worldview). So the church's role is not one of giving an ideological legitimation and a Christian appearance to such ambiguous movements. In the long run, any collaboration of Christian institutions with an idealist system is impossible. Rather, its role is one of discernment, of distinguishing between the two ideological currents and the two ideas of liberty in order to separate the Christian one from the idealist one. All these philosophies depend upon the denial of the transcendent God. Some variants present themselves as atheistic; others call themselves theistic but actually involve a kind of monotheism that makes of God a simple element of total reality (like the sun monotheism of the ancient oriental religions or the third-century monotheism of the Roman emperors). In the end, consciously or unconsciously, the idealist systems tend to be pantheistic. The Christian idea of liberty today, on the other hand, is a continuation of the biblical belief in creation and a transcendent God, which began some three thousand years ago.

Because of this very basic difference, the present debate on liberty and liberation is basic to today's expression of the problem of God.

Notice the different ways of posing the very terms of debate. According to the idealist perspective, any cultural debate rests upon the basic opposition between ancient and modern. The problem of liberation is only one aspect (although an important one) of this opposition; it is the struggle of modernization against tradition and the past. There are two stages of history, separating two kinds of people and culture. The past, the first stage, was characterized by prevailing tradition and a lack of reason, science, or technology. The second stage, the future, is distinguished by doing away with tradition as a rule of behavior and by the prominence of reason, science, and technology. The present is the time of the struggle of modernity and future against past and tradition. The decisive step within human history has already been taken by means of the scientific and industrial revolutions. The shift from a preindustrial and prescientific civilization to a scientific and industrial one has given rise to a "new human being" with a new culture, which includes a new understanding of liberty and liberation. From the traditional idea of liberty (the Christian one), humankind has passed to a more modern idea (the idealist one).

According to Christianity, on the contrary, the debates of human history have been and always will be the same. There is a permanent struggle between the same two forces: a mainly pantheistic totalitarianism and a Christian liberty. These are the two cities of St. Augustine: the City of God, present in any searching for a true liberty, and the city of humans or the devil, present within the totalitarianisms of today as it was in the totalitarianisms of the past. The material change of the world through the scientific or industrial revolution has not altered the main debate of human history. In spite of modern industrialization and all of its consequences for human beings, the same human problems continue; science, technology, and modernization have not been able to make a new "human." Consequently, to Christian thought, the debate on liberty is not a struggle of the modern idea against the ancient idea. Rather, it is the present-day form taken by the permanent struggle of the liberty of God's city against the domination of the city of humans and the devil.

Thus this analysis of development of liberation theology rests on the thesis of a very basic opposition between the Christian concept of liberty and the idealist concept. Such a thesis must now be expanded and justified.

THE IDEALISTIC CONCEPT OF LIBERTY

In this book there does not seem to be much point to examining ideas that remain on the level of pure philosophical thinking and are not embodied in historical movements of liberation. So we shall consider only these ideas that are actually present within modern society, guiding its concrete behavior.

The Ideas of Liberty and Liberation in Present-Day Culture

There are many definitions and understandings based on the idealistic framework that are various aspects of the same basic meaning. Among them are some opposites. But the idealistic framework allows for interior opposition and even contradictions. Indeed, Western culture shifts from one meaning to another. But the various meanings are tied together by a basic solidarity because they all depend upon the same framework. Such a paradox is explained by the fact that culture based on the idealistic framework swings from a radical permissiveness to a radical authoritarianism, from a complete lack of repression to total repression. It is no accident that idealism is unable to reach some stable equilibrium. The system contains no principle of equilibrium.

The same paradox can be put another way. Generally, the liberation movements of our time end by establishing a repressive system and a totalitarian society worse than the ones they replace. Does this happen by accident? Are the new totalitarianisms to be explained by the personal failures of their leaders (as in the case of Stalinism in Russia)? Is it not more a failure of the basic framework?

As proof of this statement, let us examine the various definitions of liberty common today.

What does "liberty" mean? The starting point of any definition is a simple negative idea. Everyone agrees that to be free is "to do what people want to do." "To do" here means any way of acting—thinking, expressing, speaking, moving, behaving, transforming objects, and using energy. "To do what people want" means a mere negative condition—it is equivalent to "being independent from any outer force." "Outer force" covers all possible exterior and interior pressures on the individual—psychological, physical, and social forces as distinguished from the human condition.

On this general level, there is total agreement among all philosophies. But such a general definition is useless. Such a liberty is, of course, impossible for human beings. One cannot imagine any possible society in which an individual would be independent of all coercion, rule, or obligation, because the physical world conditions human existence, and social life is based on innumerable rules and norms. Consequently, a liberty of independence is impossible. Human liberty is necessarily a liberty determined within some area of human existence. With this conclusion arise the various philosophical systems. They try to situate the area of human existence where liberty and liberation are to be sought and found, and their answers differ, resulting in different definitions of liberty.

If one tries to take into account all the areas and corresponding definitions of liberty and liberation that the idealistic system of Western culture designates, one discovers that they can be gathered around six principal categories.

These six definitions express the variations of liberty between the two extreme poles of permissiveness and totalitarianism. They correspond to the six areas in which present Western culture sees freedom, and thus involve almost the whole behavior of our world. The first four result in a permissive society, and the latter two in a repressive society.

1. Liberation is being free from all the rules and obligations, duties and taboos of the traditional society, represented by traditional institutions and families, traditional education, and the inheritance of the past generally. All areas of life are covered—sexual, cultural, economic, and political. Such an idea has deeply inspired Western culture since the eighteenth century.

2. The second idea accepts the first and continues from it. Liberation also means the creation of a "new person," free from any nature, essence, or norm. Human beings are the source of their own nature, self-creations. The idea of self-creation has been developed by the idealistic philosophies, but its accomplishment within a real society seems to be more difficult.

3. Since the second definition has proved very difficult to put into practice, liberation is being free from any coercion in order to choose the wish and impulse of the moment. Here the "new person" is reduced to the condition of someone ready to follow the first or strongest impulse. The free individual is one reduced to a succession of impulsive states without any structure, a life without institution or continuity.

4. Such a disjointed personality easily leads to the fourth definition, which represents the real position of many persons. Liberation is to become free of any responsibility defined by the patterns of traditional ethics, to break the framework of traditional objectives (concerning sexual life, political roles, social responsibility, and so on). Thus liberation is irresponsibility, passivity. (Notice that there is a practical continuity leading from the first idea of liberty to the fourth. People do not generally confess to holding the fourth idea, but it is often present under the appearance of one of the former, more beautiful concepts.)

The first four definitions express the movement toward permissiveness and the individualistic meaning of liberation. They are one pole of the idealistic system. The other is the ideas of liberty which correspond to totalitarianism. (If that sounds contradictory, remember that there is no modern sociopolitical system that does not assert itself as being the author and savior of liberty. All the totalitarian systems have been founded "in the name of liberty.")

5. Liberation means "to get sufficient power" to avoid any interference by other people in one's life. Such an idea has taught that independence means power, liberty depends upon power. Few individuals can, of course, be sure of having sufficient power to protect themselves from any interference from anybody. But the totalitarian state can promise such liberty to its citizens. This state indicates the enemies of liberty. In this way, total integration into the armed forces and the national mobilization, absolute submission to the

total strategy are the new equivalents of liberty. For the capitalist states, communism is the absolute enemy, and liberty is the submission of all activities to the war against it. For the communist states, capitalism is the enemy, and liberation is the total struggle against capitalism, even if winning it entails the most complete dictatorship. For states of each politico-economic persuasion, foreigners are enemies who hinder the freedom of the people. Consequently, the mobilization of all citizens toward total war against their enemies is another means of establishing freedom.

6. The sixth definition follows from the fifth. Freedom means not only national security, but the power to compel other nations to accept the plans and goals of one's own nation. To be free would mean to be able to manage the world, society, and existence according to one's own wishes.

These definitions have been explicated here according to the behavior they result in. People do not, of course, normally express their thoughts in such aggressive form. Generally the literary definitions are more ambiguous. Not only are the words softer; the ideas are also mixed with elements proceeding from the traditional Christian heritage. This is to be expected: idealism is not yet the common way of thinking and the definitions proceeding from it are not yet completely conscious. The idealists themselves assert that the present era is a transitional period from tradition to modernity. Modern idealism is assimilated by the person in the street (and a surprising number of supposed intellectuals) by means of ambiguous concepts which do not shock, since they are often couched in traditional language. So there is a general evolution, a progressive acceptance of the contents of the idealist definitions into the common way of thinking.

The ambiguity of thought and language goes so far that some of the modern definitions of liberation may even be understood according to either the idealist or the Christian system. For example, "to be free from the rules of traditional society" can be understood as "to reject tradition" or as "to be free from tradition not in order to reject it, but to distinguish and accept in it what is valid for all time and to give up what is not of importance and belongs to circumstances of the past." The latter interpretation, of course, may easily be Christian. Again, "to create a new person" is a Pauline expression that implies a Christian process. But for the Christian faith, creating a new person is the action of the Spirit. If such a definition is taken to mean that one is called to accept the movement of the Spirit in order to remake humankind as it had been created in its origin, the idea is Christian. But the same words can also express a very different idea.

The definitions are only an introduction to a more extensive explanation of ideological systems of liberty and liberation. Let us consider the two poles of idealism: permissiveness and totalitarianism.

Freedom in a Permissive Society. One of the poles of the present Western society is permissiveness. There is no doubt that there is a deep desire in many people for permissiveness. Such an aspiration is out of the reach of most underdeveloped masses. It is a privilege of the affluent society. It can, however, also be found in the upper classes of the poor nations, where the dominant groups are able to assimilate the way of life of the developed nations.

What is freedom in a permissive society? Freedom is individual permission to do or not do what one likes at any given moment without feeling the limits of any imposition, prohibition, or inhibition. Of course, such a freedom is never complete and remains conditioned by the economic level and power of the individual; it is always very expensive.

Permissiveness probably does help some personalities to develop their creativity (although so many creative personalities have done brilliant work in the midst of very adverse circumstances that there is no certainty a radical lack of coercion is most favorable to invention). But for the masses, permissiveness gives way to the shunning of responsibility, the disintegration of personal continuity, the lack of collective projects; without past and future, human existence is reduced to the sensual impulse of the given moment. For the privileged, on the other hand, permissiveness focuses on four areas: sex, drugs, aggressiveness, and economic competition.

For some persons, sexual freedom is paramount. By this they mean liberation from all traditional limits and prohibitions—breaking down the prohibitions on divorce, abortion, pre- or extra-marital intercourse, pornography, nudism, etc.

For other persons, freedom means free use of exciting narcotics—tobacco, alcohol, or drugs. It is well known that for adolescents the feeling of freedom is frequently tied in with the breaking of the common prohibitions concerning such products. But it is also well known that for many workers free time means more time for drinking or smoking and nothing more; inside a permissive society that does not offer its citizens any common project, freedom means more "empty" time and life becomes vacant. For the masses, permissiveness then does not give rise to creativity but only a return to an infantile condition.

Another common application of permissive freedom is aggressiveness. Many persons, above all many young persons, are unable to find any aspiration other than violence, which gives them some feeling of liberation. Such violence can find expression in sports or physical exercise; others search for it in war, crime, political agitation, or vandalism.

Finally, the most general area of permissiveness is economic free enterprise, free competition among and within enterprises and free exploitation of workers and consumers (including the freedom to waste without control or limit).

In a way, this account of permissiveness is not completely fair. The aspects cited are the most negative ones from the viewpoint of traditional ethics. There can be more positive aspects. Nevertheless, the negative aspects are very much present within permissive society, and they are the primary expectation of many people. Within a philosophy that conceives of freedom as liberation from tradition and past civilization, there is no principle that allows one to distinguish between the various kinds of repression or permission. Permissiveness means permission to create a new human existence. But for the masses, "new human existence" remains meaningless, and permissiveness leads to being ruled by ever-changing sensual impulses.

Freedom in a Repressive Society. Practically all the permissive societies are proceeding to some sort of repressive society. Nothing is more significant than the history of the twentieth century: people cannot bear life in a permissive society more than a few years. Aristotle said that, and present history confirms it. The feeling of insecurity given by permissiveness is so great that a reaction is unavoidable—there is an appeal for order and security, and a response of totalitarian power becomes inevitable.

Moreover, the very principles of totalitarianism are present within the permissive society. Complete permissiveness is impossible. Even the most permissive system is compelled to establish some rules of social and personal behavior. According to the principles of a permissive society, these rules or laws have no interior rationality; their only basis is that of the need for security and order. But in linking law with order, security, and external rationality, the permissive system is already using the principles of totalitarianism. Such principles are easily extended until every circumstance of existence is looked upon as a problem of security and order. Any rule can become repressive and absolute because the system contains no principle of limitation for rules and laws. The proof of this can be seen in the historical experience of this century, when the whole world has seen how easily it is to shift from a permissive society to a totalitarian one.

Today all totalitarian systems present themselves as the firmest supporters of liberty and claim that by establishing their dictatorship they are accomplishing the liberation of the people. Such a lie would not be possible if there was no illusion about the root meaning of liberty. Within the modern definitions, there is a hidden continuity between repression and permission. In fact, citizens have come to think that they are protecting their freedom by giving it up into the hands of a totalitarian power—in other words, that the repressive power will be the supporter of a permissive freedom. In the face of such consent, the totalitarian dictatorship asserts that it is reconciling law and liberty, order and freedom.

How is it possible that anyone can believe this? The answer is the mediation of war. All modern totalitarian systems are based on the concept of total war. They show that "enemies" stand in the way of freedom, and consequently war is the only means of achieving or preserving liberty. War means mobilization and discipline with all its well-known consequences—centralization of all the powers under the organs of security, control by the secret service, censorship, silence, lack of participation or any criticism on the part of citizens. All that, according to the proponents of totalitarian governments, is the new condition for liberty. It is through such reasoning that in Chile a dictator could light the liberty torch on September 11, 1975, after two years of radical military dictatorship. "Freedom" has become nothing but security from the enemies of freedom—it is enough to show where these enemies are and the citizens accept the war against them, even with all its repressive conditions.

It is also interesting to observe how the Marxist system has shifted from the idea of a class struggle for liberty to the idea of national security, closely resembling the national security systems of the rightist military dictatorships. At present, nothing is more like the national security ideology than the ideology of Soviet Marxism. In the course of becoming the official ideology of the U.S.S.R., Marxism has been deeply altered; class struggle has been replaced by a struggle against national enemies, resembling past struggles of the Russian nation. The struggle for communism has become a struggle against internal and external enemies, for national security and expansion. The necessities of such a war have led to all the elements of totalitarian power: centralization, control of all citizens and their activities, censorship and propaganda, and the elimination of "dangerous persons," i.e., possible opponents or critics of the system. The Soviet Marxist state is now also a military state, permanently mobilized for permanent war.

In all these totalitarian systems, liberty is the announced aim, slavery is the means. In such a manner, liberty and slavery have become identical within the idealistic concept of liberation.

The Idealistic Framework

How can we explain the paradox of innumerable human crowds running to slavery while hoping for freedom? How can we explain liberation movements leading these members to a condition of slavery? Is it a pure trick of history, as Hegel thought? There is another explanation—the continuity from permissive liberty to the totalitarian systems of today. Let us now consider in more detail the framework of the broad idealistic concept of freedom on which the continuity of such apparently different systems is based.

Even at a very superficial level, there are more points of contact between permissiveness and totalitarianism than appear at first sight.

First, there is a natural connection between totalitarianism and permissive liberty regarding aggressiveness. As we have seen, permissiveness often leads to expressions of aggression. But totalitarian systems also provide persons who seek the free use of their aggressiveness with many opportunities for satisfaction: war and repression, tortures, information service, vigilance, control of their neighbors, and so forth. With such innumerable opportunities, aggressive persons can obtain a feeling of complete freedom.

In addition, totalitarianism does not want to control or prohibit all individual activities. On the contrary, there are some areas where permissiveness corresponds to its interests. For instance, to a degree, all the armed forces manage some tolerance for quite free sexual behavior; it agrees with the needs of a mobilized state. The same thing may be said about drugs. So for citizens who find "freedom" in sex or drugs, the establishment of a totalitarian system will not change anything. On the contrary, it will justify the permissive freedom to use these excitements.

As for economic competition (which, as we have seen, is encouraged by permissiveness), there is no opposition at all between a free enterprise system and a totalitarian political structure. The experience of our century has shown that all the employer classes have no difficulty accepting a modern dictatorship. Indeed, they often want to help achieve it. In Latin America, after the Rockefeller Report in 1967, it was clear that free enterprise wanted such military dictatorship, and the local bourgeoisies would combine with international economic powers to help establish it. A dictatorship offers free enterprise more security, submission of the working class, and legitimacy.

These are not the only connections between totalitarianism and permissiveness. Both, for example, want and promote irresponsibility on the part of citizens. The permissive society leads to it. Totalitarianism encourages it because in such a system the state must be the only responsible organ in the nation and any acceptance of personal responsibility would trouble its management and probably give rise to criticism and debate.

Both permissive societies and totalitarian systems also destroy all intermediate associations between the state and its citizen. Their rights, privileges, and autonomy disappear, leaving individuals alone and isolated in the face of the state and all its power. The clearest result of any permissiveness is the destruction of associations with all their duties and rules. They are considered as oppressive structures, obviously contrary to freedom. But by their destruction, a permissive society prepares the way for the rise of a totalitarian society. After their disappearance, individuals do not remain alone: facing them are the state with its unlimited power. In this position, the human being is the weakest of all creatures, without the possibility even of thinking for oneself; the state gives people their thinking, their understanding, and their way of life. The solitary citizen can only accept the role fixed by the state; individuals have no choice but to sacrifice their own existence to the war for "freedom."

The framework for all these phenomena is an understanding of liberty and liberation from the viewpoint of idealism as a philosophy and a complete representation of the world and men and women.

The starting point and basic principle of idealism is the Big Subject— Humankind seen as a transcendental subject that underlies all cultural expression and gives meaning to the particular subjects. In this view a man or woman as an individual subject is worthwhile only by sharing in the Big Subject. Humankind is thought of as a Big Being that is permanently creating itself, growing, struggling in a continuous process. All individuals and their cultural expressions are only visible revelations of the same reality—humankind revealing itself and generating itself. History is self-creation of the Subject by the Subject itself; the transcendental Subject (Humankind) is always moving on, and its movement is precisely what gives rise to history with its cultures and civilizations. The Big Subject's movement is the synthesis, harmony, equilibrium, and meaning of everything and everybody. For that reason, according to idealism, there is a basic unity between all people and cultures; everything is an expression of the same basic process. The Subject's movement is called praxis, liberation, or praxis of liberation. The process is a movement of creation. Humankind has no nature, no rules, no limits: it is its own creation. The persons of today are only the present stage of a long process of self-creation. By its praxis, humankind makes itself, and thus history is born.

Self-creating humankind meets many obstacles, which the Subject has to face in order to overcome them. There are inert forces and coercive factors. Such forces and factors are the enemies of future humankind. They try to limit the self-expansion of people and society; it may be said that they are elements of slavery. Consequently, the struggle against these forces and factors may be considered as a liberation movement. Since self-creation has to conquer the forces that oppose it, it deserves to be called a praxis of liberation. Creation is also liberation. Humankind creates itself by means of its praxis of liberation; there is a mutual interdependence between creation and liberation. Liberation is thus victorious over the obstacles that hinder creation.

What are these obstacles? They are cultural forces (economic factors, social conditions, political structures, and so forth) above (or beneath) the impulsive, spur-of-the-moment present acts and persons. Although these forces are embodied in persons and institutions, enemies of the liberation praxis are not these particular persons or institutions as such, but the transcendental forces that lie behind such particular beings. In other words, they are not enemies as particular persons, but as representatives of the whole system of resistance. They are only the present transmitters of the enemies of liberation. The same persons and institutions may even at one time have been favorable factors in developing a liberation praxis, but now they are the instruments of regressive forces. Consequently, they must be destroyed together with the forces that they support. The praxis of liberation is compelled to destroy any factors that hinder its process; if persons or institutions stand in the way of it, their destruction is also a liberation.

Inside the same framework are several forms of idealism, divided according to the various forces opposed to liberation/creation. Within the social structures of humankind are both economic and cultural elements. Therefore, there exist both a materialist idealism and a spiritual idealism. The framework is the same—there is little difference between materialism and spiritualism. Spiritual idealism sees the basic principle of man/woman and history, and, consequently, of the Big Subject, in culture. In this variation, the struggle of human self-creation is above all cultural, and material transformations, including economic ones, are the results of cultural shifts. On the other hand, according to the materialist variant of the same framework, matter (i.e., economics) is the main principle; everything depends upon the structures of work and production. The struggle is primarily among production factors, and cultural changes are only consequences of economic change.

From our point of view these differences are secondary. What is called materialism by Marx is called spiritualism or culturalism by other authors. The emphasis here is on the common features of materialism and spiritualism.

The first point in common is that both forms of idealism understand the enemies of the liberation process as natural forces or structures and not as personal opponents. The enemy structures and forces are vanquished. They are replaced by others. The language of the natural sciences is often applied to this liberation-by-destruction because the authors believe that the liberation process is similar to a natural process (indeed, the analogy between nature and history underlies all idealism). History is seen as a succession of structures and forces, a struggle between forces, a parallel movement of vanishing and rising structures, rather than as an opposition of persons. The opposition of ancient vs. modern replaces the opposition friend vs. enemy; friends and enemies are seen only as embodiments of the basic reality of modern vs. ancient.

The praxis of liberation is presented as a struggle against structural forces, such as capitalism, feudalism, extremism, and communism, like a struggle against an illness, an epidemic, a flood, or a plague. Idealism does not look at particular persons, because they are considered only the bearers of a social structure, be it cultural or economic. The enemy is not a person or persons but a particular state of society, and the praxis aims to change the social structure. The decisive step in the praxis is the change of the structure.

The second common feature of materialist and spiritual idealism proceeds from the first. There is no possibility of changing any social structure without changing the relation of persons to nature. Resistance to social transformations is not to be explained by the ill will, lack of understanding, or impaired social sense of some individuals or groups of individuals. Certain economic structures maintain the social and cultural structure. If some citizens are opposed to changing them, the cause is not in their personal will, since economic structures depend on the possibilities of production. The ultimate principles of any change are to be found in new technology and scientific knowledge; the possibility of using and applying natural energies in some new way is the starting point for reforming the whole economy and consequently the social structures dependent on it. So, according to idealism, in the end the transformation of human beings depends on the transformation of nature. Different thinkers emphasize different elements within this praxis of liberation, but the decisive step is always the development of new technology and scientific knowledge. The self-creation of humankind first proceeds from the development of science and technology. Of course, the idealists hasten to add, the new science and technology do not produce their consequences immediately; there are opposing forces, embodied in persons and institutions. The struggle for the primacy of science and technology leads to changes in structures and, therefore, to the destruction of those persons and institutions that stand in the way of the process. But the meaning of the whole process has been given through the decisive step—the development of science and technology, the condition for a new way of production.

There is perfect agreement between Marxism and Western spiritualism. They both believe that the self-creation of human beings, the future of culture and civilization, and all ethical values depend on the progress of scientific knowledge and technical development, that humankind's transformation must be the last result of the transformation of nature. With a better exploitation of the material world, a social reformation will be possible; democracy, freedom, and happiness will be the final results of economic development, which is based on the new sciences and technology. Praxis, liberation, self-creation are various aspects of one main process: the free development of science and technology according to their own dynamics, in spite of all the resistance.

From such a framework it is not difficult to understand why liberation movements swing from permissive to totalitarian systems. In the beginning, the liberation process (self-creation by means of scientific and technological development, social change, and so on) appears as a struggle against the ancient world and society with all its structures. It is easy to find freedom in destroying the inheritance of the old cultures of humankind. Traditional society, of course, tries to resist, and that resistance is countered in the name of creating the "new human." At this moment, any struggle against any structure is a step toward progress and liberation, be it the struggle against the traditional family, associations, traditions concerning work or play, religion, law, education, or traditional art, language, and styles. Any destructive operation is considered a positive contribution to freedom since the "new human" will arise when the "old human" vanishes. In such a way idealism understands the aspirations of individualism and permissiveness as positive contributions to the praxis of liberation.

But in the next stage, individualism and permissiveness reveal their negativeness, their lack of any creative power. The hoped-for wellspring of creativity does not appear. At the same time, the permissive society makes human life insupportable. And a crucial question arises: Who will be able to carry out the work of the transformation of nature by means of science and technology?

The idealistic framework does not change, but the movement swings to the second pole. A power arises; it is usually a military power and always a candidate for leading a totalitarian system. This power offers itself as the only embodiment of nature, history, and the self-creation of humanity, the only factor able to achieve the self-creation process. Such a power believes it alone is able to make a "new human." Whether this new power is rightist or leftist makes no difference to its perceived goals or its means of achieving them. It has a military orientation and intends to carry out its task by means of the state. It conquers the power of the state by violence and considers that such violence is the first step toward liberation. Violence and power appear positive and fruitful in its hands.

Then the liberation process continues as the power of the state directs all citizens to the transformation of nature. The development of nature and the struggle against enemies are linked—enemies are seen as the embodiment of the forces trying to stand in the way of development. By compelling the citizens to work according to the new sciences and technology, the totalitarian system is now seen to operate as the incarnation of the self-creation process. Here there is no difference between Marxism and Western totalitarianism. In both cases, the praxis of liberation is nothing other than total mobilization of the nation whether through a militarized party or the armed forces themselves.

THE DEBATE ON IDEALISM

This whole framework of the idealistic understanding of liberation is, of course, opposed in many ways by Christian thinking (and in some instances by plain common sense). Before examining the points of debate step by step, however, let us review the central premise of idealism, often misunderstood because of the ambiguous language in which it is presented. The nucleus of idealism is the relation of persons to nature. It sees the chief question as the transformation of nature, and liberation as a basic process in transforming it. Some persons and institutions interfere with the process in order to hinder it, but they are not seen as the problem, only as representing natural structures that they want to maintain. By controlling the natural laws and developing its forces, says idealism, human persons will build their own liberty. When an affluent society appears, human problems vanish and there is no more reason for coercion.

As we may foresee, Christianity states the opposite position. (Indeed, the Christian understanding of liberty and liberation could almost be expressed by simply affirming the opposites of all the statements of idealism.) Let us examine in detail Christianity's chief objections to the tenets of idealism.

The Myths of Idealism. The first objection is that the basic concepts of idealism simply do not exist. The Big Subject, humankind as a historical subject, human beings as a whole process are myths. There is no total process of self-creation, no homogeneous and total development, no movement underlying the whole of history and explaining the appearance and meaning of each phenomenon within it. Such a unity does not exist. There is no Subject; consequently there is no self-creation of such a Subject. History as an integrating process does not exist. There are persons, families, associations, nations, and peoples, but humankind as a superbeing does not exist. Humankind is a constellation of competitive nations, not a unifying process.

Consequently, the praxis of liberation as a total process does not exist either. The very word "praxis" is unavoidably ambiguous. As soon as we give it the meaning of a total process involving all operations, we fall (sometimes unwittingly) into the idealistic framework.

Where then does the unity of humankind come from? It has two sources: God, and the free will of individual persons. God is the author of the biological species *Homo sapiens,* the author of the material factors that are necessary for the human subsistence, and also the author of the connections between persons and nature, author of the human vocation. This is not a question of self-creation. What all human beings have in common are their creation and the structures they have received from God; their unity proceeds not from their self-creation but from these common features that they have received.

Note that according to this view God is the author of humankind and certain structures and relationships. But God is not the author of human history. God intervenes in history, but he is not its author, except in the sense that he is the creator of all the factors present in it. History proceeds from the liberty of men and women. Nature and history are not two faces of the same process; the transformation of nature and the transformations of men and women are not the same process. The unity of humankind is not the result of a natural process but of the challenge to human liberty. History can be understood as a movement unifying all human beings, but only if the unity is understood as proceeding from the will of persons. It is a unity of agreement among several wills, not the unity of a process that involves persons. Unity between persons is not integration, but love.

The True Problems of Liberty. The idealistic framework hides the true problems: liberty is a political problem; individuals do not answer its call spontaneously.

The area of liberation is different from the areas of nature, science, technology, and development. The enemy of freedom is not tradition, but domination and exploitation. The enemies of men and women are not natural forces or a lack of natural resources but other men and women. Notice that the problem of the relation of "human being to human being" is radically different from the problem of relation of "human being to nature." Humankind does not exist. What exists are peoples and nations, classes and groups, the unequal distribution of forces and power. All persons are not cells of a superbeing, a Big Subject; they are members of peoples subordinated to states.

The wish to dominate and exploit reaches its highest level in the states, to which are put all questions concerning freedom. The state provides some citizens with the means of domination. Individuals alone would not be able to do it. But the state receives its will to power from its citizens—the weaker classes hope that it will defend some liberty while the stronger foresee the possibility of dominating others.

In short, liberty is a political problem in the strictest sense of the word, a state problem. It is the first problem hidden by the ideology of idealism.

The second problem hidden by the idealistic concept of liberty is best seen by asking the question: What makes anyone suppose that human beings spontaneously want to be free? There is no reason to identify the history of humankind (or just Western history) with a pure movement toward freedom. Certainly, there is some movement to freedom within history, but there are also many opposite movements. History is a permanent debate and struggle between liberty and its opposites.

Liberty is a calling that has to do with the relationship of persons and communities among each other. The main problem of any liberation movement is that such a calling is asleep, that persons have to be awakened to freedom. There are many other trends hindering their desire for freedom: fear, security, quiet, lack of responsibility, on the one hand; domination and exploitation, on the other. Within the idealistic framework the specific issues of freedom vanish. It sees the basic relationship as one of "human being to nature," and this is so different from the actual root relationship of "human being to human being" that the specific problems of liberty—state and nation, power and oppression, liberty as a responsibility, and so on—are hidden.

Technology and Liberty. Idealism firmly believes that liberation is achieved by controlling nature through science and technology. But historical experience has not confirmed this thesis. Certainly science and technology have increased some material and sensory satisfactions—comfort, health, longevity, and so on. But there is no sign of a parallel between economic development and freedom. Rather, material development is historically ambiguous; it has proved just as likely to give rise to oppression as to freedom. For centuries, material development has very often been related to military progress—much technology has appeared in answer to military needs. The last few decades have shown this with particular clarity: much of the scientific progress that has been achieved has been directly related to the military rivalry between nations, and much of science and technology's self-generated progress has ended by being used primarily for military aims, thus leading to an increasing militarization of life and society. Militarization has been the beginning and end of scientific and especially technological history. There is, of course, no proof that such militarization of scientific and technological achievements is unavoidable, but it is something that can be anticipated. The use of material development to increase freedom is a possibility and nothing more; such development does not proceed from a wish for freedom and, consequently, is hardly able to guarantee it.

The Spread and Confusion of Idealistic Thought. The idealistic framework originated in Europe where it has been one of the main lines of thinking for the last two centuries. But lately it has entered into the liberation movements of the Third World. Why have they accepted such an ideological understanding of the world and society from circumstances so different from their own? In many cases we may assume that they are using European language while giving it a new meaning adjusted to their own problems. In some countries this is purely a matter of fashion and literary style; in others, European culture does have some historical significance. In Africa, for example, it seems safe to assume that any European thought is purely metaphorical; the words have lost their previous meanings. In places like Latin America, on the other hand, European culture has deeper roots, and the idealistic framework is sometimes accepted for itself, more or less in the sense its originators intended. For example, the so-called Marxism of many Latin Americans who are not active members of a Communist party and actually have very general ideas about Marxism itself is simply an expression of an idealistic philosophy, drawn from one or more of its European authors.

Whatever the reasons for this widespread expression of idealistic thinking, it is a problem. In the first place, it has become so common that there is a temptation to accept it at least as the self-understanding of present society. When Christians attempt to dialogue with humankind and the world, the idealistic philosophy appears to be the evident representation of this world, and they are tempted to search for a dialogue with it in place of a dialogue with the real persons of our times. Whether or not one accepts its conclusions, the idealistic framework offers a description of the processes, movements, and values of the modern world, and it is easy to let these replace right knowledge of this world itself.

But if Christians do this, they end in the trap of denouncing or disproving a mythical process. The idealistic view of the world and persons is an ideology, not reality. If we ask about the world and modern men and women in an idealistic way, we are accepting the idealistic ideology. Moreover, if we posit the problems of church and world starting with an idealistic understanding of the world and the human beings, we will not be able to reach any theological answers. Before arriving at any conclusions, we will probably reach some impossible dilemma; if we do manage to reach a conclusion, we can be quite sure it is wrong.

This is the problem of Christians who attempt any dialogue that opposes the church. If they accept the definitions given by their opponents, the dialogue probably will show there is no place for the church in the modern world. Consequently, the first step in any dialogue ought to be a discussion about the world itself, more precisely, about the way of understanding this world and its main categories and the ideological system that is the basis of this way of understanding.

To clarify this problem, let us review some historical debates that have proceeded from accepting the idealistic framework and/or definitions and have led to impossible dilemmas.

First, the famous problem of dualism: Is there a dualism between church and world or not? Is the church a history, a process, an evolution to be distinguished and separated from world history, process, and evolution, although parallel to it? If the answer is yes, the problem arises: Should not Christianity and the church remain alien to the world and society and, consequently, do its members have any specific secular responsibility? With a yes answer, all time given to the church becomes time taken from the world, and vice versa.

But if the answer is no, the opposite difficulty arises: What is the specificity of church and Christianity? How can the danger of horizontalism be avoided? Religious concepts become understood as metaphorical expressions of a secular process. The church recedes until it vanishes and is nothing more than the world itself.

This problem of duality has been present in European Catholic theology for twenty-five years and in Latin America for the last ten. It was probably the most important factor in paralyzing Catholic theology until the appearance of political and liberation theology. For several decades all debates were deadlocked by impossible dilemmas between eschatology and incarnation, humanization and Christianization, human promotion and evangelization, and so on.

The point is that such paralysis was absolutely unnecessary. All those problems were a result of accepting the idealistic framework and its definitions. Their very existence shows how deeply the idealistic categories entered into Christian theology. The problem of dualism or no dualism between church and world is a false problem because the world does not exist; it is only an idealistic category. There is no world as a specific unit, as a process, a movement.

What exists are nations, states, political or social movements, organizations, economic development (or more) in particular areas, agriculture, manufacturing, and so on. "World" is simply a name given to the collection of movements, parties, peoples, and states. There can be no problem of a relationship between the church and a name. The real problems concern the relationship between church and state, church and economic development, and so on.

In the same way, there is no problem about faith and politics. "Politics" is a category; it does not exist. There are states, parties, political movements. Giving existence to abstractions such as "world," "politics," "faith," and so on proceeds from the idealistic way of thinking. So too, there is no problem of the relationship between evangelization and the praxis of liberation because there is no liberation praxis—it is only an idea from the idealistic framework.

When the impossibility of these debates is clear, one can also see why it is not possible to separate the interpretation of methodology and theological understanding. Theology begins with the interpretation of secular issues; of course, it cannot understand everything, but it provides the task of interpretation with ultimate criteria. In Europe and Latin America, several Christians have attempted to distinguish between interpreting methodology and theology regarding Marxism. They have said that Christianity is compatible with the methodology proceeding from Marxism, that Marxism could be a correct methodology for interpreting social issues. Later, they continued, Christian theology could give Christian judgment about a situation interpreted by means of a Marxist methodology. Actually, such a distinction is impossible; the Marxist categories in interpreting social issues use the whole system and cannot be separated from it.

THE BIBLICAL SOURCES OF CHRISTIAN LIBERATION

Now that we have examined the idealistic understanding of freedom and the whole idealistic framework, we are better able to look at the Christian understanding of liberty and liberation. And since the problem of our time is the prevailing idealism, we need not review all possible aspects of a Christian liberation theology, but only those opposed to or distinguished from aspects of idealism.

Paul's Theology on Liberation

The most complete exposition of New Testament liberation theology is to be found in Paul's epistles. (The other books of the New Testament also talk about liberty and liberation, but not in such a systematic way as the Pauline epistles.)

Pauline theology on liberty falls within two main contexts: ecclesiology, or the announcement of a new people of God (the body of Christ and the temple of the Holy Spirit); and the process of justification (salvation, conversion, human transformation, divinization, etc.) within which dynamic liberty is the end point of the whole process, the consequence of the new human condition.

One collection of Pauline verses on freedom speaks of the church, God's people, the eschatological gathering of nations and peoples, the mystery of the calling, and the coming of people from all over the world to Jesus Christ as a progressive movement until the end of time. In such a context Paul uses the word and the concept "liberty."

In one Spirit, we were all baptised, Jews as well as Greeks, slaves as well as free men, and one Spirit was given to us all to drink (1 Cor. 12:13).

There are no more distinctions between Jew and Greek, slave and free, male and female, but all of you are one in Christ Jesus (Gal. 3:28).

There is no room for distinction between Greek and Jew, between the circumcised or the uncircumcised, or between barbarian and Scythian, slave and citizen free man. [i.e., There is only Christ; he is everything and he is in everything] (Col. 3:11).

Let everyone stay as he was at the time of his call. If, when you were called you were a slave, do not let this bother you; but if you should have the chance of being free, accept it. A slave, when he is called in the Lord, becomes the Lord's freed man, and a free man called in the Lord becomes Christ's slave. You have all been bought and paid for; do not be the slaves of other men. Each one of you, my brothers, should stay as he was before God at the time of his call (1 Cor. 7:20–24).

With these verses one may compare the famous text from Ephesians:

Slaves, be obedient to the men who are called your masters in this world with deep respect and sincere loyalty as you are obedient to Christ, not only when you are under their eye, as if you had only to please men, but because you are slaves of Christ and wholeheartedly do the will of God. Work hard and willingly, but do it for the sake of the Lord and not for the sake of men. You can be sure that everyone, whether a slave or a free man, will be properly rewarded by the Lord for whatever work he has done well (6:5–8).

Paul was, of course, speaking of the problem of liberty in terms of a specific situation: slavery as it existed in his world, a social structure linked with ancient civilizations generally, and the whole Roman Empire in particular. To understand the position he was taking on slavery, one must look at the whole of his teaching.

First, Paul ignores all the metaphysical, ethical, and legal bases of slavery as they had been established within the ancient civilizations and confirmed by their philosophers and lawmen. Of course, he knew justifications of the system used by the Romans and the Greeks. But he did not cite them; that means that he gave them no value, that he did not see them as worthwhile. Neither did he use the contemporary explanations of the rules for the behavior of slaves. He does admit the distinction between slave and master, but as a contingent fact, not a necessary distinction. (The same point of view appears in the epistle to Philemon.) In the long run, such a position was to destroy the bases of the distinction. Relativism like Paul's in judging such an issue was dangerous for the institution of slavery itself; it meant that justifications taken from natural law had lost their power of persuasion and there was now room for new aspiration.

Second, it is quite certain that Paul did not even consider the possibility of a slave rebellion (although rebellions, such as that led by Spartacus, were not uncommon in contemporary history). He neither agreed nor disagreed with such action; he simply ignored the problem. This means that the gospel of Jesus Christ and the rebellion of Spartacus are situated on two completely different levels. From this we should not deduce that any rebellion of slaves is illegitimate or meaningless (or, for that matter, something of merit), but only that there was no communication between Jesus' message and the rebellion of Spartacus. The rebellion of slaves does not bring what Jesus' message brings. The rebellion of slaves in itself is not the promise of the gospel, the sign of God's people.

The reason such a rebellion is so different from the promise of the gospel is fairly obvious. Spartacus and his slaves did not oppose slavery per se; they just did not accept their own slavery. If they had won against the Romans, they would have been quite ready to make the Roman citizens their own slaves. In other words, they accepted the social institution and had no idea of changing it. Such an idea had to be born from a new point of view and a new understanding of relationships among persons.

There is a trap to be avoided here. From Paul's ignoring of the possibility of rebellion and from his expression in the texts quoted, it would be easy to conclude something like this: Paul means there are two kinds of liberty, completely separated from each other, and two kinds of slaves. There are free persons and slaves according to Christ, and free persons and slaves according to the secular city. A free person or a slave according to Jesus Christ may be either slave or free in the secular city; there is no connection between the two. It is important to arrive at liberty in Christ; the other liberty is a matter of indifference for a Christian. Slavery is not an impediment to liberty in Christ. So there are two peoples—God's people and man's people—in the people of the New Testament; the human condition is not important.

Such an interpretation of Paul's thought cannot be accepted. For it is based on the idea of a spiritual people, of persons whose souls are the only important part of them, of persons who have no connection with the historical processes and the material condition of humankind. The Pauline idea about God's people is totally different; consequently, his idea of liberty cannot be a dualism that results from the idea of two parallel peoples existing under the dualism of soul-body.

Let us look at Paul's actual understanding of the new people of the new covenant. God's people are not made only of souls, nor of mere interiority. The people of the New Testament are as visible, as material, as the people of the Old Testament. The New Israel continues the Old Israel with its history and its entire human reality. The people of God, the Christian church, continues Israel's history: such a people involve the whole of a person, interiority and exteriority, soul and body, personal and social life. Therefore, as Lucien Cerfaux said, "they are a new people in the political sense of this word."[3] The church is a political issue; it is the change of Ancient Israel to New Israel, both political issues. A new people was born in Paul's time, although it still had to increase and expand and grow up. Many centuries have been necessary to show all the political consequences of the coming of the new people; many states had to evolve before it reached the point of destroying the political units that oppose the advent of the kingdom of God. But through the Christian church, a new social and political condition has come to humankind, and eventually it will produce its political effects.

The only correct interpretation of Paul's teachings about slaves and free persons comes from placing it within the context of his complete idea of church and people of God. By announcing there is no Jew or Greek, male or female, slave or free person in the people of God, Paul does not intend to say that such distinctions are irrelevant in the kingdom of God and have lost their importance. Neither does he say that such distinctions will remain exactly the same as before. Rather, when one compares the various distinctions he included, one sees that he means none of them will remain the same. For example, Paul does not think that the relationship between man and woman would remain unchanged; on the contrary, he thought that new sexual relationships were to be established. Neither did he intend to announce that Greeks and Jews would remain in the same relation to each other; rather, he said that Jews and Greeks had to change their relationship radically. Consequently, one may anticipate that a new relationship between slaves and free will also be reached through Jesus Christ's advent.

Paul did not announce what that relationship was going to be or exactly how it would come about—he did not know future history. But since an entire new people, not merely a new soul, is concerned, the secular problem of slavery and not merely the problem of interior liberty has to be involved.

So Paul did hope for a social change. What would be the way to such change? He does not tell us in this first group of texts, but some ideas are suggested in a second group, which say that the opposition between slaves and free persons can be abolished only through the "new man" that God creates through his Spirit. A mere insurrection or law is not sufficient; a radical change within "man" himself is necessary. Let us look at the "man" who is the new creation.

The idea of a "new man" is commonplace in most present-day philosophies, Christian or idealistic. The difference between frameworks is the way of this new creation. For example, Marxist dialectics require a "new man" who is the proletarian class, not by virtue of its class, but because the proletarian class is above all the other social classes. The proletariat is the expression of humankind itself.[4]

According to Christian revelation, the origin of salvation and liberation is in poor and lowly people. But it is not by reason of their dominated position or by means of the dialectical evolution or the contradiction between production forces that liberation is to be found there, but rather by virtue of a divine calling. Christianity believes there is no social class which will automatically be the author of true liberation, only those who are called.

Human beings have been called to form the new people, and their first expression of their renewed freedom is simply to accept the calling. Before creating a new social structure it was necessary to establish a new people of free persons. But this new people is a historical group, not an invisible assembly of souls. Consequently, the new people cannot suffer social patterns that are incompatible with the new calling of humankind. The creation of the new people announced many future revolutions, although Paul could not anticipate the exact succession of the multiple issues that were to make such revolutions.

Let us now consider the second group of Pauline texts about freedom, those that use the context of the new creation and the "new man" who results from it.

The first passage is chapter 6 of the epistle to the Romans. In this chapter Paul describes the new human condition after Christ's atonement through his death and resurrection.

You were once slaves of sin, but thank God you submitted without reservation to the creed you were taught. You may have been freed from the slavery of sin, but only to become "slaves" of righteousness (6:17–18).

Under the law, human beings had been slaves of sin and the body's desires, although sin and law lead to death. Now they have been made free first from sin, then from law, then from death. On the other hand, such a freedom is also slavery. Liberation is changing from the slavery of sin to the slavery of righteousness, grace, Christ, and God that leads to life, not to death. Such is the structure of the new creation.

So, freedom is service or obedience. What service? That is not specified until chapter 8, where Paul completes his own idea and shows how Christian freedom proceeds from the Spirit. The Spirit makes us free from sin, law, and death and guides us to a new condition—obedience to a new law that is a law of life:

the law of the spirit of life in Christ Jesus' law of sin and death (8:2).

The whole creation is in solidarity with men and women and has been called to a new condition of freedom; all material beings share in the liberation.

The whole creation is eagerly waiting for God to reveal his sons. It was not for any fault on the part of creation that it was made unable to attain its purpose; it was made so by God; but creation still retains the hope of being freed, like us, from its slavery to decadence, to enjoy the same freedom and glory as the children of God (Romans 8:19–21).

Notice that human liberation does not depend on material transformation; on the contrary, material transformation depends on human liberation. The sharing of the whole universe in the liberation process shows that that process is not merely spiritual. Any transformation of the material universe is necessarily material.

These texts tell us about the starting point of liberation: freedom from sin, law, and death. The next group tells about its end point: a freedom for apostolate. The connection between this beginning and end is quite clear in the epistle to the Galatians, whose subject matter is freedom from law.

. . . the liberty we enjoy in Christ Jesus (2:4).

The Jerusalem above, however, is free and is our mother (4:26; cf. 22–31).

When Christ freed us, he meant us to remain free. Stand firm, therefore, and do not submit again to the yoke of slavery (5:1).

My brothers, you were called, as you know, to liberty; but be careful, or this liberty will provide an opening for self-indulgence. Serve one another, rather, in works of love (5:13).

The last verse (5:13) is the most concentrated form of Pauline theology, matched only by

where the Spirit of the Lord is, there is freedom (2 Cor. 3:17).

These texts are very rich, and commenting on all their contents here would be impossible. Let us consider a few points based on the exegetical studies of theologians of all times.

1. Christian liberty is a calling. It is not the human condition, or a part of it, or the automatic result of the Spirit and its gifts, or the effect of a transformation of universe, society, culture, or economy. Its advent depends on the free choice of a person: such a choice of becoming free is the first free act.

2. The ultimate principle of any domination lies in the will of the individual person. Only a change of the will, therefore, can generate freedom.

3. Because the basis of domination or freedom lies in the individual will, law is not able to emancipate persons. By the word "law," Paul meant not merely Jewish cultic law, but any law—the legal systems, customs, and rules of all peoples and nations, cultures and civilizations, including new laws made by revolutionary movements. Laws may show the way to life, but they cannot operate the transformation able to bring about liberation. The hope of civilizations has always been liberation by means of a new legal system, structural reformation by means of power. But according to Paul's theology, law is never able to set people free. On the contrary, it is a form of domination and slavery, and in trying to liberate, even reformed or revolutionary law gives rise to some new forms of slavery.

4. Freedom is a new life, a new behavior. Its principle lies within the human person; it proceeds from his or her will, from the Spirit living within each person's heart. The new behavior is not unreasonable; indeed, it is reason itself; the "new man" is guided by the Spirit, which is a new law, a law of love. All ancient and modern theologians have understood that the law of the Spirit is love (a glance at St. Thomas Aquinas, for example, is instructive). And Paul said it explicitly: "the whole of the Law is summarized in a

single command: love your neighbor as yourself" (Galatians 5:14). Freedom and love are equivalent. Love is free, and freedom produces love.

5. Law creates new ties, which are ties of service to neighbor. Such ties are so tight as to be called a new slavery. But this is a voluntary slavery, a new law that people give to themselves. There is no doubt as to Paul's concept of the content of love; chapter 13 of 1 Corinthians is clear enough. Consequently, freedom is far from corresponding to the corruption denounced in 2 Peter:

With their high-flown talk, which is all hollow, they tempt back the ones who have only just escaped from paganism, playing on their bodily desires with debaucheries. They may promise freedom, but they themselves are slaves, slaves to corruption; because if anyone lets himself be dominated by anything, then he is a slave to it (2 Pet. 2:18–19).

Paul's command to love and freedom is the same as that expressed by 1 Peter:

You are slaves of no one except God, so behave like free men, and never use your freedom as an excuse for wickedness. Have respect for everyone and love for our community (1 Pet. 2:16–17).

Being a slave of God is loving one's neighbor. The idea of love provides the connection between the two ideas of freedom, the negative one of the epistle to the Romans and the positive one of the epistle to the Galatians. Freedom from sin is freedom for love. Indeed, love and sin are opposites: sin is the breaking of social ties; love is the making of new ones.

In summary, Pauline theology can be condensed into the following principle: freedom refers to the relationship of persons with each other; it is a way of relating to other persons. Freedom has nothing to do with loneliness, individualism, or selfishness. The principle of freedom is not a new bond with nature, but a new bond with other persons.

Some people misunderstand the meaning of service to neighbor, which is the new slavery of love. The service of love is not a subordination to the aspirations or desires of the neighbor, but a service to liberating the neighbor from his or her own slavery. Therefore, the service of love is exactly the same as the apostolic mission. Such a mission requires the most absolute liberty; in serving others, the apostle imposes his or her own liberty. He or she wants to be free of being a slave and acts accordingly in a manner received from the inspiration of the Spirit.

I personally am free: I am an apostle (1 Cor. 9:1).

So though I am not a slave of any man I have made myself the slave of everyone so as to win as many as I could (1 Cor. 9:19).

In Paul's context, there is no contradiction between "not a slave of any man" and "slave of everyone." He does not intend to reject his own advice: "do not be slaves of other men" (1 Corinthians 7:23). To be "the slave of everyone" is to be the slave of the "new man" who is created through God's word and grace, rather than the slave of the "old man" who lives in the midst of sin, law, and death.

Such a radical change from sin, law, and death to life, love, freedom, and free apostolate cannot be reduced solely to a religious experience. That would be a "modernization" of Paul's theology. For Paul, the language of freedom is perennially political and public. The language of liberty was originally Greek and as such had a political sense. It entered into the Greek Old Testament with its political connotations and was used by the authors of the New Testament, especially Paul, with all its political connotations.[5] This was no accident: the transformation process (justification, conversion, salvation, etc.) is not only a personal but a social change; it refers to a people, Israel, becoming a universal people open to the heathen nations. Freedom from sin and law and death is freedom from Israel's sin, Israel's law, and Israel's death, and the heathen people had shared in the condition of the people Israel. Love as a "new man" is a social disposition—a social tie, responsibility, and solidarity within the new people of God. All Pauline theology talks about the fate of Israel's people. Freedom is the bond of mutual service among the new people. Love is the energy that creates a new people.

Jesus' Message of Liberty and Liberation

Although the Pauline language of freedom was Greek, Paul's message was not Greek. That message proceeded from Jesus (or, more precisely, from the Bible and Jewish history, which converged in Jesus and reached its perfection in him). Paul used the Greek language in order to express Jesus' message. With this language he could express the scope and the importance of freedom at the center of Christianity. But the content of freedom he was speaking of refers to the Christian experience—to Jesus' life. In other words, Paul should not be separated from Jesus; he used the language of freedom to express Jesus' experience but not to replace it.

There was a good reason for Paul's use of the Greek language of liberty. The Jews had no abstract words to explain the human condition. They lived life but they did not talk about it. So Jesus, speaking in Aramaic, had no words to express his own way of life. The Synoptic Gospels, therefore, do not relate any speech about liberty, and Jesus' message is to be encountered in the acts of his life, not in speeches. But although Jesus did not talk about his own life, comparison of his action and Paul's language shows that the language of freedom is well adapted to express what Jesus did not say because of the nature of Semitic words.

Luke is the author who makes the connection between Jesus and Paul. Remember that Luke's intention was to give his readers a summary exposition of the meaning of Jesus' life and that he was writing for readers who would not immediately understand Jewish categories. For the Jews, the connection between Jesus and Israel's fate was clear enough, but for a Greek audience it was necessary to specify it. And Luke made it very clear. The whole of Jesus' mission was related to the accomplishment of Israel's calling. Jesus was a new Moses, the liberator of his people. The liberation of Israel was a new creation of the people, or a returning of them to their prior condition. Free from sin, law, death, and all their consequences, Israel could return to its calling. Jesus' mission was to make Israel a "people of God," as it had been the mission of Moses. But the scope of Jesus' work was more radical than Moses' work—the renewed Israel would be the perfection or consummation of ancient Israel, accomplishing the promises of the prophets.

There are several passages in which Luke explained the meaning of Jesus' life. First, the prophecy of Zechariah:

Blessed be the Lord, the God of Israel, for he has visited his people, he has come to their rescue, and he has raised up for us a power for salvation, in the House of his servant David (Luke 1:68–69).

Then Anna the prophetess also announced:

. . . to all who looked forward to the deliverance of Jerusalem (2:38).

Luke gives to Jesus the words of Isaiah:

To set the downtrodden free, to proclaim the year of the Lord's favor (4:18).

So, too, the disciples understood:

. . . our own hope had been that he would be the one to set Israel free (24:21).

Jesus was not a philosopher, or a wise man talking and teaching for his disciples or even for the world generally. He did not direct his words to souls or to isolated persons, but to the members of his people. His promise referred to the salvation of his people; he was the new founder of his people who had been destroyed by the Pharisees, the priests, and the masters of law.

Does the liberation of Israel include liberty in the sense used by Paul and the Greek language? The model of life given in the Synoptic Gospels allows us to answer that there is a basic concurrence. Jesus delivered his people by founding a free people; he did not deliver them merely from exterior enemies, but chiefly from their inner corruption, from their lack of real freedom. His deliverance is the founding of a free people in the Greek sense.

Of course, Jesus did not want to restore the kingdom of David to what it had been in the past, though that was what the contemporary Zealots were trying to do. To Jesus, the goal of the Zealots was not the true deliverance of

Israel, but simply a new expression of law and domination. Re-establishing the kingdom of David would be a step backward, since David was the past, not the future, of Israel. Even if victory had been possible against the Roman Empire, repeating the victory of David would have been a defeat of the kingdom of God.

For Jesus, delivering Israel was the fulfillment of his calling. Like the prophets, Jesus reminded Israel of the meaning of its calling and existence. But Jesus was far superior to the prophets, since he did more than announce or promise; he was able to achieve the real goal of Moses and the prophets. Roman domination was only a sign and a consequence of the real slavery of Israel. The "people of God" had given up its true nature. Instead of living as a free people according to the covenant and relying on God's love, Israel had been deceived by false leaders and careless shepherds—the Pharisees, the lawyers, and so on. Jesus was the true shepherd who led his people to the reality of true happiness.

How has Jesus delivered his people? The nature of his acts showed the nature of his plan. His acts were the acts of a free person undertaken to set other people free. Indeed, all the acts of Jesus' ministry may be summarized under three categories: his struggle against the law; his struggle for the unity of all Israel against discrimination; and his struggle against the devils. These three struggles were the starting point of creating a new people free from its traditional corruption, so they are worth examining in more detail.

1. By means of the law, the Pharisees, lawyers, and other Jewish leaders deceived the people and separated them from their true calling. Jesus engaged in, continued, and completed the debate of the prophets against the legal mentality and the social and cultural system that is called law (prevailing material cult, legal regulations, the placing of diplomacy and strategy above faith and love, and so on). Like the prophets, Jesus made clear the opposition between love and law. The mission of Israel was love; Israel had been called to form a people based on a covenant and the respect of the rights of each individual. What Paul called liberty was for Israel the covenant, the fraternity of the twelve tribes, the supremacy of love and mercy above law and forms. Over a period of time, law had come to be used by the false elites in order to legitimize privileges and to oppress the poor and powerless. Such a law could not save; rather than delivering from sin, it was increasing it. Jesus wanted to re-establish the true law, the law of love and mercy (which is the new law, although it is as old as Israel). The Sermon on the Mount was simply the publication of the new law. All Jesus' teachings, not only his controversy with the Pharisees, were part of the struggle against law and legalism. He was preparing the advent of the renewed people, the covenant of the tribes based on love and respect. Such was and is the freedom of Israel.

2. Power and state struggle against division by laying down rules and by eliminating the members of the community who do not submit to law and order. The law of the Pharisees gave rise to discrimination, established many

second-class citizens or rejects, and marginalized the many members of the community who were not able to obey all its regulations. By so doing, they rejected the poor, the oppressed, and the powerless from the people of God. But Jesus replied: "I was sent only to the lost sheep of the House of Israel" (Matthew 15:21). He gathered the lost sheep whom the Pharisees and other leaders of the people had rejected and lost. For him, delivering Israel was a task of reconciliation. A free people is a people in which there is an open door for everybody, especially for the lost members of the community; the very act of deliverance from sin and law is the calling to them to enter. Jesus not only told the lost members the doors were open; he traveled from one village to another to call them in—the sinners, the tax-gatherers, the poor, the sick, the prostitutes. His controversies with the Pharisees concerned this calling: they condemned him because he dealt with sinners, and Jesus condemned them because their law rejected sinners from the people of Israel. To Jesus, dealing with sinners, tax-gatherers, prostitutes, and so on was not simply an expression of pity or comprehension; it was a political activity involving the true nature of the people of Israel. In rejecting all the poor and marginalized persons from the community, the Pharisees and the doctors of the law had deflected and destroyed the real meaning of Israel as a people of God.

3. The signs of Jesus' mission were summarized in his own words:

Go back and tell John what you hear and see; the blind see again, and the lame walk, lepers are cleansed and the deaf hear, and the dead are raised to life and the Good News is proclaimed to the poor (Matt. 11:4–5).

All that was part of the struggle against the kingdom of the devils, whose works are illness, death, and contempt of the poor. In addition, the Gospels record many incidents of Jesus' expelling devils directly.

These signs are difficult for many modern readers to accept. To the secularized mentality of today there is a radical difference between illness and the power of the devils. Modern culture understands the problem of illness as a merely material problem: we are ill because there is some trouble with our bodies. People do not accept the idea that their own state might carry any responsibility for the sickness of another. Even mental illness is considered a mere material problem for which no one is responsible. And if there is no question of responsibility, there is also no question of the interference of the devils. Recently, however, some persons, including scientists, are re-examining this denial. Without denying the interference of many material factors, such as microbes, germs, viruses, and so on, they are observing that the same material factors do not always produce the same results in everybody. They are concluding that here are also some personal factors involved in illness, that personal disposition is of importance not only in mental but in physical illnesses. They are seeing that there are many connections between sin and sickness, and some between virtue and health.

Sin provokes many disturbances and diseases and is responsible for many kinds of mental and physical weakness.

The Jews, including Jesus, emphasized the other aspect of illness—its ties with sin and responsibility—to such an extent that they easily forgot that there were any material factors involved. Their viewpoint was as partial as today's secular idea, but there were reasons for Jesus to take it. He was not a physician and did not want to look at sickness like a physician. In illness, he saw the work of sin and the devil, against which he was powerful. He knew that health was a kind of liberation from human beings' enemies, the devil and sin. And his liberation was not only a spiritual one; it reached the body as well as the soul. Jesus was searching for a people of Israel free from any enemies, free to love.

So all the Savior's acts had the same goal: remaking, restoring, and gathering together the free people of Israel.

Jesus knew that he was not going to complete this goal in his lifetime, that it was not his mission to accomplish the whole of God's plan for humankind. He also knew that his own death would be a necessary stage in and factor for the history of the restoration. Consequently, he knew that after his death new stages would appear; he did not know what those changes were going to be or how they would come about. But since he had not received the task of revealing the future steps of the kingdom of God, he knew that after his death great changes had to happen.

And, of course, after Jesus' death something new did happen. Paul was the most lucid witness of these new events and has given us the right interpretation of the new and definitive step of the kingdom of God. There is, however, a continuity between Jesus' activity and Paul's interpretation of the extent of Christ's work. The same people of God are involved, and Jesus and Paul have the same idea of this people. The only difference is the extension of these people. Jesus saw the people within the limits of the Old Testament; Paul sees them as far more extensive, since the Spirit is sent to all nations and peoples. The renewed Israel is universal, open to everybody. The liberation of Israel is a universal calling from the slavery of sin, death, and illness to the liberties of a free people of God.

Paul and the first Christians understood that Jesus' death was a decisive factor in the change from the people of the old covenant to the universal people. They realized that through his death all the barriers of discrimination, law, and privilege had fallen, that the new covenant was open to everybody. Jesus had destroyed all the principles of the separation of Israel from other peoples. The only step lacking was the effective calling of the nations—that was the task reserved to the apostles, the task which Paul revealed.

So Paul received the idea of liberty from Jesus (and the Jewish tradition) and added one new element: the effective calling of the heathen nations, the introduction of the new communities into the people of God. Notice that the "new" idea was really one of fulfillment: the calling of all peoples had been a promise for Jesus; it was an experience for Paul. But the two had exactly the same idea of freedom; the difference between them was only a question of vocabulary and time.

Now what about the political meaning of their message of freedom? Many authors have been deceived by the silence of both Jesus and Paul on the Roman Empire. Both the Gospels and the epistles make some allusions to Rome but contain no doctrine about it. From such a silence these authors have deduced that Jesus and Paul were indifferent to the political aspects of life, that their message was mainly "spiritual," or "interior," or "religious." Such a conclusion is false because it does not put Jesus and Paul into their proper context. For both, the political unit was Israel. For the most part they did not deal directly with the Roman Empire because they were living in Israel and experienced the reality of the Roman Empire only in a secondary way. Consequently, their political meaning (or the lack of it) must be examined within the context of their idea of Israel. If their conception of Israel lacked political consequence, one may conclude that neither was interested in political issues. But if their idea of Israel included or implied some political change, one has to admit that their message was meaningful from the political point of view.

The position of both Jesus and Paul toward Israel was clearly political. They announced and provoked the most important revolutions within its social and political structures. They stated clearly, in several different ways, that Israel would disappear as a political people, that the inheritance of Israel had to survive outside the frontiers of ancient Israel.

So there were definite and important political implications for Israel in both Jesus' and Paul's messages of freedom. But as for the Roman Empire, neither established connections between it and the liberation of the people of God. They did not yet see how the Roman Empire could be an obstacle to freeing, calling, and gathering the new universal people. It seemed to them that the people of God could be born, grow up, increase, and fulfill its purposes within the Roman Empire. They considered the empire as if it were a simple accident, almost a physical setting like mountains and roads, sea and cities.

Jesus told the Pharisees that their concept of the Roman problem was irrelevant because it included a wrong idea about Israel. The problem of Israel, he said in effect, was not its dependence on Roman tax collecting or the manner in which those taxes were collected or even the existence of those taxes; the problem of Israel was law or love, privileges or mercy, righteousness or sin. But Jesus did not enter into the problem of the Roman Empire in itself. At that moment he did not consider the Roman Empire important.

In the same way Paul solved the connections with Rome pragmatically. He asked the early Christians to be obedient and submissive to Roman laws and power in order to show that they were good citizens. Disobedience and indifference would deceive the Romans as to the true meaning of the Christian message, and Paul wanted it made clear that Christianity was not trouble or insurrection or anarchy. But the problem of the empire remained outside the consideration of the epistles. So, for instance, Paul did not consider the intervention of Pilate as causing Jesus' death. The Gospels give Pilate no importance; he had been an instrument of the Jewish leaders.

In short, until A.D. 80, the Roman Empire was not considered as part of the mystery of salvation. All Christians were still living within the perspective of Israel and were thinking of the mission of Israel all over the world, without interference from Rome, as if Rome would remain a spectator, looking on indifferently at the advent of a new people. Neither Jesus nor Paul could foresee that Rome would not remain indifferent. This was the message of the last of the apostles, John, the survivor of the first generation, in the last years of the first century. A greater political change cannot be imagined.

John's Message on Liberty and Liberation

John's message showed that the repercussions of Christianity were of importance to the Roman Empire as well as to Israel. It was John who grappled with the problem, for Christianity, of the political meaning of the common structures of the heathen nations of the world. Indeed, his primary subject was the encounter of the people of God with the structures of the heathen world. And he showed how the earlier principles taught by Jesus and Paul could be applied to the situation of the Roman Empire, that there was a possible translation from the Hebrew world to the Greek world, that the message of liberty and liberation, which was valid for Israel and the traditional problematics of the people of God, was also meaningful for the condition of the Roman Empire.

John's Gospel, the book of Revelation, and the three Johannine epistles were written roughly around the same time and certainly reflect the same stage of development of the church. Their main perspective is the same.

As for their language, the biblical idea of the people of God is present throughout, and Revelation shows perfect continuity with the chief statements of Paul. The word "free" itself is used in only one passage. But that text is placed at the center of the Fourth Gospel and is connected to John's chief theological concepts, so that it expresses the nucleus of his message. It comes at the climax of the controversy between Jesus and "the Jews" (who are the Pharisees and doctors of law of the Synoptic Gospels). Jesus denounced that false definition of their differing positions and revealed the true positions:

> If you make my word your home
> you will indeed be my disciples,

you will learn the truth
and the truth shall make you free.

They answered, "we are descended from Abraham and we have never been
the slaves of anyone, what do you mean 'You will be made free?' " Jesus
replied:

I tell you most solemnly,
everyone who commits sin is a slave.
So if the Son makes you free,
you will be free indeed (John 8:33–36).

Then begins the debate about sin. Jesus denounces "the Jews" as living in sin.
What does he mean by this? The sin of "the Jews" is the one of the serpent in
paradise, the lie that leads to death. Like the serpent, they are guided by a lie;
this lie leads to murder, as is proved by their desire to kill Jesus. The sin of
"the Jews" is rejecting truth, searching for a lie, killing their own Savior, the
bearer of truth who is able to liberate them from falsehood. The lie makes
people slaves; the truth, which Jesus brings, sets them free.

This text continues the teachings of the Synoptic Gospels. Truth, according to John, corresponds to Jesus' wisdom, Jesus' new law. The truth of the
Fourth Gospel is not a philosophical truth, but the truth about God's plan, the
kingdom of God. The lie is a lie about the kingdom of God, the true Israel,
the people of God. Jesus defended his truth by setting forth his teachings
about the new law of love; in like manner, "the Jews" defended their lie by
defending their own traditions, laws, and customs.

This was clear enough in the Synoptic Gospels. From John's perspective,
however, the understanding of the controversy between Jesus and the masters of the law becomes more complete. In that controversy, John saw the key
that opens the way to an understanding of the conditions of the church in the
last years of the first century. By that time, the first important struggle
between the church and the Roman Empire had appeared, and to John, Jesus'
controversy with the Pharisees spoke to this new situation, as well as to the
specific situation of Israel at the time of Jesus.

In the Fourth Gospel, "the Jews" signify the whole world. What happened
in Jerusalem signifies what is continually happening—the constant drama
enacted on earth. Neither the Synoptic writers nor Paul moved beyond the
area of the Jewish people, but John entered into the entire universe. And, of
course, in his day and place, the most concrete and evident feature of the
universe was the Roman Empire.

How is John's account of Jesus' controversy with the Jews applicable to the
universe? In John, the whole of Jesus' words make up one "testimony,"
and this testimony is truth. One may say that Jesus came to give his testimony to the world, to all peoples and all times. From John's perspective, the entire world was the peoples that made up the Roman Empire,

and it is to them that Jesus addressed his testimony of truth.

John clarified this idea as one of extension. Jesus' teachings to the Jews were public and were addressed to the Jewish people as such; in other words, they were given to the Jews as the "public people of God." John used this characteristic of publicness and extended it to the universe; he chose the idea of testimony to express the public character of Jesus' message for the peoples. To John, history is like a court of justice, and Jesus pronounced his defense before a world tribunal. In this context, Jesus' condemnation by Pilate takes on a special significance alongside the sentence of death from the Jews. Jesus facing Pilate signifies a lasting situation. The church, too, faces Pilate. And, like Jesus, the church may say: "I came into the world for this: to bear witness to the truth" (John 18:37). (In a way Revelation continues this concept, taking the opposition between Pilate and Jesus as a key for the condition of the world.)

In short, in John testimony and truth are political units; they are the origin of liberty, which was the calling of the Jews but which they had lost. This calling for liberty was now addressed to all men and women of all peoples within the Roman Empire. The cause of such a liberty is Jesus' testimony accepted and lived.

From John's viewpoint, such truth and testimony were able to change the political condition of humankind, in particular (for him) that of the people within the Roman Empire. Jesus did not create a new political system or a new political ideology. But he was not indifferent to the political condition. "Mine is not a kingdom of this world" (John 18:36), he said. At the same time, his kingdom has come into this world. Consequently, truth and testimony cannot be indifferent to the political units of this world. Truth and testimony are not opposed to the political world as such, only to that political power which is the servant of falsehood and sin (as Pilate was a servant in allowing the murder of Jesus). That is the continual danger or temptation of political power—that it will act as a servant of the devil, quite possibly unconsciously, by becoming an instrument in the hands of the enemies of truth and testimony.

The book of Revelation confirms the outlook of the Fourth Gospel. The enemy of God and Christ is not the Roman Empire as a political system, but as a political power manipulated by falsehood and injustice. For example, under the emperor Domitian, Rome became a servant of falsehood and murder by persecuting the church. The true enemy is the serpent of Genesis, Satan, who, according to Jesus, was guiding those who persecuted him. Revelation 13 shows Satan acting on the heathen peoples by means of the two beasts. The first beast is political power as a system of domination; the second, political ideology as a factor that makes the first beast worshiped and followed. The first beast was particularly present in the Roman Empire per se and the second in the imperial ideology and the cult of Rome; both beasts represent the domination of the devil, lies, and murder. Such beasts were the historical reality of the Empire at the time of the Johannine writings, the concrete way in which the devil acted against the church. For John, the persecution of Christianity under Domitian was a meaningful event; it was the present revelation of an eternal struggle—the devil against God and Christ. The Roman Empire and its ideology were the instruments of Satan; the martyrdom of Christians was the testimony of Christ and the force of God.

There are two opposite forces: on the one hand, the testimony of God, and on the other, the servants of Satan, who use political power and political ideologies. Political power per se is not the instrument of Satan, but it becomes such an instrument in its concrete acts of submission to domination and lies and sin. Satan gives rise to domination and slavery; the testimony of God and Christ leads to liberty.

As John saw it, such liberty is related to the political condition within a system of domination such as that of the Roman Empire under Domitian. And the testimony of the church aims to overcome the domination of the Roman Empire (and hence all domination). Liberty and testimony appear as two new units that were beginning to operate inside the whole political system. Through its testimony, the church acts as a political factor to produce liberty.

How does testimony produce liberty? To explain this, John employed the biblical concept of prophet in the twelfth chapter of Revelation. There are three stages in which prophet-witnesses carry out their challenge in the face of power and domination: word, death, and resurrection. Through his death, the prophet becomes a martyr: the complete and logical end of his opposition to Satan is his own death. John principally develops this negative aspect of testimony: martyrdom does not change the world or give rise to a new world. Rather, it generates the church. The church is born from the testimony of the prophets; faith is the answer to the death of the martyrs.

There is, however, a more positive aspect of testimony. The word of the prophets of the New Testament is also resurrection and new life; it is able to generate a change in public life and society. How does the testimony of the apostles enter into history and the structure of the world? The New Testament does not say, since revelation ends where history begins. But we know that Christ's word enters into history through the Spirit and his guidance, so we may say that the history of the Kingdom of God in the world manifests the ways of God's testimony. The prophets were free in their testimony and their opposition to the beasts until their martyrdom; indeed, martyrdom is itself the highest act of freedom. But liberty is not only present under the forms of opposition and martyrdom. Liberty is also the experience of a new human-kind, created by the Spirit and following the way of testimony and prophetic words. This second aspect of testimony was not developed in the New Testament, but in the subsequent history of the church and Christianity.

But the New Testament certainly does remind us that the first aspect of testimony—opposition and martyrdom—is a permanent constituent of the struggle for liberty. Liberty will not be a tranquil evolution overcoming established domination and slavery by means of a quiet explanation of the truth. Truth challenges established domination radically and will sustain that fundamental antagonism even to the martyrdom of the prophetic church.

THE SPIRIT AND THE HISTORY OF FREEDOM

With the biblical sources of the concept of Christian liberation firmly in mind, it is possible to examine the same concept as it has been revealed in the history of the church. As we have seen, this revelation is not specified in the New Testament. But that does not matter. The truths of Christianity are composed of the revelation both of Jesus Christ and of the Spirit. Both divine persons are necessary; they are the two hands of the Father accomplishing his plan. Without the Spirit, Jesus Christ reveals but does not accomplish. Without Jesus, the Spirit accomplishes but does not know what is to be accomplished. Jesus reveals the idea of liberty. The Spirit gives rise to liberty in history.

Moreover, the Spirit is the author of a new history inside history: the Spirit gives rise to a new guidance of history and, simultaneously, to a new meaning for everything—including history itself. There was history before the coming of the Spirit, but without the Spirit it remained without direction or significance. With the Spirit, meaning and sense have entered into history.

For example, before the coming of the Spirit, people understood history as a succession of empires, dominating powers, and dynasties. And their understanding was correct. That is exactly what history was then—a succession of patterns of domination, the evolution of the sin and corruption of humankind. Such a history was and is real; the Spirit does not deny that. But the Spirit makes it apparent that such a history is the presence of sin and corruption, and as such the Spirit denounces its very nature. Thus, for St. Augustine the history of Rome was the history of sin, for the Roman Empire was nothing but a great robbery (*magnum latrocinium*). The Romans could not perceive the true reality of their historical process, but the Christians could see it in the light of the Spirit.

The Spirit accomplishes and simultaneously manifests what it is accomplishing. What is the new aspect of history it accomplishes and manifests? It is the positive shaping of a new world, the development of liberty over domination and sin. History is still sin and domination, but with the advent of the Spirit it has also become struggle against sin and domination, the beginning of liberty and truth.

Modern times have seen the introduction of yet another new concept of history: history as a development of economy or the material conditions of human life. Such an evolution is very interesting, but it does not replace the more radical reality of history. Changes within the material condition of life shift the context of the problem but not the challenge itself. The first problem of humankind and history remains the problem of sin and liberty, with or without material development. Material development changes the conditions but not the nature of the challenge of history. The target of human life and history remains liberty, not comfort or sensory gratifications.

Since the advent of the Spirit, human history never has been and never will be as it was before. Never again can it be viewed as a mere succession of dominating powers or even material improvements. With the coming of the Spirit, history became a search for a new people, the people of God who live in liberty and constantly liberate themselves. Since the advent of the Spirit, liberation has made history.

The contents and implications of such a liberation, moved by the Spirit and guided by Jesus Christ, need to be examined carefully.

Creating a New, Free People. First, liberation is the shaping of a new people. Liberation has to do with the relationship of person with person. Now, as we have seen, modern idealism emphasizes the relationship of persons with nature. But this is a result of the relationship of persons with persons, not the cause. So Christianity opposes the modern idealistic pattern. Relationships between persons are not the results of material forces as, for example, the production of material goods may be the result of new technology. Neither are they the effect of a will to power. Empire, state, king, or dictator can impose some kind of social relations, but not liberty. Many relationships are the effects of material causes, but not the shaping of liberties within society. A relationship based on liberty and free agreement is exclusively a problem of human responsibility. Matter, economics, and power are indeed conditions that challenge the Spirit and the human calling to freedom, but they are unable to create such a freedom. Only human responsibility is able to replace the ancient relationships of domination with the creative relationships of friendship, agreement, loyalty, and service.

This change is the conversion announced by the message of the New Testament. Indeed, according to Jesus and Paul, liberation is to be free from sin, and sin is a lack of love of neighbor. If God's command is love, sin cannot be anything but a lack of love. Sin is a breaking down of relationships based on friendship and agreement and a creation of new ones based on domination and rivalry, individual selfishness, and the exploitation of others. The New Testament reveals that such a sin is present within humankind as a whole and in every person as a responsible subject.

Sin does not reach only the outer social structures. If it did, it could be removed simply by the will of the political power, or by the elimination of the individuals most responsible for maintaining those outer structures. On the other hand, sin is not only a personal disposition. If it were, a radical change of personal disposition would be sufficient to remove sin from the world and society. Rather, sin is present in everything—in all personal behavior and in all social structures. The very organization of life and society is based on sin and domination. We cannot do anything without sinning: customs, social patterns, social roles, environment—everything obliges us to share the collective sin of humankind.

But, in spite of that, the message of the New Testament announces a liberation from sin and domination. How can this be, given the ubiquitousness of sin in the human condition? The answer lies in the nature of liberation.

Liberation from sin means more than simply removing a prior situation. Sin has no positive content; on the contrary, it is a lack or absence. But there is no means of removing a lack. So liberation from sin can be nothing other than the creation of new ties and agreements among persons. Liberation from sin is possible only by means of shaping a new society.

This conclusion must be emphasized. It means that according to the Christian definition, liberty cannot even be imagined as the individual disposition of a person alone, isolated from the others, independent from any ties and commitments. Rather, liberty is a new kind of common life, a mutual relationship based on equality and cooperation. Solitary persons cannot be free; their liberty would remain without content; they might be independent but they would have no reasons for acting. A human existence without ties remains empty. (The founders of the monastic orders took notice of this problem. They accepted the ancient monastic way of life into Christianity but made some important additions—the common life and hospitality. Hospitality became the highest duty of the monks: by this means, they show their otherwise isolated lives as integrated within the Christian liberation movement.)

In all societies, there are several levels of common life with its agreements and covenants. The most universal is the family. With faith and Christianity, the family ceases being a mere biological or psychological unit. It becomes instead a community of persons, a royal community. Man, woman, and child are united within the same divine calling to love and loyalty.

On the more complex levels of common life, we meet varied kinds of associations. The history of liberation movements is a constant source of new associations. Such associations create a true people; they are the structures and the material of a state of liberty.

Finally, the state or nation is the highest level of common life. Liberty in the nation (and indirectly in all the associations within it) depends on the institutions of liberty being established as the structures of national life. There is no liberty without the institutions of liberty (a parliament, congress, or some form of popular representation; constitutions; courts of justice independent from repressive or military power; charters, etc.).

Moreover, freedom is not only in the objective structures of the common life, but also in the way such structures are made up. The social structures are free only because they proceed from the citizens' free decisions and struggles for freedom. And unless they continue to proceed from free persons, associations and agreements cannot continue as guarantees of liberty.

A process of liberation leads to liberty when it proceeds from the free will of each person. It is not enough that it proceed from a collective movement or a political party. As Paulo Freire has said, no one liberates anybody else; citizens must make themselves free or they will never become free.

The Call to Freedom. That thought leads to the second chief concept of the Christian idea of liberty: Who is the person who wants to be free? On what level of the human being is such a will to become free to be found? Certainly, that will is not easily disclosed by the methods of psychology, sociology, or the other human sciences. For the human sciences, at present, the individual human being does not exist. Scientific observations disclose culture and social structure, but never a human being as a unit. Such a human being is regarded as a projection of language or imagination meant to satisfy some individual or collective needs; it is not regarded as meaning anything. "Man" is a myth of utopia. (If this were true, the liberation of "man by man" would be a myth of utopia, too.)

Actually, neither scientific observation nor common sense allows us to think that human beings are really searching for liberty. They usually have several other goals—security, comfort, quiet, personal ambition, collective dreams, and so on—but liberty has never been the most evident aim of peoples and societies. So how can we talk about a human will to freedom? What is such a human being?

It is easy to understand why the revolutionary parties identify the true human being with the party member. For Marxism, the proletariat and the working class are the members of the party; the very will of the proletariat is to be disclosed through the will of the aware members of the party, and the awareness of the workers is the awareness of the party. So the party expresses the reality of the human being. Such a definition is very clear and does not allow for any doubt. But how can the charge of being unscientific be avoided? How can a member of such a "liberation" party be distinguished from an object of manipulation? Can one's awareness of freedom be anything other than the mere projection of the plan of the party?

According to the New Testament, the calling for liberty is not the projection of a party but God's presence within the individual. Only God is able to create a movement toward liberty without manipulation. So liberty relates unavoidably to God. Human beings and their ultimate meaning are given by God. Even though statistically the will to freedom may not be representative of humankind, the calling that proceeds from God and leads to freedom is truly the seed of a new humankind, growing and increasing. As such it is a promise and hope for the future; it expresses the deepest meaning and the chief movement of humankind. God's calling allows us to select, from all the units of human experience, the most decisive one. And although weak and threatened, the will to freedom is increasing, for God's calling is eventually effective—the Spirit gives it life and strength. The liberation movement is as weak and as strong as its participants' obedience to God's commands, for obedience and liberty are identical and make one unit. Human existence cannot be signified by mere statistical data, but only by that most profound calling, which unifies all the particular attempts to create a human order. Liberation does not remain on the level of a mere myth, because the Spirit is active in the world and produces signs of the kingdom of God.

If God and the Spirit are the principles of any will to liberty, one may deduce that they are also the sources of any community based on a covenant, an agreement, love, and loyalty. Indeed, all real communities, from the family to the state or nation, are expressions of the people of God. Where the will to freedom is active, we may assume the presence of the Spirit. The ties uniting the members of communities—the loyalty and love that make up their agreement, the mutual acceptance that creates their association—are steps to the increase of the kingdom of God. The ties that bind such communities are not simply the present inclinations of the members, because such inclinations of will and emotion are intermittent. Rather, God gives them the beginning, the continuity, the energy, and the shape.

For example, God gives strength to a family, strength that binds its members together into a stable unit. And that stability is stronger than the individual dispositions of the family members. In the same way, from the will for liberation a people (and all intermediary associations) receive a kind of stability greater than the normal human disposition. This happens because the desire to make community and common life—which is equivalent to a liberation movement—is more than a psychological disposition; it is the kingdom of God. Vatican Council II emphasized the sacramentality of the church. As a sacrament of the kingdom of God, it is the seed, the first approach to the future kingdom, a sign of the invisible reality of the future; simultaneously it is also an instrument in God's hands for promoting the kingdom. The same thing may be said of all communities. The family is certainly a sacrament of the kingdom (the Catholic and Orthodox confessions specifically recognize it as such). But other, larger communities, too, are sacraments of the kingdom. The common life based on freedom is a sacrament of the kingdom, and the people of God is sacrament in all its expressions.

Such a sacramentality does not imply that all free associations are as firm, lasting, and unvarying as the family or the church. The Spirit is the author of history and makes it variable and pliable; from the Spirit rise evolution and revolution as they are guided toward liberation and liberty: It changes and creates new shapes of human common life adjusted to new time and conditions as they occur. With every new phase of the kingdom of God, some shapes have to be adjusted to the needs of the time. For example, the Latin American church has come to think that the basic communities are the actual expression of the liberation movement, proceeding both from the Spirit and from human freedom, that this movement constitutes a people as a people, that it is a continuation of the signs of the covenant given by all the prophets from Moses to Jesus.

Freedom from Law and Power. The third aspect of Christian liberation which is to be emphasized is the freedom to be free from law and power. The law of the Pharisees did not vanish when the church cut its contacts with the Jewish people. As we have seen from the Johannine perspective, the old law survived in all its power within non-Christian civilizations, especially the Roman Empire and its successors over the centuries. Any domination or ideology of domination is an analogical repetition of the Jewish law. So liberation must be an ongoing struggle against new shapes of law and power.

Liberation itself does not intend to establish a new kind of power. On the contrary, it seeks to overcome all power and domination as a way of common life, since any power gives rise to a domination. The testimony of liberty intends to break the vicious circle of violence and domination. It intends to create a free association of persons facing all powers and dominating forces as a people. Thus, viewed as the struggle against power and domination, liberation can be seen as a movement to control, limit, and contain the scope of any power. It often uses new institutions to do this, but its other aim is to contain power and domination within the limits of a real social service.

In the fourth century, when the Catholic bishops decided to collaborate with the emperor Constantine, their agreement was based on the conversion of the emperor, which they believed to be sincere and definitive. They assumed that Constantine (and by implication, his successors) was accepting the role of Saul or David, that a Christian emperor would be the true protector and defender of the Christian people and its liberties. In short, they based their agreement on an assumed change of the imperial role. Actually, of course, that was a serious misunderstanding on the part of both bishops and emperor, a misunderstanding that led to innumerable conflicts. The tension continued for centuries (in some places to the present day) because the ecclesiastical authorities keep thinking imperial power has been converted. That is always the basis of any agreement between church and state: the state (or emperor or king) restricts itself to defending the laws and liberties of the people; it may not change the laws of the people, since it is only the caretaker of the laws, not the author of them. That the state has almost never played its role truly (even in medieval times when all society was based on this principle) does not in itself invalidate the idea of a Christian state. But it is enough to make would-be liberators think carefully when the state offers cooperation.

Since the liberation movement seeks to win guarantees that power will limit itself, liberation can also be seen as a struggle for guarantees, for a certain degree of individual autonomy, for certain rights for persons and associations, for certain "liberties." Without "liberties" there is no liberty. When power and state are concerned, the liberty of an individual citizen is a myth. Without the rights of associations and popular institutions, there is no liberty. Only a developed communitarian life is strong enough to contain power's apparently spontaneous trend to increase itself.

Conclusion. Of course, there is a great difference between the Christian principles, as explained here, and the historical practice of the churches. In fact, one can say that the very history of the church is the ongoing debate and struggle between church and Christianity. On the one hand, the church is drawn by its Christian constitution and the necessities of playing the prophet and the call to liberty. On the other hand, the church exists among actual social structures; its members and its authorities are submitted to the pressures of their environment. (This is often unnoticed, since individuals live within their environments and are not aware of their influences.)

Christian mission, which is created by the Spirit, and environment, which is created by culture and the state, has shaped the variations of the history of Christianity and will undoubtedly do so until the end of time.

8

Mission and Strategy

The problems of the Latin American church have become those that most awaken the conscience of the Catholic Church, especially since the Synod of Bishops held in Rome in 1971. The same is true of the Protestant denominations (at least those represented by the World Council of Churches), especially since the WCC Conference in Geneva in 1966. More and more church people everywhere have become aware not only of the specific problems of Latin America but of the universal significance of their repercussions for the meaning of mission and self-consciousness of the church in the world.

In Latin America, the church does indeed need to know what its mission is, and many theologians and ecclesiastical authorities are searching hard for answers. It has been said that the intention of Vatican II was to answer the question: "Church, what do you say about yourself?" In contrast, the present question of the Latin American church is, "Church, what are you supposed to do? What are you going to do?" In other words, ecclesiology that is searching for itself is by nature also a theology of mission.

It is in the search for mission that all the strands this book has previously touched on come together. Into the theology of mission must be woven the meaning of revolution and liberation, the reality of the present-day situation, including political structures, the relevance (or lack of relevance) of freedom for the development of the people of God, the meaning and success of the various pastoral initiatives taken in Latin America during the past decade, and so on. We have already dealt with many of these strands at some length. In seeing how they form the warp and woof of the various possibilities that exist today for a new theology of mission, some repetition, however, is not only unavoidable but helpful to enable the reader to become well aware of the interconnections.

"NEW" FACTS

There was a general meeting of Latin American theologians in Mexico in August 1975. During this encounter the scholars involved brought into the

166

center of their discussion a clearer expression of their unique position as they described the current problems of the church in Latin America. In this description, three facts about the present situation became clear. They were not entirely new, but they had never before been perceived in such a lucid way, nor had their connection with the theology of mission ever been made so clear. They are (1) a political fact, (2) an ecclesiological fact, and (3) a "mixed" fact (both political and ecclesiological) about revolution. At the same time, the many connections between the first and the second fact became evident.

The Political Fact

The political fact is the new structure of the state in Latin America. The national security state has come to power through the influence (and often with the help) of the present center of the Western world, the United States of America, acting variously through its military chiefs-of-staff, its CIA, its State Department, the multinational companies, and its universities. The new state has been firmly established in Brazil since 1964. It tried to establish itself in Argentina in 1966 and provisionally failed there in 1972, but it has prevailed in Bolivia, Uruguay, Chile, and in most of the countries of Central America. It seems to be ready to establish itself in Colombia momentarily. In a somewhat different shape, it has taken over Peru and Ecuador. In short, the whole of Latin America (except for Mexico and Venezuela) is now dependent upon this new structure.

The Ideology of the New States. The new state is a military state. But militarism far from defines its complete essence. Some military dictatorships are transient phenomena and do not really alter the country's political institutions; after some interval, as the constitutional order is restored, the nation can begin to operate as it did previously because its roots were never destroyed. But the current Latin American militarism is entirely different. It is the beginning of a new political order that intends to stay in power and is enabling itself to do so by systematically destroying the traditional roots and patterns of society. It not only severs constitutional order, but also the means for setting up any new state patterns in the future. Thus it dictates a new pattern for the whole of society.

The new state is no mere issue of some "political pragmatism," as many military like to suggest or pretend. Civilians who collaborate with the military governments often have recourse to the argument that such governments are the result of "military pragmatism." They use this argument to justify their own collaboration; by it they would give the military the privilege of being able to act without ideology, with only devotion to the cult of efficiency. Of course, this is by no means true. The new military state is commanded by a specific ideology—the ideology of national security, which is also the ideology that has guided the world politics of the United States since it became the dominant power of the Western world after World War II.

The national security ideology includes a theory about the state (it considers the state the basic reality) but it does not stop there. It also offers a whole understanding of person and society, a real *Weltanschauung* in which person, society, and history appear radically dependent on the state, first and last reality of the human condition. According to this ideology, the human person exists only within the state and by means of the state. Without a state, persons are totally unable to survive because their basic need is security and only a state is able to give security.

Concerning the state itself, the ideology says its essence cannot be deduced from a philosophy; it can be understood only from history. And the most general science that describes this reality "state" is geopolitics.

Geopolitics and States. Geopolitics discloses the "reality" of humankind and state. Humankind is an abstraction. As a concrete reality, humankind is a constellation of about 150 nations, which are separated and rival powers, competing with but simultaneously needing one another. Peoples do not subsist without nations, nations do not exist without states, and states do not exist without power. Therefore, human beings cannot exist without power. (Of course, the human being is both the agent and the subject matter of the power.)

Geopolitics goes further. Since states are in constant competition with each other, if they want to survive, they have to struggle against their competitors. Life is war; peace is only another name for war. But alone states cannot win. They are compelled to find allies. Consequently, the distinction between friend and foe is the basic human reality. Since geopolitics is the science that seeks to know who are each nation's friends and foes, it is therefore the science of the basic reality of social life. And since persons exist only within and because of states, it is also the science of the basic reality of the personal life of any man or woman.

Geopolitics admits that any nation is composed of territory, population, and various material and cultural factors, but it sees all these elements as passive. Only the state gives them some capacity for action. The state is the only active element of the nation. It takes over territory, population, and material or cultural factors and makes of them a real power for acting, conquering, and dominating. Consequently, the state is the only active principle and the only norm for nation and people. Further, the state may not accept any principle or value above itself. As General Golbery do Couto e Silva, the chief ideologist of the Brazilian military revolution of 1964, said, the state is either an absolute being or nothing.

The state has its own goals, called national objectives, the most important of which are survival, security, increase, and the conquest of additional territory for further expansion *(Lebensraum)*. Expansion is not always immediately possible, but survival and security (or the preconditions for survival) are always the supreme goal of any state and all its citizens. In order to preserve its own security, the state needs to use national power. Power is the chief quality of every reality within a nation. Men and women, territory, and material or cultural goods are valuable according to their capacities for power.

The management of national power for national security is the subject of the total state strategy. Today politics is only an aspect of, or another name for, strategy. Strategy has become the most general practical science, the most general synthesis of the human or the social sciences. Everything is a matter of strategy, since war has become the total, permanent reality of the human condition.

The evolution of the concepts of total war and strategy are typical of the pervasiveness of the national security ideology. Lundendorff's original concept of total war was only a mobilization of all citizens and national resources, doing away with the old distinction between civilian and military, and between ordinary and war budgets. At present, total war also means a universal war among all nations, a war against a total enemy, and a continuous war without any intervals of peace. It does away with distinctions between neutral and fighter, war operations and normal human activities, war and peace. Any nations not fighting for us are fighting against us. All actions relate to war and are of strategic value. Every human being is related to war. Accordingly, strategy seeks to control every human activity—economic, political, psychosocial, and military—in order to protect national security, both internal and external. Moreover any activity has to receive its meaning and scope from strategy.

Such a view of man and society is not entirely new. Even the empires of classic times were modeled on similar ideologies; in a way, the Pax Romana was another name for imperial security. And in the seventeenth century, Thomas Hobbes set forth themes so close to those of today's national security that its ideologists acknowledge him as one of their chief forerunners.

More recently, European fascists have set up what could be called national security states. Some of their ideologies were quite similar to the national security ideology of today. But they were full of emotive and affective elements. The fascist state wanted to be the true representative of a mythical people. It sought, therefore, to disclose a historical identity between people and state. The fascist ideology wanted to become the spontaneous and unanimous thought of the masses, to convince all the people. It embarked, therefore, on intensive propaganda campaigns.

On the contrary, the present ideology has become free from any emotive or affective need. In a way, it is more technical and scientific. In order to convince, it depends on its own efficiency, and in the meantime it thinks that it can reach sufficient popular consensus by means of supplying what it believes to be the major stimulus for social order—fear and a desire for security—through total repression and a system of control. It takes care to apply that major stimulus and no other, since it does not want mass demonstrations or popular liturgies; the police are enough to awaken fear and the desire for security, to convince the people that it is the only means of meeting their needs.

East-West and North-South Antagonism. In Latin America, two variants of the national security ideology are available. Both are, of course, based on eternal antagonism between nations, but there are presently two views about the priority of one kind of antagonism over another, and geopolitics changes according to the view taken. (From each kind of geopolitics proceeds a somewhat different strategy.)

At the present time, geopolitics perceives two major antagonisms: East-West, and North-South. (The first is the antagonism between the West and communism; the second, between the developed and the underdeveloped worlds.)

If a national security state gives priority to the antagonism of East-West, it is taking the Brazilian model, the most common in present-day Latin America. According to this model, the state's strategy is directed mainly against communism in the sense of a total war, conducted within the overall strategy of the United States and the other Western capitalist nations. In this condition, when it is decided that the primary objective of strategy is the defense against communism, any state (especially any underdeveloped state) has to adapt to dependence on the Western metropolis. Consequently, the dependent state limits its own economic interests and control so as to avoid any conflict with those of the metropolis. On the other hand, such a state becomes exempt (habitually) from any direct military strategy against the principal enemy, the Soviet Union. Because the United States is ready to deal militarily with the opposing metropolis, the Soviet Union is not a problem for the dependent states. But the dependent states do have to face the major enemy in its infiltrations inside the nation. Their problem is the internal front. (Strategy always supposes that there is a very dangerous internal front.) The dependent state must forever fight against communist infiltrators by completely repressing any dissent or questioning of its actions and by achieving perfect control of all social and cultural life.

Two other points about the Brazilian model of national security ideology are worth noting. First, it is considered unnecessary to try to convince the lower classes that this type of state is desirable or in their interest. And, of course, it is very much not in their interest, since that is totally submitted to the interest of the metropolis. But the conflict between the interest of the masses and the interest of the great metropolitan power is unavoidable and has to be accepted by the elites as a condition of the geopolitical model. Consequently, it would be useless to set up any propaganda system; fear and desire for security provide sufficient cooperation.

The second point involves the dictatorship's acceptance of being a dependent state. This seems somewhat surprising in light of the geopolitical imperative to achieve power. It is, of course, explained in the ideology as a pragmatic step in obtaining allies, which are necessary for security. However, it must be noted that within any empire various degrees of importance are alotted to dependent states. Several nations usually manage to win important, although subordinated places. Geopolitics encourages this scramble for place as part of the fight for survival and power. For example, Brazil seeks to be the leader of the South Atlantic, under the primary leadership of the United States.

This Brazilian model of the national security ideology is the most common, but a new military state can also choose the Peruvian variant (although, since August 1975, it is not at all certain that this model is going to be able to survive in Peru itself). The main difference lies in what is perceived as the primary antagonism. According to the Peruvian model, this is the antagonism between North and South, not East and West. The war between the developed and underdeveloped nations is seen as more important than the battle between the West and communism. Naturally, Peru is a member of the Western world and may not get out of the West. But without going out of the world to which it belongs, Peru tries to create a third way between East and West. Without forgetting that it is a part of the Western world, Peru may seek a new position that does not greatly increase the power of the Soviet Union, nor endanger the hegemony of the United States, but does achieve a certain degree of freedom (see Appendix).

The difference in aims means differences in strategy. For the Peruvian model, strategy consists in increasing connections with the other peoples of the Third World so as to form a common front against the industrial nations. And since struggle between East and West is relatively less important, the battle for internal security loses a great deal of its importance. There is also less danger from infiltration: the lower classes hope for more advantages from the government than from the opposition, and leftist or communist parties are anxious about causing too many problems for the government. On the other hand, security must worry about greatly increased dangers of external aggression. The primary threat comes from American hegemony. Even if the metropolis does not wish to step in directly, it can provoke local disagreements between neighbors should it wish to put some pressure on a client state it feels is becoming too inconvenient. For a state like Peru, this is a real danger; even the possibility of open war between Peru and totally dependent states, such as Chile, Bolivia, and Brazil, is not entirely theoretical.

Within the Peruvian model, the state aims at increasing its control over national economy; this is possible only by taking away some of the powers and privileges of the multinational corporations. In order to balance the power of the corporations and their allies, the local oligarchies, the state tries to awaken a popular response: the appeal to the masses offsets the hostility of the elites.

The development of the national security state—in either variation—is the political fact that has conditioned the whole Latin American evolution for ten years, although this is just now becoming apparent. At the time of the Medellín Conference and the beginnings of liberation theology, the situation was not yet clear, although the Brazilian model was already complete. Most Latin Americans did not want to believe that the occurrences in the Brazilian model could possibly announce the probable future of the whole continent. It took the events of September 1973 in Chile to open the eyes of many people.

The Ecclesiological Fact

The new political structures and ideology now paramount in Latin America have forced the church there to shift its strategy and consider its mission carefully. This is the new ecclesiastical fact. Most Latin American theologians would explain it this way. The church cannot live outside the state, and the state always conditions the mission of the church. It is impossible for the church to deal with the salvation of the people without taking into account the state and its strategy. This is always true, but given the present political situation, it has special importance, since that situation is such that there can be no ecclesiastical expression that does not touch state strategy and power. At the time of Vatican II and the Medellín Conference, Catholics had forgotten the reality of the state. They talked about the mission of the church—while forgetting the state; they seemed to believe that the state does not condition the church. Events during the intervening years have forced realization of the truth. At the present time, every person or institution within the Latin American church feels the presence of the state. This realization is forcing a re-examination of the mission of the church, since the constant presence of the political system makes two appeals.

The Dilemma of Security. On the one hand, the church realizes that the absolute, totalitarian state provokes a strong response. Its very presence is an invitation, almost a demand, for the church to renew its prophetic mission by taking such actions as publicly championing the rights of human beings or the universal principles of justice and peace. One group of Latin American bishops, priests, pastors, and laypeople are already expressing such a challenge.

On the other hand, there is a problem of security for the church. This problem always exists, although not always consciously. In Latin America today, however, church people are very conscious of it. They are well aware of the price of the prophetic word. By speaking out in defense of something such as the rights of the human person against the geopolitical and strategic interests of the state, the church runs the risk of losing many material and cultural goods, including many opportunities of acting on behalf of its own people. The cost of the prophetic word is pressure, persecution, threat, and finally death. In the present situation the church is realizing that the word of God may be dangerous to its own security. If Christians speak, the power of the state reacts against them, and may silence them forcibly. If they choose to remain silent, they choose survival, but they feel they may be betraying their own mission.

This dilemma is deeply lived by all the churches and religious persons and communities in Latin America: either to choose the prophetic role and then to accept persecution, to be put out of the national society, and to give up the security of the church for the future; or to remain silent in order to ensure the security of the church, but with the risk of betraying the very reason for the existence of the church—the prophetic word that it ought to announce.

In short, the church has as much of a problem of security as the state does. And there are no easy answers.

What is the meaning of security for the church? How should the need for security affect its mission? One answer is obvious. For a human society, it is possible for security to be the highest and most urgent value because survival is the precondition of all other values. But for the church the question is different because there are other values for Christians. They have the example of Jesus Christ and martyrdom as a constitutive aspect of the church. Above achieving security in order to survive, there is the necessity to remain faithful to its mission. There are circumstances in which the church has to achieve its own mission without worrying about its security or survival (the survival of persons or the survival of institutions).

But that evident answer leads to a paradox. Martyrdom is not the totality of the church's mission. The survival of persons and institutions is necessary to achieve other aspects of its mission—for instance, preaching the gospel and inviting to conversion. Jesus himself stood up against Jewish and Roman power in a radical way only after several years of preaching. He experienced the essence of the present dilemma of the church and adopted a strategy to deal with it.

At this moment, in Brazil, in Paraguay, in Bolivia, in Uruguay, in Chile, in Central America (except for Costa Rica and Panama), there is practically no bishop, pastor, priest, or active layperson who is not living this dilemma in his or her daily Christian mission. Each must choose either to speak up and die, forfeiting any opportunity for further action, or to remain silent and survive in the hope of taking future action (or at least continue present ones).

Some minorities have chosen to speak. In Brazil and Paraguay, such minorities have succeeded in influencing whole episcopal conferences. The institutional Catholic Church in these countries has chosen to defend human rights against the arbitrary power of a totalitarian state, especially the arbitrary power of the secret services. And at the present time in Latin America, there is no doubt that the ministry of human rights of the human person is a prophetic function. Defending such rights inside the protected assembly of a Roman synod or some other international meeting can be done without danger. The same thing cannot be said of an institution—much less an individual—acting in Latin America today. Reprisal springs immediately from the state security agencies. State and power are able to prevent all expression of such a prophetic word, and to isolate a prophetic church from any communication with the people.

If the voice of the church as an institution cannot be heard by the members of the nation and state, how is the church still able to accomplish its task? This is the problem usually cited by those church people at all levels who would choose silence over prophecy. For them, it is of the utmost importance to ensure the survival of a church as an organized institution able to express its voice publicly within the state. And so they arrive at a paradox opposite to that of those who choose prophecy. In order to retain its means of speaking, the church remains silent. But it does not use its means of speaking, because if it did, it would probably lose that means. The church can save its freedom to speak out only by not using it.

So the problem of security is a true dilemma. But it is not at all new, although the churches in the West have managed to remain oblivious to it in recent times. For instance, the concept of security is not mentioned in Vatican II's *Gaudium et Spes* (Pastoral Constitution on the Church in the Modern World) or in the modern papers of the World Council of Churches. That is why these documents seem so idealistic: they have placed the church in an ideal, ethereal world; they lack the concrete realism that comes from the resistance of history. In Latin America in recent years, however, the resistance of state to church has reappeared in such a way as to be unmistakable. When the dilemma posed by this resistance becomes part of daily life, it becomes clearer and clearer that one of the main lines of history is the permanent tension between church and state, and that church history is the history of the debates between church and state, because relations with the state determine the whole behavior of the church.

The Connection Between the Political and the Ecclesiastical Facts. The problems presented by the demand for security of state and the demand for security of church are not at all independent. On the contrary, there are many contacts between them.

This is to be expected because the church does not live outside the major antagonisms of the contemporary world and cannot remain neutral to them. Today it is not outside the structures created by geopolitics, and consequently it does not remain indifferent to the security problems of the nations in which it exists. The Catholic Church, for instance, is geopolitically situated: it belongs to the West and mainly to the North or the metropolis of the West. (Most Protestant denominations belong to the same geopolitical area.)

The East-West Antagonism and the Church. Particularly since 1945, it has become evident that the Catholic Church understands that its own security and survival are tied to the security and survival of the West. (In the last ten years, the Catholic Church has tried to improve its relations with the communist nations, but only insofar as such actions do not weaken its affiliations with the West.) The church has many means of strengthening its political ties with the West, and it makes good use of them.

First, the church does not allow its members to belong to any Communist party. Insofar as communism is concerned, Catholics are simply not permitted political freedom. Second, the church uses its institutions to strengthen Western ideology and serve as agents in stimulating and strengthening anti-Communist parties. For example, the Vatican and some European episcopal conferences have been powerful factors by promoting the Christian Democratic parties and the European Common Market, which have served as defenses against communism. To take another example, Pius XII and the Latin American Catholic churches officially decided to share the struggle against communism in 1955 (at the Eucharistic Congress in Rio de Janeiro). The pope asked for help in order to save Latin America from the communist danger, and the European and North American churches responded with an outpouring of "aid."

It is important to realize that none of these actions has been undertaken to protect the doctrinal position of the church or the faith of its members. The stated position of communism is indeed antithetical to all religions, and association with communism may very well make living the faith difficult for Christians. But the reasons the church joins the battle against communism so willingly are neither doctrinal nor pastoral; they are geopolitical. The church exists in the West; the West seeks security in fighting the East (communism); so the church seeks its geopolitical security in doing the same.

This point may be easier to understand with the help of an example. In recent years the international movement Christians for Socialism has questioned this geopolitical stance of the church and encouraged political collaboration with groups of the left, some of them communist in name or ideology. Ecclesiastical authorities are not supposed to permit any political or social movement that shows any connections with a communist ideology or practice. Therefore, since the beginning of Christians for Socialism, the Catholic Church has been attacking it in order to limit its expansion and to alienate it from the Christian people. And if the church does not succeed in its goal by means of its present pressures, there is no doubt that it will intervene officially, forbidding priests at least, and perhaps others, any participation in the movement.

If an official declaration occurs, the stated reasons for it will be of a doctrinal nature; taking part in Christians for Socialism will be considered as support of some heresy or doctrinal error. But such an argument will be completely beside the point. In many other cases, political and social collaboration with non-Catholic movements is not considered as a support of heresy. For example, extensive political collaboration with the Protestant churches is not considered as heresy; participation in the one Christian Democratic party of West Germany (which is essentially Protestant) is not only allowed, but recommended and firmly supported.

In short, the true reason for forbidding similar collaboration with Communist or Marxist parties is not doctrinal, but geopolitical. It is not a problem of heresy but of security and survival. The church authorities and most Catholic laypeople think that communism is dangerous for the external security and survival of the church. They think that God is not enough to ensure the security of his church. He is able to save the essence of the church, its internal continuity; but he is not able to ensure the survival of the institutional system in a given nation or state, that institutional system which gives the church its public presence and ability to proclaim the voice of the gospel. The external security of public ecclesiastical institutions requires an ecclesiastical geopolitics.

So there is a specific complicity between the political goals of the church and those of the West: the security of both is based on the same foundation.

Such a political condition determines the actions of the church and every member of it. Many bishops, pastors, priests, and laypeople feel that the actions possible for them at any given moment are limited by the problems of security. They know that the security of the church is tied with the security of the state. If they question any policy of a national security government, this government answers with a powerful argument: security. If they denounce crimes of the security agencies against human rights, the state appeals to national security. Any charge against the government becomes a support of communism, a help to the enemies of both nation and church.

And the majority of church people support this attitude. They say: "This government is our security against communism. If we speak against it in any way, the communists will use our words. The prophetic mission of the church strengthens the power of communism and weakens the defense of the West. Prophets speak the truth, but the truth can be used by communists, so truth may be dangerous." Such an argument has been heard thousands of times in the past decade.

And so in Latin America as in other nations, the church takes very different actions against totalitarianisms of the left and of the right. Against leftist totalitarianism, there is total, unlimited opposition. Against rightist totalitarianism, such as that of the national security states, the prophetic voice of the church is limited. Moreover, the Catholic Church (and the Protestant churches too) maintain far-reaching connections with these states, generally more important than those maintained with the former liberal governments; there is much cooperation in relief, social works, hospitals, and public ceremonies, including military celebrations.

This cooperation is undertaken in the knowledge that its precondition of anticommunism limits the freedom of the church to undertake its prophetic mission. And this limitation is not necessarily forced on the church by the state. The church chooses silence for reasons of its own external security. It agrees with the state's security policy before any coercion by the political authorities becomes necessary.

In addition to the problems caused for the church's mission by this solidarity of ecclesiastical and state geopolitics, there is also the side effect of creating many problems for the churches living inside the communist states. This phenomenon is, unfortunately, no newer than the common cause of church and state for political goals. When the Christian bishops accepted alliance with Emperor Constantine, all those Christians who lived outside the Roman Empire and were citizens of other political units were persecuted. In the same way, at the present time, the churches in the communist world are considered as the fifth column of the West. Geopolitical opposition increases the persecution, and the increase of persecution justifies the fear of communism and need for security on the part of Western churches. The circle is perfect.

The North-South Antagonism and the Church. The church continues to place its major geopolitical emphasis on what it conceives to be its interests in the East-West antagonism. But the church does not ignore the North-South antagonism, either. It does not consider it to be as important as the East-West antagonism, nor is it quite so tied to state policy. But it is not neutral: this would be impossible.

At the time of the colonial empires, the Catholic Church (and the Protestant churches, too) was tied to the colonial power. The church conceived its mission as acting in connection with the colonial policy of the metropolis. After decolonization, the survival of the church required a type of nationalization. This meant making some changes in its institutional system and, even more, entrusting part of its authority to national members of the church. As time went on, survival also required a certain change of geopolitics, a shifting of its international policy. It began to defend the interests of the South to some degree, although until very recently it was considered wise to do so only when those interests were not directly contrary to the interests of the metropolis, because the major commitment of the church was already with the North. Today the church favors the independence of new nations and the promotion of the South only when they are not contrary to the policy of the traditional metropolis. The cases of the Portuguese colonies and Vietnam have shown that the church is still limited in its southern policy by the danger of breaking the privileged ties with the metropolitan states.

Today the church also perceives another limit to its solidarity with the countries of the Third World—the danger of communism. If the policy of a less-developed state threatens to strengthen the communist world or even connect the nation with communism, the church prefers to stand with the metropolitan centers of the West (as it did in the case of Vietnam, Cuba, Cambodia, and others).

In short, the church's position on the antagonism between North and South is somewhat ambivalent and tends to shift pragmatically. It realizes that the future lies in the Third World, but it is a remote future. The authorities and most Christians believe that if the church depended upon the Third World for its security today, their geopolitical position would be very weak.

For the immediate future then, the voice of the metropolitan powers is generally preponderant. This tendency is reinforced by the preceived need of fighting the communist danger, against which the church believes the Third World cannot provide sufficient security.

This interplay of ecclesiastical and political situations is the ecclesiological (the second) fact: the church is discovering the reality of the security problem within the implications of the geopolitics of nations and blocs.

The Fact of the Disappearance of the Opposition

The third new fact is more specifically historical and needs only brief discussion because it is a negative. The fact is that revolutionary movements have been eliminated from Latin America for the present. Such an occurrence obviously affects both political and ecclesiastical strategy.

The Political History. Starting in 1959 the example of Cuba brought about the formation of various revolutionary movements in almost all Latin American countries. They intended to seize political power as had been done in Cuba. The leaders of these movements believed that a prerevolutionary situation existed in their countries, that the revolutionary forces were present there, and that they were ready to create a successful revolutionary front. They thought that the active presence of a small revolutionary group would be a symbol sufficient to gather all dissident forces around it, to awaken the unhappy masses, and to sweep into power. Because the basis of the idea was the small, active group, these were called focuses; from there the movement came to be named *foquismo.*

Today it is quite clear that *foquismo* has no future. In almost all countries the repressive action of the security forces has already eliminated these political revolutionary movements. They still survive in Mexico, Argentina, and Colombia, but without any political success. Indeed, their only contribution to history was accelerating the creation of the new rightist totalitarian systems. *Foquismo* is dead, politically dead. Regis Debray, the movement's main ideologist, has acknowledged the fact in his book *La critique des armes.* Even Fidel Castro has given up helping such movements and accepted the Soviet thesis of their inefficiency in Latin America. The revolutionary minorities of Latin America—Marxist or not, violent or not, clandestine or not—have been swept from this period of history.

How can such a radical failure be explained? The answer is clear: these movements ignored the state. The case in Cuba was quite different. Fidel Castro faced the government of an almost nonexistent state; Batista's armed forces were not organized as a modern efficient corps, its soldiers did not resist, and their officers preferred to run away rather than fight. Many people believed the conditions of Batista's Cuba existed in other Latin American countries. But there the state was present as a real state. Revolutionary Marxists (or leftists, *foquistas*) thought that class warfare could be developed from theory into practice without problems. But the state reacted violently in the face of attempts to do so. The revolutionary groups believed they were able to challenge the power of the state and the armed forces. They learned that any challenge to a modern armed state is suicide if the army is in the hands of a state committed to defend a national security system.

After this virtual elimination of revolutionary groups or parties, the political possibilities became clearer: no political action can succeed without the support of the armed forces. Any political action must take place inside the state and the existing political system. Any attempt to destroy the political system is an idealistic, utopian dream.

The Ecclesiastical Repercussions. This political fact has also an ecclesiastical aspect. The *foquistas* and other, similar revolutionary groups included some Christians, which had an enormous influence on the Latin American church. The number of Christians who actively worked in the movements totaled just a few hundred, but they were generally well-known people who had been members of Christian movements, mainly student movements. So the work of these few persons had strong repercussions in the church, stronger than it probably deserved. It led Christian movements of both the left and the right to organize propaganda out of proportion to the real importance of events. For all those groups searching for a change in church or society, the participation of outspoken and well-known Christians in the revolutionary movements became a symbol to be used as an appeal for a more general change. On the other hand, the Christian conservatives organized propaganda (much more violent than that of the left because they could rely on more means) claiming that the participation of Christians in such movements showed how vulnerable Christianity was to Marxist infiltration. Consequently, for fifteen years a few hundred persons became the center of the major debate within both the Catholic and the Protestant churches. Many people (for instance persons in Rome and in many ecclesiastical institutions) got the impression that the guerrilla movements were the most important problem for the church, and some saw them as a real alternative for the church to follow. Thousands of times, the position of the guerrilla (especially Camilo Torres) was condemned; many times, too, it was praised or made to appear legitimate.

The revolutionary minorities were perceived as constituting a danger to both political and ecclesiastical security. The reaction of both church and state was radical. The danger was, in fact, remote and overestimated because the guerrillas had no support from the people, but the system reacted as if it were imminent.

It is important to understand this situation. The danger to the church was overestimated (since the *foquistas* had so little chance of success) but it was real. Most of the Christian revolutionaries believed they should and would be able to reform Christianity without and against the church, and they intended to challenge the ecclesiastical system by starting from an independent Christian position. They believed that the ecclesiastical system was to be destroyed, just as the state was to be destroyed, and that such a destruction was the absolute precondition of creating any pure Christianity. Therefore, most revolutionary Christians ran away from the institutional church. By so doing they increased the gap. They rejected the church because it did not accept their policy; the church rejected them because they rejected the institutional church. It was a closed circle, and given the relative strength of the revolutionaries and the institutional church (supported, at least in part, by the state) it eventually spiraled out of existence.

Now, after years of experience, almost all Christians realize that they have no power, no expression, no voice, no ability to survive outside the institutional churches. Only a church united around its institutional system has some capacity to assume its prophetic mission. The temptations of separatism have disappeared. The debate within the church about revolution has been erased by history, made impossible by the struggle between state and church.

There is, however, today a division within the institutional system as to ideology in the sense of doctrine about relations of church and state. This is not (at least not yet) an opposition between base and authorities, but a vertical division; each side includes episcopal conferences, clergy, religious institutes, and laity. One group believes that the security of the church is best served by following its prophetic mission no matter what limits are imposed by the state; the other, that Christianity is better served if the church cooperates with the state, at least to some extent. Given the political situation and the institutional church's own geopolitical imperative, this division was probably unavoidable. Nevertheless, there is no question that the conservative side was strengthened by the reaction against the revolutionary movement. Some of the occurrences, especially in 1972 to 1975, have been similar to those that gave the military access to state power. For example, there was a real coup in the General Assembly of the Latin American Episcopal Council (CELAM), in Sucre in November 1972, when a new group took power with a plan of fighting for ecclesiastical security by emphasizing measures against communist infiltrations. Since then CELAM's main ideology has been developing and maintaining a new security system against communism.

At any rate, the revolutionary episode has shown that it is impossible to reform church and Christianity outside the church itself, and that any non-institutional Christianity is utopian.

The Captivity of the Church

The three facts discussed in this chapter—concerning the imperative of the state, the dilemma of security for the church within the state, and the failure of Christian revolution—make more apparent what is really the permanent condition of the church, namely, "the captivity of the church." This condition is based on the logical consequences of these three facts.

First, Christianity and church live inside a state, and consequently their existence and evolution are bound up with the geopolitical and strategic policy of the state. Christianity is always confronted by the state's priority of security; the church is the captive of the state's need for security.

Second, the search for security is not imposed by the state alone. The institutional church also needs security and limits its mission according to what it perceives as the requirements of security. In other words, the captivity of the church does not derive only from outer causes but also from its inner essence. The church seeks its own captivity.

Finally, any Christianity or Christian action in the world outside the institutional system is utopian.

Consequently, captivity is the unavoidable condition of the church. The idealist and optimistic ecclesiologies of the rich churches of the developed West try to cover up such a condition; they have convinced themselves they are "free" churches because they do not want to see their own condition. In Latin America, the screen of idealism has been torn, perhaps because the captivity of the churches there is no longer a golden captivity.

But if captivity is unavoidable, an ecclesiology that includes that fact must be developed. Such an ecclesiology must be able to explain how captivity and freedom are compatible, and how the church is able to accomplish its mission in a condition of captivity.

The ecclesiology of the people of God is basic to meeting this need.

THE ECCLESIOLOGY OF THE PEOPLE OF GOD

Present trends in Catholic and Protestant ecclesiology are converging (take, for example, the work of Moltmann and Pannenberg), so one may start with either and end in more or less the same place. Since I am dealing with the situation of Latin America, whose countries are strongly Catholic, it is convenient to start with the texts of Vatican Council II.

The idea of the people of God was taken by Vatican II as the center and the main reference of Catholic ecclesiology. Probably the future of the Latin American idea is to be found in that idea, but only with an extension toward a more historical perspective. An extension is necessary because the ecclesiology of Vatican II is not complete enough to deal with real situations in a real world. For example, *Lumen Gentium* (the Dogmatic Constitution on the Church) does not explain the present condition of the church in the world. And *Gaudium et Spes* reflects the idealistic view of the developed churches of the rich world. It does not speak of states and power, but of the world and society in a general sense; its generalizations often make it ambiguous; its idea of the people of God has to be completed. For this reason the following considerations are a continuation, or extension, of Vatican II ecclesiology, not a simple explication.

The Temptations of the Present-Day Church

As far as Latin American theology is concerned, conciliar ecclesiology is so general that it can be explicated to cover several quite different systems. The conciliar idea of the people of God is ambiguous enough to have three possible interpretations. And in a way, these three conflicting interpretations lead to the theological controversy of today.

Accordingly, this extension of conciliar ecclesiology starts with an examination of these three interpretations, or concepts, of the people of God. These three concepts are related to three theories about the church, three ways of life, three manners of being Christian in the Catholic Church. (There are undoubtedly parallels in the Protestant churches.) From a Latin American viewpoint, these concepts are the three temptations of the present-day church.

The first temptation comes from the contestation movements. Such protest is now impossible in Latin America, but it is possible in other countries, for instance in many of the developed nations. A theology of contestation starts with the idea of the people of God and gives it a more specific content. The people of God is considered as the opposite of institution/authority/ hierarchy, so the distinction between them becomes the major axis of the ecclesiology.

A theology of contestation develops such an opposition in order to point out and to glorify the people of God in contrast to institution/authority/ hierarchy.

On the one hand is the people—the base, the spiritual church, the church of the laity, which is the church engaged with the world and secular values. On the other hand is the institution—the organization and its bureaucracy, the system, the church of the clergy, the church engaged with the social structures of the establishment and the repressive system. In other words, the basis of a theology of contestation is the horizontalist church in opposition to the verticalist church. Within this theology, promotion of the people of God means a democratization of the traditional church.

Such an ecclesiology is very appealing to certain revolutionary groups who see the future of the church in an ecclesiastical revolution similar to a cultural revolution, which would derive from the base and destroy the domination of the upper classes and structures of the church. Such movements have been known in Latin America, especially from 1967 to 1973, many of them, at least in part, an imitation of the developed world's New Left, counterculture, student movements (such as those centered in Berkeley and Paris), the general rebellion of youth, and so on. Some of the Latin American protest groups also had various connections with the revolutionary movements (Ação Popular in Brazil, Camilo Torres in Colombia, MAPU in Chile, JP in Argentina, Tupamaros in Uruguay, etc.).

During their height, the protest groups did have some effects in the Latin American church. Nevertheless, most of them, especially those linked with the *foquista* revolutionary groups, did not actually want any renovation of the church. Their goal was not the promotion of the people of God. What they wanted was to weaken the whole social system, and they attacked the ecclesiastical system as a part and a support of it. Glorifying the people of God in opposition to the institutional church was a useful tactic for weakening the latter.

In Latin America, at least, such an ecclesiology has been swept away by history and has only theoretical interest at present.

The second temptation, secularization, arises as a consequence of the theology of secularization. According to that theology, the people of God is the federation of "living communities" of "true Christians" led by an "authentic faith"—"adult communities" of "adult Christians." These Christians have a personal and communitarian experience of faith. For them, "people" means "elites" grouped in "small communities." The main feature of such communities is the communication of their religious experiences in a kind of personalist intersubjectivity. The church should be a federation of similar small groups.

Most of the members of such groups are undoubtedly sincere. The problem is that their communities are only accidentally linked with the people and nations, their history and struggles. These communities live inside the states, but without contact with them, relatively indifferent to their fate, like the Jewish synagogues inside the Roman Empire. They apply the concept "people of God" to the federation of communities in a metaphorical sense as the word "flock" applied to the church in the Bible. To them the word "people" means only "a large number," or, at the very most, the existence of some structure among the small communities. "People" used in such a context cannot be compared with the historical peoples. The concept excludes from the "true" and "authentic" church the popular religion of the lower classes. To the members of these groups, the "true" church is their small communities coming together with a religious fervor that is far from popular superstition. But they also remain far from the temporal history of the peoples, their struggles for liberation and justice. From more general concepts of the "people of God," they retain the idea of "active participation of laity" and nothing more. And even their "active participation of laity" is understood in the sense of an "active participation" in the religious experiences of their communities.

This elitist ecclesiology is present today in the Latin American church, especially among some of the Catholic bourgeoisie and other areas suffering from the influence of modern European or North American cultural and secularization movements.

The third temptation is separatism. There is another metaphorical understanding of the concept "peoples," and this one is related to the third ecclesiology and the third temptation. To most conservatives, the church is a people in the sense of the *societas perfecta* of Cardinal Bellarmine, the master of post-Tridentine Catholic theology. According to Bellarmine, the church is a people in the English sense of the word "nation" or "country," the organized whole of the human masses living inside a specific geographic area, and the unity of this whole derives from institutionalized powers. In short, the *societas perfecta* has population and territory, just like the modern nation-states. Within the church is an equivalent of the state, powers which make up the church as a *societas,* as a "people." "The People of God," to Bellarmine and his followers, means an organization of the crowd through the hierarchy and its powers.

The emphasis on hierarchy is the best-known aspect of traditional Catholic ecclesiology. But another aspect of the same idea is no less interesting. Bellarmine compared the church, the *societas,* the people of God, with the other peoples or *societates* of the earth. And for him the church is a people beside the other peoples but separated from them. The church has its own history parallel to or independent of the history of other peoples. It has permanent connections with them, as every people has connections with its neighbors, but there is nothing more. The people of God is a truly separate people, like, for instance, the Jewish people living within medieval Christendom. For Bellarmine the fundamental image of the people of God would be the Papal State, a state separate from the other states. In a way, he sees all Catholics as belonging to the Papal State; they are the representatives of the people of God—the people of the pope—scattered among the other countries of the world, just as the Jews of the Diaspora were the extension of the people of Palestine.

Bellarmine's idea is not so different from that of General Pinochet, who thinks that the church and its ecclesiastical policy are very similar to the Soviet Union and its policy. According to Pinochet, the Catholic Church, like the Soviet Union, has a territory and a population. The Vatican State is the center of the people of God, and the extension of the Catholics outside this base is the principal force of the people of God. All over the world, according to Pinochet, Catholics act as true members of the Vatican State, just as communists all over the world act as citizens of the Soviet Union. Consequently, Catholics have a sort of dual nationality. One part of their life belongs to a secular people, and the other part to the people of God. The boundaries between the jurisdiction of the secular nation and that of the spiritual nation are fixed by the Catholic Church. Among the areas the church claims as its own are the sectors of education, social promotion, relief, marriage and the family, hospitals, and matters of doctrine. These areas of jurisdiction are recognized by any reasonable state (or church); however, boundary disputes are unavoidable and are the matter of both church and civil histories.

The Idea of the People of God Now

After examining the three current interpretations of the ecclesiology of the people of God and finding them all to be temptations to falsity, we must look for hope elsewhere. We must search for a new view of the people, one that can be applied to the special condition of Christianity in Latin America. As the reader must have observed by now, we tend to start from certain events of the last few years, but over and over again we find that these events oblige us to return to the very meaning of the New Testament.

What does the New Testament really say when it is read liberated from the ideologies of the past or temptations of the present? It displays three major ideas about the people of God which, when developed, constitute a response to the challenge of a Latin American ideology.

The Church as the Continuation of Israel. First, the New Testament says clearly that the church is a people because it continues the history of Israel. The people of God is the continuation of Israel; the church is Israel continued until the end of any history. There has never been a break between Israel and God's people, between the Old and the New Testament; the same people march on. True, a part of Israel has been unfaithful and severed itself from the people of God (without losing the promises, according to the mystery revealed in Romans, chapters 9 to 11). But the church has never separated itself from Israel. Indeed, when a part of the Jewish people separated themselves from their king and savior, Jesus, the king of Israel, they were also separated from their ancestors—Abraham, Moses, David, and the prophets, who gave testimony to Jesus. The disciples of Jesus continue the call of Israel; the twelve apostles will be the judges of the whole Israel. All the New Testament sets forth such an idea of people of God.

With Jesus Christ, the people of God did not pass from being a historical people to being some "suprahistorical" people or purely religious, mystical community. The relationship between Old and New Testaments is not at all the relationship between matter and Spirit or secular/temporal and religious/eternal; neither is it the relationship between image and reality (as Bultmann and his innumerable disciples think). The Christ and his church are as historical, as material as the people of old Israel. For instance, Paul was always a Jew and always understood his life and ministry as a task within the people of Israel. As an apostle of Jesus, he was a successor of the prophets. Up to his death, he wanted to be faithful to his Jewish condition and calling, which was always rooted in the reality of the people.

But part of the confusion has arisen because some authors seem to impute to Paul a strange ecclesiology, a half-gnostic theology. It is possible to imagine a Pauline ecclesiology inspired by gnostic concepts (although that never was the thought of the apostle). One can imagine Paul developing an ecclesiology something like this: the people of God is an archipelago of small groups of disciples scattered all over the world, united by the same faith in the same Savior, by the same hope while expecting the advent of their Savior, and by some solidarity. It is like the Isis communities, the Mithras communities, or the other oriental cults of the Roman Empire. Among each group of communities there was some communication and circulation, but they never intended to form a people, and they remained indifferent to the fate and history of the empire and its sixty peoples.

In the abstract, it is a possible system, but such just never was the ecclesiology of Paul. Most probably, he never even suffered the temptation of such an ecclesiology. His Jewish origin, his Jewish education, his Jewish faithfulness protected him. For him, salvation could not possibly be conceived of outside the people, specifically the people of Israel. There is never a merely personal salvation. Therefore, his theological concepts defining the Christian church are either the same concepts used by the Old Testament to define the people of Israel or come from them. His few extensions of Old Testament concepts were not from the religious gnostic world, however. Rather, they came from the political vocabulary of the Greeks, people who rarely let loose from their firm connection with political realities.

For example, Paul used the word *ekklesia* (the political assembly of the Greek city) as the equivalent of the Hebrew Bible's *qahal* (the assembly of Israel). By choosing the word *ekklesia,* Paul and the Septuagint maintained (and intended to maintain) the political meaning of the people of Israel. The Christian *ekklesia* is the continuation or accomplishment of the political meaning of Israel.

Many of Paul's other vocabulary choices were also deliberately political. The word *laos* also means a people organized as a political community, a free people independent from any domination. And the word *soma* (as in *soma tou Xristou),* body of Christ, also has a Greek political reference: the body of the citizens of the city (i.e., the citizens are the body of a city). He used *leitourgia* for the whole of the acts of the Christians; for the Greeks it was the public ceremony of the Greek city. Freedom, *eleutheria,* which is the calling of the church, is never simply an internal, subjective, or personal reality. It is the freedom of a people, the freedom of the Greek city and of the people of Israel freed from the Egyptians. Even charity is not simply a subjective quality; Paul uses it to mean faithfulness to the social agreement of the people, faithfulness to the covenant with the other citizens and members of the community in order to shape a people.

Paul's theology of history conveys his idea about the church even better than the words and themes. For him, the people of the Hebrew Bible—the Old Testament—simply continued. The people of the Old Testament reached its true reality and its fullness with Jesus; Israel became universal and open to all the peoples.

Paul's ecclesiology remained faithful to Jesus himself. There is no doubt that Jesus understood his mission in terms of Israel and Jewish history. His mission concerned Israel, its history and fate. He had not come to speak to humankind in general, to the world in general. He had come in order to save Israel, his people. He had come in order to continue the work of the prophets and to achieve the history of his people. He was not speaking to souls or even individual persons, but to members of his people, and through those members, to the people of God.

Luke showed he understood the same thing by writing the history of the beginnings of the church as a continuation of the Hebrew Bible, Israel's history. Jesus is the link between the two stages of Israel's history.

Finally, according to John, the church is the true Israel opposed to the false Israel. And that false Israel was not a metaphorical Israel, not something different from the historical Israel, but a historical reality. The historical Israel was rejected not because the times of a historical people had passed away, but because it had been unfaithful to its calling.

Israel as an Ecumenical People. The second feature of the ecclesiology of the people of God made clear by the New Testament is that although the church and Israel are the same people with the same history, there has been a change. What is this change? Very simply that, thanks to Jesus, Israel is called to become an ecumenical people, a people open to all peoples, nations, tribes, and languages. Such a fate had been announced by the prophets. They had foretold that the true Israel would go beyond its ancient frontiers, territorial and biological or racial. In the New Testament, Israel calls to all peoples all over the world so that they may enter into the one people of God.

This change has several aspects that are pertinent to developing a better understanding of the people of God.

The first is its universality. Jesus and his disciples asked for an opening of Israel's frontiers so radical that Israel would disappear as a singular people, isolated from other peoples. They asked that it give up its unique personality in order to become the center and axis of a new universal people. But the necessary condition to becoming such a universal people, the *ekklesia tou theou,* was the disappearance of the old form of Israel. In a way, Israel had to achieve the work of the Diaspora. The Diaspora had a providential meaning; it was the first step in the task of the apostles in the extension of the people of God all over the world. It is significant that Christians have always acknowledged the important role of the Diaspora as a stage from the Old Testament to the New Testament. The Christian Bible was the Bible of the Diaspora, the Greek translation of the Septuagint. And the Jewish communities of the Diaspora were the starting point of the apostles when they traveled to the peoples of the ecumenical empire. The apostles proposed a new step to Israel: Israel ought to give up its own territory, renounce its race and biological origin, give up its own communities and synagogues, its customs and traditions, in order to meet other persons of all the peoples.

The New Testament collects all the particularities of Israel under one concept—the law—and announces that Israel ought to give it up as the thing separating Israel as a singular people from the other peoples. The law is a collection of customs, behaviors, rites, and duties that makes the particular civilization, way of life, and identity of the Jewish people. Jesus' message was that the law is overcome; it has ceased being necessary. The new and definitive stage of the people of God is not a law, but the accomplishment of all laws by giving up any law and creating love instead of law. The specificity of Israel now is not law but love. Naturally, the accomplishment of the law does not mean that the peoples no longer need any laws. But they need not accept the old Israel's traditional system of laws in order to become a people of God. In joining the people of God, they do not have to adopt any particular law, because the law of this people is to have no law but love. All people may keep some laws, customs, or traditions if they are ready to submit them to the supremacy of love. But the people of God as a people no longer imposes any law on anyone, and the sign of this new condition is the abolition of the ancient law of Israel.

In consequence of the abolition of the law, Israel has stopped being a separate people, similar to other peoples but alongside them. (The existence of a Jewish people after Jesus is a mystery explained by Paul in Romans, chapters 9 to 11.) The true Israel is now open to every individual in the world. All humankind may belong to the people of God.

The idea that Israel (or the people of God) is not a separate people contradicts Bellarmine's ecclesiology. Bellarmine's system establishes Catholicism as similar to a new Judaism. He sets the church alongside the nations and peoples as a separate people, without any real connections with them. Such an ecclesiology does not allow individual members of the people of God the freedom of being both Christians and persons within their own people and its history. Rather, it makes them agents for another people, responsible for another history. According to Bellarmine's ecclesiology, the people of God is neither secular nor spiritual; it is a mixed people that is not allowed either the freedom of the Spirit or the freedom of the peoples. Like the Jews in the times of Jesus, the Catholics of Bellarmine's school have two affiliations; they are the people of the pope and the people of their state. Like the Jews, they have Caesar and God, and they must try to give to Caesar what is Caesar's and to God what is the pope's, with no connection between the two.

But the New Testament concept of the people of God is quite the contrary. According to it, the people of God is living and growing within all the peoples of the world. Christianity is not a new condition alongside the condition of citizen or member of a people. It is a new manner of belonging to a people or nation. Christians continue to belong to their own people, but they receive the mission of calling this people to participate in being a part of the people of God. The people of God is not the meeting of many human persons, but the meeting of all the nations and people. By virtue of such a calling, every nation has within it the beginning of a radical change; all the peoples enter into a process of conversion. The people of God is the ancient peoples continuing after a process of conversion. Such a process is not yet finished and will never be finished: it is constantly increasing inside every nation and people. One might say that the people of God constantly ferments every secular people. Its eschatological condition hinders the complete identification of any people with the people of God. But all peoples of the world have the beginning of identification with the people of God. By virtue of its past, each people is still a pagan people; by virtue of its calling, each people is a part of the people of God. Each people is the people of God moving toward its full condition.

Consequently, the people of God is the eschatological unity and reconciliation of all the peoples. The unity of the people of God is not produced by reducing all the peoples to the same way of life, the same system, the same law, but by a communion among all the peoples, a convenant of all the peoples.

Naturally, the eschatological people of God is present not only in the beginning of a conversion of the peoples, but also by means of signs that anticipate the future. There is a community of hope, expressed by meetings, sacraments, and other visible signs. But the people of God is not only, not even mainly, the system of ecclesiastical signs. It is primarily the conversion of and the beginning of a new life within the peoples of the world. The signs of the future people are services subordinated to the real people of God. The most important aspect of the people of God is not the signs of the ecclesiastical system—no matter how many Christians (and others) think that the church is such a system and nothing more. The right concept of the historicity of the church is derived from the continuing conversion of all peoples. The historicity of the church is deeper and more radical than most theological ideas of historicity. The church has no separate history of the peoples; Christian life is sharing the historical process of the nations. Every individual calling is a part of the fate, process, and challenge of a nation or people, a fragment of the history of that individual's people (or another concrete people if he or she is a missionary or an immigrant). The Christian life as exemplified in particular Christians does not offer a universal model, nor does its application in a concrete situation provide a universal model (although such a distortion has been attempted so frequently that it seems to be almost unavoidable—ecclesiastical institutions tend to repeat the same model of congregation, community, spiritual method, rites, catechisms, and so on). Actually, each person in every generation is called to perform, in a concrete nation and a specific historical process, a limited number of acts, gestures, or expressions. Within one lifetime each human being is able to perform perhaps ten or one hundred or one thousand important acts; some persons may accomplish a little more, others a little less. The point is that since each individual's life is limited by time and geography, the acts he or she is called to perform are limited in number, conditioned by the historical context, and to be selected according to the discernment of the Spirit. Additionally, such acts have to be adjusted to the conditions of every period. Charity today does not require the same acts as it did in the Middle Ages. Each period contains its own challenges. Each member of the people receives a particular role in the history of salvation.

On the other hand, one's personal actions are never insulated. We all act within collective movements. Our acts are connected with the collective behavior of our family, group, class, and nation, and are conditioned by geographic and historical context. A Christian conversion is never strictly individual; it is a step or fragment of a more general movement. We all become Christians on behalf of our people. That is not only a fact, but a requirement of the people of God. Because a Christian conversion includes a total conversion of the whole person, nobody may offer to God only his or her internal life; the offering must include the totality of one's human relations, work, and social existence, including the future of one's people. Conversion means radical change—immediate or virtual, present or potential—of the whole of civilization. Every new Christian undertakes the duty of changing the civilization and way of life of his or her people.

Another aspect of the same fact is that a personal conversion is not an isolated act. It takes place as a continuation of other conversions of other persons, whether they be of an earlier or the same generation. Nobody remains independent of other Christians. Nobody could arrive at faith and Christianity alone, as a result of an individual evolution. Consequently, after several or many generations, the integration of the various processes of faith, hope, and love produced a certain Christian heritage. Such a heritage is a way of thinking, feeling, living, and acting within an appreciable number of schemes and structures. It is true that an authentic conversion is a personal fact, the effect of a personal option. But it is also the continuation and reactualization of a social heritage. Through such a heritage, people become progressively and dramatically Christian in themselves, in their social patterns.

Such a historicity of Christianity has received a name: it is Christendom. The people of God cannot subsist without Christendom. Christianity constantly generates Christendom, and any personal faith leans on Christendom. Far from Christendom, Christian individuals are condemned to lose their faith (except in the case of some unusual individuals). Christendom is the continuation of the historical people of Israel, the new Israel.

Some ancient and modern authors have understood Christianity as a religious association, like a gnostic movement, without any real continuity with the Jewish people (take, for example, modern Marcionism). For them Christianity is a religious contact with God, received and lived within small groups, independent of the dynamics of global society. In a way, the Christian communities of the pre-Constantinian era did look something like the gnostic cult associations. It is true that they had few connections with the Roman Empire as a social and political structure or with the Hellenistic civilization as a way of life. Nevertheless, the resemblance to the gnostic cults is more superficial than real.

A closer model, although still not the correct one, is the synagogues of the Diaspora. A Jewish synagogue, no matter what its distance from Jerusalem, never forgets its connection with the whole Israel (*Kol Israel*). Even (or especially) after A.D. 70, the synagogues continued to look forward to the time of the final gathering of the twelve tribes of the people of God. The Christian communities did not look to Jerusalem. The hope of a future advent of the Messiah was not the center of their faith. They knew the Messiah was already present, and some elements of his kingdom had begun to appear. His kingdom was effective in the world—the real world, not just some communities or religious groups isolated from this world. All the religious communities were a reference to the kingdom of Jesus in the world. They knew that a religious assembly is only a sign, a symbol, a figure of another reality—the kingdom of God, the real church, the people of God.

The early Christians' understanding of their agreement with Constantine was derived from their ecclesiology. In the ancient church the conviction prevailed that Constantine's conversion and the consequent Christianization of the Roman Empire were an effect of the kingdom of God in this world. Owing to Constantine, Christianity received its first opportunity to get out of the synagogue and to share the public existence of the Roman Empire and its sixty peoples. The conversion of the emperor led to some integration of the church with the empire. Such an integration involved countless problems— problems for that time and problems for all subsequent periods of church history—since the basic structure of the empire was conquest, violence, and the cult of power and domination. Such a situation was a terrific challenge for the church, but such a challenge is the continuation and the active presence of Jesus Christ's incarnation in this world. The ancient Christians believed that they had no right not to accept the integration because it involved problems. The synagogue had been a transition period. The Constantinian church was only a first step in the permanent problem of church vs. world. But at least it revealed a definitive aspect of the kingdom of God: the church is as extensive as the frontiers of the peoples. Christendom means problems, but its problems are the expression of the worldly condition of Christianity. The church cannot be present in the world by avoiding the problems, but only by facing them.

In other words, as necessary and joyful as Christendom is, it is also the captivity of the church. By getting immersed in the peoples of the earth and all their sins, the church binds itself to their fate, history, and struggles. It may try to conduct and to inspire them, but it is not able to control them. The church is both the promise of and the appeal for peace and justice.

From the time of Constantine through the present day, the Christian church has always existed in a state of Christendom. Even the most extremist Protestant communities, which want to remain absolutely independent of politics and public life, are in fact connected with the culture, way of life, and public institutions of the country or countries in which they exist. Except for a few regions of the world where Christianity is almost unknown and the church insignificant, there is always a connection, generally a far-reaching one, between Christianity and culture, church and state. Some writers claim that this connection was broken by the secularization of so many countries, starting in the late eighteenth century. But "liberal" constitutions of the states, with their official secularization and formal separation of church and state, are legal fictions. Such fictions are significant and even helpful as a protection for religious pluralism and the guarantee of some religious tolerance, but they do not convey the real condition of the church vis-à-vis the state in those countries.

One amazing fact is how many Christians have accepted these fictions for truth. The theology of secularization accepted the idea of separation, a liberal theme, as a theological postulate. By so doing, it destroyed the idea of Christendom, though not its actual existence, and tried to claim the idea of a nontemporal and unhistorical church without influence from or on state and power—a church that is pure faith, pure personalism, free from any historical contamination. Such a theology accepts, justifies, and seeks the deportation of the church from the concrete history of peoples and states.

Unfortunately, up to now Christendom is not universal; it remains a Western condition, and so church history is mainly a Western history. There are, of course, some Christian groups and communities in other civilizations all over the world. But that is not enough to make Christendom exist. The people of God really exist in a country when it is making history in that country by acting and reacting on the national ideas, norms, traditions, customs, and so on.

And using this definition, one can detect several signs that Christianity is beginning to shift from a Western axis to a more universal one.

It is important to understand, however, that although the people of God exists (or will exist) within all nations and history, influencing all countries with which it is connected, there is a very definite antagonism between it and secular power. Indeed, one feature of the people of God as a people is that by nature it is opposed to state and power. Being a people means autonomy of the citizens, social life based on horizontal connections among individuals, covenant, agreements, alliances, and loyalty among the members of the community. Although no social life can subsist without some kind of power, force, and coercion, human persons have some ability to regulate their own social life by reason, dialogue, and persuasion. Order does not have to come entirely from the state; much of it can start from the initiative of the citizens. There is no opposition between freedom and social living; on the contrary, a "people" is directly related to "freedom."

Historically, the origin of the idea (and reality) of the people as a covenant, a horizontal agreement, is Israel, the biblical people of God. Christianity then received, developed, and universalized this idea. As Christendom and the Christian tradition spread throughout the world, with it came the idea of the people as a free association, independent of power and domination.

Many will point out that in fact the Christian churches have often struggled against the reality of a free people, rather than promoting it. This is true, but when they have done so they have gone against their own message, not disproved its truth. Other critics will say it was the Greek city and the Roman republic that provided the basis for the existence of a free people. In the sense of setting some historical precedents and inventing certain institutions, this is also true. But the Greek city and the Roman republic were aristocratic states in which freedom was for a few rich or high-born families, persons corresponding to our bourgeoisie. Their systems included neither freedom nor the possibility of being a people for the slaves and the workers, who constituted an overwhelming majority of the population. But Christianity, on the contrary, following biblical tradition, called all men and women—free and slaves, "Greeks" and "barbarians"—to make a people.

As a social reality, "the people" was born in Israel. What is a "people"? It is much more than a population, a crowd, or a tribe, which are groups gathered by virtue of necessity, custom, or the will and power of a lord, personal or abstract, a king, a state, an empire. A people gathers together in order to cooperate by means of free contracts or agreements. The idea of covenant is the basis of any free people. "Sharing" or being free means being faithful and accomplishing the duties that the covenant calls for. Love (*agape,* which is also loyalty) replaces obedience and submission.

Such an idea of freedom runs head on into the problem of state and power because it implies that the state cannot be the origin of any freedom. Christian anthropology denies all the modern theories that seek the origin of freedom in power. The state is called to limit its own power in order to respect and protect its citizens' liberties, but it is not able to originate them. On the contrary, freedom has to be conquered by each person in an ongoing struggle against state and power.

Remember, of course, that "state" and "power" in this context are not purely external, objective realities. The struggle against them is not simply a struggle against external units. State and power are first present within every human being. The first enemy of liberty is in the hearts of every man and woman. Every human being has a disposition to submission and slavery. The lords, dominators, and powers have been internalized in each individual. The struggle for liberty is the struggle of all human beings against their own psychology. Each person has a fear of liberty and a wish for security—a fear of any risk and of all other persons as possible dangers. The constant temptation is to fly from responsibility and to seek the protection of a powerful sovereign. The strongest support of dictatorship and tyranny is fear. The idea of liberty necessarily includes some prospect of martyrdom. The struggle for freedom, therefore, includes some risk, even a risk of death. It also has to overcome all the lesser irrational factors—aggressiveness, rivalry, envy, desire for tranquillity and amusement, and so on—which separate human beings from their vocations.

After taking notice of this inner, subjective problem, one must admit the objective problem, one must admit the objective obstacle to liberty—the state, which is essentially a power. All civilizations have known some kind of power and state. In our time, all the peoples have adopted the structure of the nation-state because such a structure has proved to be the most powerful one for gathering all possible material resources and for facing other peoples. The nation-state is, for the moment, the most powerful agent of security and power.

Of course, the subjective yearning for security and power mentioned above is what has made possible the establishment of nation-states. But the will to freedom is totally opposed to them in their complete form. So a real, ongoing conflict between the calling for freedom and the structure of a nation-state cannot be avoided. Such a conflict is the external projection of each person's inner conflict between the desire for freedom and the fear of insecurity.

Nevertheless, a certain power structure is unavoidable, even though it constitutes a limit to freedom. Neither Christianity nor the church can overcome any use of power, violence, or coercion in social life. Neither Christianity nor the church is able to create a permanent condition of peace and justice, since the kingdom of God is limited by the kingdom of sin. Therefore, all Christian churches have always accepted some kind of state and power, some kind of established violence. But the message of the kingdom of God is not compatible with a stabilized power, a state that is not making any progress toward liberty; still less is it compatible with any kind of regressive power and violence. Thus, the present growth of power and state, the terrible concentration of power in the modern nation-state is an unavoidable challenge for the gospel of the kingdom of God. The present nation-state presents as important a problem as did the Roman Empire with its slavery and domination of sixty peoples.

Of course, destroying such a power is not the task of the institutional church. The church is too linked with its structure to have the independence, energy, and ability to undertake such a task. But Christianity, as a force coming from the word of God and the presence of the Spirit, can awaken and bring about a new reality of a people. And such a people is a unit independent of the state. The effect of true Christian preaching is precisely the appearance of a people as a new reality different from the state.

Such a new, free unit does not come from any power above the human beings who create it. A people comes from human beings and nothing else. A people is the social support of a human being or, to put it another way, the social existence of a human being as an autonomous reality. Such a people builds limits, boundaries, and defenses against the state and power. To some degree, it is an antipower. According to the gospel message, Christianity includes a conversion of the state so that the state is the servant and not the owner of the people. This idea clearly appeared in the first years of the fourth century during the first serious meeting between church and state—between Emperor Constantine and the bishops of Nicaea. As we have seen, the bishops accepted and supported Constantine not because he made an individual act of faith but because they thought he was going to be accepted in the church, and supported by the church, if he was ready to change the role of emperor to that of *episkopos tou ektos,* the defender of the people of God against the outside world.

Of course, the bishops of Nicaea were naive about the willingness of power to subordinate itself. Nevertheless, Constantine became the model for the Christian state, and the endless struggles between church and empire suggest how determined Christianity was to cling to its ideal. Some eight hundred years passed before the Western Roman Empire was destroyed by the Gregorian popes. Progressively the calling for freedom of the Christian church produced a political change as the people asserted themselves vis-à-vis the absolute power of the state.

The state is, by its nature, dominating and totalitarian. Its purpose, like that of any power, is to increase its power. It attempts to make of its citizens the agents of its growth. (The present national security system is the new incarnation of such a political reality.)

In short, the state has never accepted the role of servant without being compelled to it by the active resistance of a responsible people. Such an active, antipower people is the people of God. Nor is there any real people of God if Christians are not in the process of becoming a people, an assembly of free persons struggling against the state and its powers. The church as an institution is Christian only if it supports and defends such a people. The church as an institution is legitimate only if it is a system of symbols able to anticipate and represent the hope and struggle of the people of God. The ecclesiastical meeting is an anticipation and a message of the future peoples of God; it announces the advent of the people of God and calls every person to be converted to that people. As such, the church may and must produce some ferments and historical stimulants.

In the Middle Ages, several Christian institutions anticipated the modern tendency to freedom. For example, the common life of the Franciscans and Dominicans and the democratic model of the guilds and brotherhoods prepared the principles of modern democracy. After the Reformation the congregational model found in the Anglo-Saxon countries became the background and immediate source of democracy. Indeed, modern democracy could not have appeared without antecedents such as these.

In this manner the church is present in every people that is becoming a true people. The kingdom of God is simultaneously the congregation that antici-pates and prepares the model of a new community and the political and social institutions that come from Christian inspiration.

The church as an institution—as a congregation—shares the kingdom of God as a prophetic promise and a visible sign, as a process of conversion of person and society; it is primarily a symbolic presence of the kingdom—real, but real as a symbol. The true material presence of the kingdom of God is the present transformation of personal and social life in the world.

In such a manner, Christianity is a way to freedom—a way to a free people—which does not come from any power or state. Any church as an institution, therefore, faces a terrible temptation. The temptation of the church is to consider itself as the real presence of the kingdom of God and the end of its activities.

But the church is means and not end. If the church considers itself an end, it becomes a kind of state. This was the temptation of the Roman church after defeating the German emperors, and since then it has been the constant temptation of the Catholic Church (and of all the established churches that imitated the Catholic Church's way of relating to the world). In the struggle against the totalitarian state and the defense of the *libertas ecclesiae,* some church people think that the best and fastest way is to give the church power similar to what it is fighting. Then its power balances the power of the state. Such an ecclesiastical power is conceived as power for liberation, and it can become a power that protects, supports, and defends the oppressed peoples. But such power is outside the proper role of the institutional church; it is also very dangerous.

For example, in Latin America, the friars and Jesuits were the sole protec-tors of the Indians; the "reductions" of the Jesuits and the "lands of the church" were the "reservations" for the Indians. That condition was ambiguous—with both good and bad results—while it lasted. The danger became evident with the coming of independence and the consequent end of the power of the church. The Indians lost their lands, their freedom, and their protectors. The church's loss of real estate meant the total oppression of the people. Thus, compassion for the oppressed can give rise to ecclesiastical power and, in a way, legitimate its existence in history, but dependence on such power places the oppresssed in a position where their lot can easily become worse than before. Power is also dangerous for the church because it can oppose the church's mission by generating many terrible abuses, such as the Crusades and the Inquisition. The secularization movement initiated at the end of the Middle Ages was caused (and justified) by countless abuses of ecclesiastical power.

Perhaps the best conclusion of this exposition on the people of God is to say that the church has not received the mission of being an institutional power against the power of the state. But Christianity has an important political mission, which must be supported by the institutional church. This mission is to be active by creating a people as a people, as an autonomous reality. The people of God exists as a people when it becomes conscious of its own existence facing any power and state; such a consciousness stems from the biblical message. For ordinary people, such a consciousness has never existed outside the biblical tradition; it is the Christian contribution to human society.

THE CHURCH AND GEOPOLITICS

Any discussion of the people of God and the world cannot, however, stop with a delineation of mission. It must include a discussion of the geopolitics and strategy of the church for achieving its mission. This imperative is forced on the church by its nature and the conditions of its existence. The Christian people live within a world of powers and struggles for power. Today the church is present in the middle of some 150 hostile states, gathered into blocs opposing each other and often the church itself. The church cannot possibly exist alongside such powers and states: the church and the Christian people are immersed in their antagonisms. Consequently, one must deal with the church's and Christianity's own problems of geopolitics and strategy to see how they can accomplish their mission.

Many Christians think that the question of the church's geopolitics is irrelevant, that the church is able to remain angelically pure and free from any contamination of power or geopolitical aims. For them, the church is only the loyal servant of Jesus Christ; it accomplishes the mission it received from Jesus Christ and nothing else. Its actions receive their principles only from heaven, not from earth. The motivation for its actions is pure obedience to Christ and the Spirit, without any interference from human factors such as geopolitics or strategy.

And indeed, one can imagine an evangelical mission whereby Christians, sent by a heavenly inspiration, would go throughout the world to all the peoples, announcing the same message with the same words, indifferent to the different results of their preaching. Is such an evangelization possible? Perhaps in theory, but it certainly does not seem to exist. (Although only the Catholic Church is referred to here and throughout this section, the other churches seem to be in a similar position.)

Because it is evident that an angelically pure church and mission do not exist, it is equally evident that there has to be an ecclesiastical geopolitics. The Catholic Church defines its mission in the world from a geopolitical viewpoint. That statement requires some explication, for neither the hierarchy nor the theologians like to speak of such a subject. The books of ecclesiology do not make any mention of it.

Why such silence? One probable reason is that the Vatican's diplomatic service, like the diplomats of secular states, think that foreign policy is not a matter to be publicly discussed; secrecy is a guarantee of success, and the ordinary citizens need not have any understanding or information of world affairs. Moreover, the Roman Curia, like any secular state, likes to justify its various acts regarding foreign relations in such a way that they appear to come from the abstract principles of ethics or theology, from its Christian calling. It can always find transcendental reasons to explain contingent decisions.

The hierarchies, too, like secular officials, prefer that their decisions appear to be based on principle. They want Christians to believe that all their decisions are based on Jesus' gospel and inspired by the Spirit. So the church gives its clergy and missionaries (not to mention the laity) a theory of mission that explains its universal principles and nothing more. It gives them no explanation of the concrete planning. Seemingly, it is better that missionaries not be aware of the plans, strategy, and geopolitics that are the background of their activities; it is better that they refer all their operations directly to the ultimate purpose, the kingdom of heaven, and raise no questions about the contingent planning of the authorities. Theology functions as an ideology and furnishes a spiritual motivation for all decisions. It is rather like every army in the world. The chiefs of staff never explain or discuss their geopolitics, strategy, planning, or tactical motivations. It is enough that the soldiers believe that all their acts are directly aimed at saving freedom and happiness. (If the soldiers knew the strategy of their officers, they might have some doubts about the real significance of their sacrifices.)

In short, the geopolitics of the church is covered in such a way that there are almost no documents on it. So one can do nothing but induce what that geopolitics is from the facts, the concrete practice of the system. Throughout the political acts of the church, it can be supposed that there is some logical connection or plan, and any plan presupposes a geopolitics. But neither the laypeople nor the priests nor the bishops are aware of the geopolitics of their institution as a whole. (Indeed, even the decision-makers are probably generally unaware of it, since geopolitics is more powerful if it remains unconscious.) Within their own small sector of autonomy, bishops and pastors have also their secret geopolitics, but in a very naive way because their decisions are never of importance.

One wonders whether the participation of laypeople in the church claimed by Vatican II requires some knowledge of the institution's geopolitics, or not. What participation is possible in decision-making if laypeople are ignorant of the geopolitical views underlying the planning of the church? It is easy to understand why church officials are reluctant to permit laypeople much participation in matters such as liturgy or doctrine. But geopolitics and strategy seem to be especially suited to the capabilities of laypeople, since these sciences require knowledge of history and human sciences that many laypeople probably have a better grasp of than most clerics. Nevertheless, secrecy remains the rule generally observed by ecclesiastical authorities.

It seems to me that this rule of secrecy is the result of the influence of the secular state (or perhaps of the same psychological tendencies and "will to power" that guide state officials). Certainly there is a close parallel to the way in which the state maintains its secret policies. But is not such an imitation of the secret policy of the states a real mistake? Do the ecclesiastical authorities mean that their geopolitics is so scandalous or shameful that it cannot be publicly discussed by the members of the church? Why are decisions a secret of the Vatican Secretary of State? Why cannot Latin American Catholics know what plans the Vatican has for their future? Why is there such similarity between hiding the foreign policy of the church and that of the states?

Security and Church

Ecclesiastical geopolitics exists primarily because the church as an institution has a problem of security. Some Christians believe that the church by virtue of its spiritual nature should not seek security; that, like Jesus, it should be ready to become the victim of the world. And it is true that the biblical idea of mission does not include any idea of security or its defense. Therefore, if the church dealt only with announcing the kingdom of God and proclaiming the word of God, if it relied only upon the gospel and faith in order to ensure its own security, if it entrusted the risks of the future only to the Spirit of God, there would be no argument for any policy based on security. But, in fact, there is no church that relies only upon the strength of the gospel to ensure its security. As a guarantee for the future, the churches have properties, gather capital, seek legal defenses, influence public opinion, and seek to win a position of prestige in the establishment. They try to enter into the cultural and social structure of society—partly to evangelize and change that structure, partly in order to rest on it. A pure spiritual church would seek only the support of its conscious, faithful members. But, in fact, any church also seeks the support of public opinion and social pressure, so that many people will remain under its influence even if they have lost faith, religious interest, and obedience to the Christian rules of behavior.

The subject of security is survival. The survival of the church as a faith in the gospel of Jesus Christ, a hope in the kingdom of God, and the possibility of charity is not a problem. Nothing can force a Christian person to lose such realities. The problem of security is the survival of all the material and cultural objects that the church believes are and will be necessary for accomplishing its mission. In a way, through such goods, the church is trying to foresee and guarantee its future. In short, there is a problem of security in the church because it is not able to apply Jesus' words: "Look at the birds in the sky. They do not sow or reap or gather into barns; yet your heavenly Father feeds them" (Matt. 6:26).

So the present condition of the church is a contrast between the requirements of the gospel of Jesus Christ and human weakness. The church seeks its own way between the need for security and the calling to freedom. It is permanently free by virtue of its calling, but captive by virtue of its security, a captive of its own security.

General Principles of Ecclesiastical Geopolitics

The general principles of the church's geopolitics, which determine its strategy, seem clear enough not to need any demonstration, even though one must deduce them for lack of documentary evidence.

Anticommunism. There is no doubt at all that the first geopolitical (and therefore, strategic) principle of the church is the struggle against communism. This is true not only of the Catholic Church, but of most Protestant denominations as well.

This is a strategic struggle (a political action), not a doctrinal one. Clearly, communism as a doctrine is incompatible with Christianity and has to be rejected by the church as heresy or error, like liberalism or fascism. From a doctrinal condemnation, a church does not necessarily deduce that it should take political action against some parties, governments, or states. The necessity of political action does not immediately result from the doctrinal exclusion of communism.

So why is the church determined to promote an anticommunism that is not a mere doctrinal condemnation but a political action?

The answer has to lie in geopolitical considerations. This becomes more obvious after a little consideration of history. Over the centuries, the church has been confronted with numerous doctrinal heresies. Sometimes it has seemed evident to ecclesiastical authorities that a given heresy should be fought strictly on doctrinal grounds. In other circumstances, it has seemed equally evident that a political struggle was called for. And this decision (which always seems so "evident") has changed drastically over time. For example, after the Reformation it was "obvious" to both Protestants and Catholics that a political war was the necessary conclusion of their doctrinal separation. At the present time, the opposite conclusion is just as "evident," while an all-out fight against communism seems to be necessary.

Again, in the nineteenth century, the Catholic Church deduced from the errors of liberalism the necessity of a political struggle against it. Today the same church does not, although the problems of faith created by liberalism have never been solved and are as dangerous now as in the past. Innumerable Christians are losing their faith and Christian loyalty to the church because of liberalism. Indeed, it is not clear that there is less faith and charity in many communist countries—say Poland—than in the liberal states of the West. Liberalism probably gives rise to more crises of faith than communism. The problem of communism is not immediately connected with the problem of the future of faith. Why does the church consider that the errors of liberalism do not justify a political struggle, and that the errors of communism do? The most probable answer seems to be the church's desire for geopolitical security. In the nineteenth century, the church perceived liberalism as the most dangerous enemy of ecclesiastical security. Today it does not. Today it sees its most dangerous enemy as communism. Consequently, it has chosen to emphasize its geopolitical antagonism toward communism, leaving its antagonism toward liberalism in a secondary place.

In the West, all the political parties supported by Catholics have been encouraged as the most potent enemies of communism. All the various kinds of Catholic organizations have been given the struggle against communism as their main task. Unions, schools, and social organizations have to engage in the anticommunist struggle before working toward their own goals—cultural, social, political—and their goals have to be controlled by their compatibility with the main task of anticommunism.

Such strategy is derived from the geopolitical view of the ecclesiastical authorities. But naturally the authorities have received the support of many powerful sectors of Catholic opinion. In many cases, Catholic organizations and individuals have even anticipated the warnings of the hierarchy. The Catholics of the upper and middle classes did not need any papal exhortation: they were prepared to be more anticommunist than the pope himself, and they have spontaneously guided the Catholic organizations toward an anticommunist strategy. So there has been a convergence of the practices and goals commanded by the ecclesiastical authorities and desired by many organizations. The greatest problem arose with the Catholic worker movements, which had to be invited (or forced) to limit their social programs in order to avoid any collaboration with communists. The authoritarian attitude Rome adopted toward the Catholic workers' movements was typical.

In all the debates of our times—peace movements, independence movements in the Third World, the problems of the worker-priests in France, Catholic Action—the attitude of the Catholic Church has been authoritarian: no infiltration or possibility of communist infiltration can be tolerated. When anyone or any group shows the slightest tendency to be helpful to a communist movement, the Roman response has been and still is immediate and terrible. With those who display liberal leanings, there has been much tolerance and patience (for example, the Dutch theologians, or the Swiss theologian Hans Küng). But for theologians who show any liking for Marxism (such as Giulio Girardi), exclusion is immediate.

Concerning Latin America, the Roman church has taken an even stronger position of anticommunism than it has in the metropolitan West. During the 1950s, the calls from Pope Pius XII to "save" Latin America meant saving it from the "communist danger." The Roman Curia supposed (and still supposes) that Latin America's social problems had to provoke a communist attack there. The Medellín Conference, therefore, caused even greater anxiety in Rome, because ecclesiastical officials took it as opening a door for communist infiltration of the church. Since then, the Roman Curia has tried to control the Latin American Episcopal Conference (CELAM) and, in a way, succeeded when its staff was "renewed" in a sort of coup d'état in November 1972. Since then the new staff of CELAM has carefully manifested that its main care is the struggle against communism and, above all, communist infiltration of the church. The various national episcopal conferences share the same geopolitics and strategy: communism is a top-priority problem for them in a reflection of Rome's preoccupation with it.

Thus, because of the church's anticommunist geopolitics, the action of its prophetic minorities against the new rightist totalitarian systems has been limited and controlled. Any prophetic action has to affirm and manifest clearly that it has no connection with any communist infiltration because such a charge is a constant threat (or reality). The institutional church is more tolerant toward rightist totalitarian states than toward leftist states because the former are firm barriers against communism.

What is the church defending by means of this geopolitics? Primarily, its external security. It wants to save the heritage of Christian civilization—all the cultural and material goods that give Western men and women a Christian heritage even if they remain unaware of it. It wants to defend its present cultural context and all the power factors underlying that context—language, laws, customs, mass media, schools, hospitals, social relief, and so on. And there is no doubt that it would loose all these factors under a communist system.

The North-South Antagonism. The church's second geopolitical principle has to do with the antagonism of North and South and is much less straightforward than the all-out fight against communism. From the actions of the church, the guiding principle may be deduced to be something like the following: the independence of the new nations of the South is to be favored if—and only if—it is compatible with the struggle against communism and tolerated by the ruling nations of the North. In the Third World, all the churches created by the metropolitan churches are nowhere near economic or cultural independence. They all depend upon the "aid" of the metropolitan churches. This dependence is convenient, so the geopolitics of the Roman church is based on maintaining it. In other words, the strategy does not consist of trying to prepare the churches of the Third World for a more genuine independence, but, on the contrary, of maintaining their basic dependence. It is supposed that a certain degree of dependence favors the unity of the institutional church as a whole.

Avoidance of Conflict with Governments. The third geopolitical principle says: the church has to avoid any problem with the governments in power if faithfulness to the word of God does not make a conflict absolutely necessary. The church must accept many sacrifices in order to keep its prestige and maintain its access to and favor with the upper classes (which support the governments). Prestige and favor with the lower classes is not so important because these classes do not support the governments. The governments (and consequently the ruling classes) are the groups that are best able to give the church security and power; therefore the church relies upon them. (Such a principle, of course, makes the church dependent on changes of governments.)

Social Unity. The church relies on government support to protect its heritage of Christian culture and civilization—in other words, to provide it with external security. But the church also seeks internal security. Primarily, this means holding out against any and all factors that might trouble its internal unity since, like any human institution, the church considers unity to be in permanent danger. From a strategic viewpoint, maintaining government support is perhaps the principal way in which the church attempts to protect its internal unity; anticommunism is also important, since communism is seen as a stronger, specific threat to unity.

From the church's concern for unity, one may deduce several conclusions. The most important is that the church, quite correctly, sees class warfare as more dangerous than wars between nations. The latter do not create any danger for the unity of the institutional church; on the contrary, they tend to strengthen the unity of all national institutions. In many cases, the prestige of the church actually increases during a war. (This was true even in the Soviet Union during World War II.) Therefore, the Christian churches have accepted, approved, and helped the wars of their nations. Class warfare, on the contrary, divides the church because it gives rise to conflict among the classes within the church itself. Therefore, the church tends to strengthen all movements that encourage social unity.

The Support for Ecclesiastical Geopolitics. All these geopolitical principles cannot be explained merely by some Machiavellian tendency of the ecclesiastical authorities. Rather, by using them, the institutional church is representing, defending, and promoting the corporate will of its members of the church; the authorities are defending the interests of their "people."

It is evident that the majority of Catholics—the faithful and loyal parishioners—fear and hate communism. The anticommunist geopolitics of the hierarchy expresses the anticommunism of the Catholic masses. Similarly for the majority of the members of the Catholic church in the Western world, the problems of the Third World are secondary; such problems do not create troubles for their own existence, and although, as men and women of good will they would not mind seeing them solved, they do not wish the solutions to cause them personal inconvenience. Neither does the majority want trouble between their church and their government or social disunity in their ranks.

It is clear that the Catholic Church (like many Protestant denominations) is defending the viewpoint of its majority—the middle class of the developed Western countries. But there is a contrast and sometimes a contradiction between the interests of the ordinary members of the church and the interests of the people of God. The problem arises: Is there a sufficient convergence between the interests and ideals of the middle-class member-ship and the movement of the people of God? Can the Western middle-class desire for security be connected with the movement to freedom of the Spirit that is the calling of the whole people of God all over the world?

Expansion of the Church

So far we have considered the church's principles for the first essential of any geopolitics—security. But beyond security, there is another possible geopolitical goal—expansion. Has the church projects of expansion? Is its geopolitics oriented toward expansion?

The answer varies in different parts of the world. The established churches of the metropolitan West have, since the nineteenth century, been preoc-cupied with the attacks of modern culture—rationalism, liberalism, sec-ularism, and now communism. They have been compelled to a merely defensive strategy at the expense of expansion. In the Catholic Church, any increase has come exclusively from population growth (Holland, for in-stance) or immigration (United States). The established churches see their task as defending their past and their survival in the future. They have no geopolitical plan for expansion.

In the rest of the world the situation is different. During the last four centuries there has been a movement to expand the established Christian churches in the non-Christian countries—the so-called missionary move-ment. Such an expansion followed the norms and recommendations of geopolitics (conscious or unconscious) and continues to do so today, al-though in a slightly different guise.

Since the sixteenth century, the expansionary geopolitics of the church has been conducted under a simple principle: to settle the church all over the world by following the roads opened by Western colonization. In almost all cases, the missionaries accompanied the conquerors. Almost without excep-tion, the expansion of the church resulted from agreements between a colonial power and the Roman or national church.

The churches (Catholic or Protestant) have never blamed, forbidden, or tried to hinder colonization. Such an idea was discussed only by the Domini-cans and Jesuits in the sixteenth century; after that, the churches agreed. They often encouraged colonization, since they supposed that such an expan-sion of Western or European power would provide Christianity with the best opportunities of increasing all over the world. They accepted the colonial ideology—the idea that the white peoples were "civilizing the savages." They helped the ideological position of the conquerors by attributing to their military and political superiority the value of an ethical superiority and sometimes of a Christian mission or divine blessing.

Since the expansion of the church was part of colonization, the new churches the missionaries founded in the conquered countries were simply copies of the metropolitan institutions with the same religious system, the same doctrine, the same rites and religious expressions, the same laws and customs. So the foundation of copy-churches became the principle of the expansion of Christianity.

And that made things easy when the era of colonialization came to an end. The goal had to be changed, but not very much. The new principle seemed to be (and still is): the heritage of the colonial period is to be saved by entrusting to the copy-churches the survival and progress of the new communities. In other words, the nationals are called to continue the European settlements. Saving the heritage of the colonial period is their primary task. Saving the past is more important than trying to conquer something new; there is to be no serious approach to a new form of Christianity.

The reason for this imperative is easily understood because it works back to the first motivation of any geopolitics—security. The church is afraid of any "evangelical risk." Colonial missions were (and are) without dangers; since the new churches of the colonies were copies of the metropolitan churches, there was little risk they would change the traditional patterns. That was geopolitically desirable; if the new churches created new patterns and new ways of living Christianity, they could lead to troubles in the metropolitan churches themselves. Innovations might give rise to discussions about the absolute value of the traditions in the metropolitan church. For that reason, the Roman church did not accept the new rites proposed in the eighteenth century. By virtue of the rigidity of the institutions in the old churches, the new churches were not allowed to create any new models of a Christian way of life. The "Chinese rites" might cause perturbation within the European churches; such a danger ought to be avoided.

The principle is still in force today. The Catholic Church is suspicious of any new mission that runs the risk of troubling the heritage of the past. Suspicion exists even within the metropolitan countries, which shows how closely it is related to several of the geopolitical principles aimed at security. Take, for example, the case of the worker-priest in France and other countries. Such a mission to the working class endangered the traditional alliance with the bourgeoisie. The upper classes were not ready to suffer such a betrayal of a sector of the church. The whole system was upset by that visible presence of the church among the working class, so the mission was stopped.

Theological Judgment

Examining the church's strategies in expansion leads back to the questions: Is the use of geopolitics justifiable for Christians? May the church simultaneously rely upon the gospel and geopolitics? Is there a difference among the various kinds of geopolitics? If some geopolitics is legitimate, are there any criteria to discern between good geopolitical principles and wrong ones? Such questions deserve extensive consideration. Here we can only anticipate some ideas with a view to a future statement on the problem.

In the first place, the security of the church is more complex than the security of the nations. The secular peoples have within themselves all the resources necessary for maintenance, reproduction, and rejuvenation. The culture and the material resources of nations continue by virtue of inner factors. So the problem of secular security is just a question of protecting and promoting these processes against dangers from outside. The state that guides a nation may rely on the spontaneous processes of corporate life.

The problem of the church is more difficult. A Christian church cannot survive only by virtue of its connection with spontaneous social processes, at least not for more than a few generations. To survive, the church requires a periodic renewal of faith. And faith does not continue by virtue of social process. It is not the result of a natural evolution, and it does not depend merely on structural laws. In a way, faith is a personal activity and a new beginning in each person. Parents have no guarantee of being able to communicate their faith to their children. Therefore, it is not enough to protect faith against external threats; it must be created anew in each generation (or each period of history). So the church cannot rely on geopolitics to ensure its future. It must have a frequent revival of its mission in order to give rise to a new support of faith. Pure survival of the past means death for the church.

From these considerations, we may conclude that geopolitics alone is not sufficient for the security of the church. But they do not allow one to say whether it is unnecessary or harmful or desirable. To do that, one must examine two hypotheses: either a geopolitical consideration is a positive contribution to the future of the church and in accord with its mission or it is a negative contribution and an obstacle to mission.

The first hypothesis creates an alliance between church and state. In such a case, the church accepts the geopolitical worldview of the state; it seeks its security by means of the alliance, and its future depends on the future of the state.

Such an agreement with political power practically guarantees the safety of the institutional system of a Christian civilization. But by virtue of the same factors that ensure such safety, such an alliance can produce a separation between the church and the lower classes. Then any preaching to the poor becomes impossible. This has happened in the past. It was from the realization that this had occurred that Bartolomé de Las Casas made his condemnation of the church-state alliance in the sixteenth century. He said that preaching to the Indians was impossible because of their domination by the Spanish. The *encomienda* system made impossible any conversion. Consequently, Christians had to share the struggle with the Indians for their rights and independence as a prior condition to any possible preaching to them.

If a geopolitical security policy hinders the conversion of the poor, how can the church remain the church of Jesus Christ called to announce salvation to the poor? Such a policy destroys the very mission of the church.

Similarly, if the church shows masses that it is supporting the states and elites, and these states and powers are oppressing the poor, there is a contradiction within the church. Christianity is a calling to freedom and love, so a church that supports oppressors emerges as a refutation of its message. In the nineteenth century, the European churches lived such a contradiction, and in consequence many members of the working class rejected the churches and Christianity.

In Latin America today, many aware Christians are afraid of a similar occurrence. In the past, the church has defended the poor Indians and the peasants, and has been their ultimate protector. The faithfulness of the Indians to the Catholic Church until now is to be explained from such a past position. But how will the church react to the recent changes in society and church, to the new contradictions of the neocolonialist condition of the Latin American peoples? Will it remain faithful to its own past?

If the church chooses the geopolitical strategy of seeking the protection and favor of the new totalitarian system, and such a system is the new oppressor of the Latin American masses, the external security of the church will be saved, but not the faith of the people. Just as happened in nineteenth-century Europe, the apostasy of the masses will be the price paid for the security of the ecclesiastical establishment. And if the poor leave the church, is the church still Christian?

When it is allied with the upper classes, the church tends to assume their prejudices. The upper classes are prone to believing that the lower classes are easy to manipulate by propaganda and indoctrination. So the clergy come to believe that the problem of faith of the lower classes is a problem of indoctrination and catechism. They assume that the poor are merely passive receivers of a catechistic system. However, the facts show that the lower classes, like everyone else, do not accept any doctrine so easily if that doctrine contradicts their own aspirations. The poor look at concrete reality and can see whether the church is struggling with them or against them. They will trust the ecclesiastical message if the church announces to them their liberation and freedom, in other words, if the church is faithful to its own message.

Therefore, many Latin American Christians are anxious because they know that the options which the church chooses now will determine the future for many centuries, and they are not sure the church is ready to stand with the poor. They are afraid that the church will ignore its mission and follow the secular principles of strict geopolitics in its search for security.

On the other hand, mission and geopolitics will meet if the church entrusts its security to the peoples, the masses, and especially the peoples of the Third World instead of to the totalitarian states. Of course, the peoples do not have the power to guarantee the continuity of ecclesiastical privileges. The support of the poor is not as lucrative as the support of the state and the upper classes, but it is a sufficient protection against the anger of the upper classes, as has been shown in the past (for instance, in Mexico during the persecution). The people are able to maintain the continuity of the church even in the face of persecution by the whole power system.

STRATEGY AND CHURCH

Having examined the geopolitics of the church, one must also look at its strategy. Geopolitics and strategy are not independent. Any strategy is based on a particular geopolitical view of the world—its forces, struggles, and powers. Geopolitics becomes efficient by means of a strategy; a strategy is a plan for reaching the goals of security and expansion set by a geopolitics. Actually, the church's strategy has been touched on in our review of its geopolitics. But the subject is important enough to require a direct examination as well.

In the present condition of the world, the church must choose among three strategies that are possible and one that can be imagined in theory but does not appear to be practical except in a few areas. The Latin American context is a good one in which to examine these models because today they compete there rather more openly than in most other parts of the world. (Notice that each of these strategies relates directly to one of the previously described concepts of the people of God. This is because strategy is so closely tied to worldview.)

The Conservative Strategy. The first possible strategy for the church is the conservative strategy. It consists of using all available means in order to save the heritage of the past, especially the structures and institutions of the past. It assumes that salvation is to be understood in the sense of maintaining and not changing; it supposes that the present change in world and society is a transient crisis. Consequently, the basic objective of the conservative strategy is to be able to save as much as possible of the Christian heritage while awaiting the end of the crisis. Its proponents think that after the "crisis," all conditions will go back to the "normal" position—the former one. To them the problem is only to remain firm, resisting and waiting.

But since it is evident that the spontaneous evolution of society is presently destroying many ancient structures, laws, customs, and religious and social patterns, how is such resistance possible? The conservative strategy accepts and often seeks the support of a conservative state. It favors, whenever possible, the advent of more conservative governments and political structures. That is why the conservatives support the national security states in Latin America; they are willing to close their eyes to the totalitarian doctrine and systems of such governments. These governments give the church very privileged conditions that no democratic government would willingly give it. Without the rightist dictatorships, the national churches would have been unable to maintain or recover their privileges.

What are these privileges? In the first place, they include various social advantages, the maintenance of many features of the past within the social structure. For example, the civil law of the conservative authoritarian governments actively supports many ecclesiastical laws concerning the family and sexual morality. The teaching of religion is brought into the national education system. The clergy are an influential class, invited to public functions and given good seats in the public administration, the army, and the university; they also receive various immunities (from certain customs duties, taxes, and fines; from conscription; etc.). The mass media are censored in part according to the rules of ecclesiastical morality. By such means, the conservative governments try to save the social prestige of the church, which, by itself, is unable to maintain such a prestige.

In the second place, support from the conservative governments brings many socioeconomic advantages. The civil authorities are willing to support various ecclesiastical institutions, especially those giving educational, hospital, and relief services. Many persons receive help through these social services, so a church that can offer them receives great social prestige and appears to be an immense paternalistic power. Thus by setting the church in the distribution line of its utilities, the state gives it a reputation of being a wonderful benefactor.

Finally, owing to the control of all information sources by totalitarian governments, the church (when it supports such governments) receives many opportunities to use the mass media to spread its message.

The Strategy of Secularization. A second strategy is best called secularization. To a degree, it is the continuation of Catholic (or Protestant) liberalism of the nineteenth century and is the normal reaction of that sector of the bourgeoisie which remained loyal to the church during that period (or came back to the church in the second half of that century). According to the ideology of the dominant bourgeoisie, the secularization of the whole of society is the most important religious fact of our times because it is the typical event of modern society, urban and industrial, scientific and technological. For them, the secularization of life is an irreversible process, and any serious strategy has to begin by recognizing such a fact.

The strategy of secularization has two faces—one positive, one negative. On the latter side, it is a negative task. The Christian bourgeoisie believes that the modern world will never accept Christianity if the church is not willing to "modernize" itself. In order to make the church more compatible with the "modern" way of life, the bourgeoisie invites the clergy to do away with all the religious expressions and symbols tied to old-fashioned rural society— language, rites, customs, laws, and relationship. For them, the future of Christianity starts from a new catechism, a new liturgy, new ministries, new communities—all patterns suited to the scientific and technical language and customs of the new society. For them, the main obstacles to faith and Christianity today are the external forms of traditional society that survive in the church. When the church is adjusted to modern life, they say, modern men and women will come back to it without difficulty. Such a strategy implies a change in the church, but only a peripheral change.

In many Protestant churches this adjustment to secularization began in the nineteenth century. In the Catholic Church of Europe and North America it has been applied since Vatican Council II, where it has resulted in an immense simplification of external apparatus. For many persons, this simplification deserves the name "destruction" or "ruin." Others say that it is a shift toward Protestantism. And it is true that many of the changes carried out by the Protestant churches under the name of Reformation are now accepted by Catholics as a result of Vatican II, so, in a way, the strategy of secularization has looked like a "Protestantization" of the Catholic Church.

This modernization of the external apparatus of the church was an adaptation to the requirements of the bourgeoisie and did not take into account the feelings of the popular classes and their attachment to certain traditional customs. The Catholics of the upper classes, especially the intellectual class, controlled the modernization according to their own tastes. A religion of pure interiority suits them; therefore they reduced worship services to a simple expression of words. The lower classes feel that their sensitivity has been rejected as a norm for the church; many continue to practice their religion in their traditional ways, but half-secretly.

Some claim that the present decrease in religious practice and in vocations, the crisis of Catholic publishing and Catholic education, and the fall-off in religious teaching and consciousness of affiliation within Catholic families have been caused by the liberal modernization of the church. The supporters of secularization argue that such a process of decrease in the externals of religious practice was unavoidable because it is the product of a total evolution of all Western society. Moreover, they believe that any delay in adjusting the Catholic Church to the present society would only increase such phenomena in the future.

Of course, this argument is based on two postulates: (1) the shift to the present modern society and way of life was unavoidable and is now an irreversible process; (2) there is a close connection between modern life and secularization. Several years ago, both postulates were taken for granted by sociologists. Now, both postulates seem more debatable than evident.

Some recent authors have pointed out that these principles are too general and too abstract to provide sociology and other social sciences with a real-world explanation of what is happening. As for the first postulate, they say, traditional society cannot be described as totally nontechnical, nonscientific, and rural and nonurban. On the other hand, modern society is to a degree pretechnical, prescientific, and rural. Actually, since the beginning of any civilization, human society has been partly based on science, technology, urban life, and rationality. And it is probable that, in the future, all peoples will always partly know rural life, irrationality, and a pretechnical and prescientific mentality. Between the different ages of humankind, there is a difference of degree, not of nature. Consequently, the transition from a traditional life to a modern life is a process as old as human history and does not explain particular occurrences of the present time. It is difficult, therefore, to justify a process of modernization of the church from the "principle" of the irreversible modernization of society. Such a principle must at least be completed by other, more comprehensive ones before extensive changes, so upsetting to many persons, are based on it.

The second postulate is no stronger than the first. It is not clear that the secularization of cultural life (which here includes religion) is a necessary consequence of the material modernization of life. The connection between secularization and modernization that is presently made by most sociologists may be the product of three centuries of liberal bourgeois propaganda. It is not easy to perceive a really necessary connection between the two phenomena.

At any rate, the negative side of the strategy of secularization may be summed up by saying that it is based on the conviction that the way of life of the bourgeoisie of today is the model for every people in the future. Such a conviction relies upon the feelings of the Western intellectual elites. It supposes that the opinions of the lower classes are not of importance because their religion is retrograde and superstitious, and it surmises that popular religion will eventually disappear, that sooner or later the lower classes will imitate the upper classes in their behavior in religion, as they are supposed to do in all behavior.

As noted earlier, however, the strategy of secularization also offers some positive opportunities. The means for a positive strategy of secularization are the conditions given by modern society. Secularized society is not totally nonreligious; on the contrary, it provides the church with certain open sectors, religious appeals, and ways of acting. It does limit the action of the churches in many areas, but it allows them much in others. In short, religion is given an opportunity to respond to the voids of modern society.

In the first place, because the scientific and technical society does not provide any absolute value and has no ultimate reference, it is unable to give an absolute meaning to human existence. Such a society often produces feelings of despair and void. Many persons pursue a successful profession or otherwise spend ten or twenty busy years and then become conscious that their activity is pointless. At that moment, a religious conversion may occur. At that moment, religion succeeds if it is able to give the individual a feeling of an absolute value. For today's bourgeoisie, religion is called upon to offer a kind of religious experience that can be perceived immediately. The bourgeoisie seeks an immediate satisfaction. Therefore, any church's movements of conversion, charismatic revivals, and so on can expect a great future because they give an immediate and intense religious experience. In a secularized culture, access to God by means of reason and rational arguments is very difficult to accept; the more popular way is that of intuition and irrationality. The church can answer this need by offering the biblical faith in the form of religious experience. The Protestant denominations adjusted to a bourgeois public many years ago; they learned to offer their clients religious revivals and religious experience. For the Catholic Church, such models are a novelty, but becoming more common every day.

The second opportunity for the strategy of secularization is the ability to provide counseling. Modern society leaves men and women devoid of ethics, norms, and values. They live without guidance amid a plethora of products, models, and appeals. What is to be done, accepted, sought, or avoided? Where is the distinction between right and wrong? What is the way to peace, truth, and happiness? Everybody searches for guidance and counsel. Some call upon psychology, others upon astrology, the occult sciences, or oriental wisdom. But religion remains a privileged cure. At this moment, spiritual cure and moral counseling are successful sectors for an understanding church. Even the most conservative religion can rejuvenate through this strategy.

Another area for the strategy of secularization is the provision of community and communication. The modern way of life substitutes functional and impersonal secondary groups—enterprises, factories, schools, hospitals, unions, clubs, political parties, social movements—for the primary ones of the extended family, neighborhood, and so on. Such a social structure gives rise to a feeling of loneliness. It makes difficult real community and communication. In such a society, education prepares women and men for competition, not for love and communication.

Under these circumstances, religion may be the ideal place in which to experience intersubjectivity, communication, and social relations. The churches provide lonely people with "real" communities. A church will succeed if it is able to organize meetings, encounters, social dynamics, communication; indeed, in the present state of our technical, urban society, community cannot be a common or spontaneous experience of daily life. Community is a particular experience resulting from a difficult and sophisticated mechanism. The church is one of the few institutions able to plan and arrange such experiences.

The benefits of these various opportunities still tend to go, however, to the upper classes, who support secularization in the first place. In Latin America, for example, the strategy of secularization was introduced by foreign priests (or Protestant pastors) and some native ones who learned it in the schools of Europe or the United States. They imported the problems of the cultural and intellectual elites of the Western metropolis, and then they provided Latin America's small groups of elites with the new look of Christianity worked out to meet the needs of the sophisticated elites in the metropolis.

This imported secularization caused serious problems in Latin America. Many priests and religious left the ministry. Thousands of young Christians were cut off from the traditional church because the imported secularized culture made contact with the popular religion and heritage intolerable.

Some upper-class groups accepted the inspiration of charismatic methods and the formula of religious experience. But such sophisticated religious experiences cannot be transmitted to the masses. In short, the strategy of secularization has meant more separation between elites and ordinary persons, more separation between upper and lower classes, more separation between clergy and lower classes.

The Utopian Strategy. Not completely unrelated to the strategy of secularization is a strategy that is not really possible for the church in Latin America today, except perhaps in Cuba. It has, however, been defined and discussed by small groups of priests and laypeople (mostly students and intellectuals) and attracted some attention, so it deserves mention. It may be called the utopian strategy. If it could exist it would be a strategy of total *kenosis,* or external disappearance of the church as a social system.

Such an idea starts from the following fact: a part of the working class has accepted the program of Marxism (more correctly, Marxism-Leninism). To the fact, the strategy builders now add a postulate: this part of the working class is representative of the option that will eventually be chosen by the entire working class, and that option shows the way to liberation for all the dominated peoples of the present world. The way has already been chosen by the peoples; the church cannot seek another. It must accept the way the dominated peoples have already adopted, so there is no point in even discussing another.

Now, continues the theory, the working class is (or will be) completely secularized. It is unwilling to accept interference from any other ideology (such as religion) with its Marxist movement and ideology. Marxism is incompatible with any other ideology; it is a complete system in itself. Consequently, Christians must recognize that Marxism is the ideology and movement of the working class, the only possible guide for social action. When Christians are integrated within the Marxist praxis, their religion as a doctrine cannot furnish any guidance for social action, but it can add a supernatural meaning to the autonomous system. This Christianity would not intervene in the Marxist movement. Rather, it would be purely an inner reality, a separate sense added to an external project. The church would be the transmitter of a pure meaning and nothing else. Expelled from public life, it would survive only in the form of small communities that did not interfere in public affairs in any way.

Naturally, such a Christianity seems to lack any motivation. The other members of the revolutionary movement can live without any supernatural meaning added; why do the Christians need it? Christianity appears as an arbitrary and subjective need of a small group.

A few Christian groups, however, think that such a process could be a source of rejuvenation for the church. Some Christian Marxist movements (for example, Ação Popular in Brazil and MAPU in Chile) have suggested such a strategy. But they have not been able to create a stable movement.

Every time they try, there is quickly a separation into the theory's two elements, Christianity and Marxism. On the one hand, the geopolitics of the church remains anticommunist and incompatible with any strategy based on an alliance with a definite form of the communist system. All strategy based on Marxist ideology and institutions is immediately denounced or rejected by the ecclesiastical institution. A Christian Marxist group is insulated, condemned, and deprived of any opportunity of defending its position in the church. The members of such a group are isolated from any contact with Catholic institutions or masses. On the other hand, Marxist Christians also suffer the pressure of the radical secularization of the Marxist movements as a whole. They feel the helplessness of their religious system being reduced to a pure sense that has no efficiency. They realize that nonreligious Marxists are freer from any alien influence and able to concentrate more on their own ideology.

The members of Marxist Christian groups all end by forsaking their impossible Christianity. Two tendencies converge to drive them out: the Marxist groups leave of the church, and the church expels them. After a few years there is always a complete separation, even if there has been no explicit condemnation from either side. In short, the utopian strategy is simply the ideology of a transition from Christianity to a communist movement. It is not a possible strategy for the church.

Strategy of Liberation. There is, however, another strategy for the church in Latin America that is possible. It consists of making a radical change, which can be expressed something like this: instead of relying upon the upper classes and the state, the church seeks the support of the people, the lower classes, the traditional people, who remain faithful to the traditional church in spite of its many problems, lacks, faults, and betrayals.

The first advantage of such a strategy is that it is based on the heritage of ancient Christendom. According to the intellectual and bourgeois elites, popular religion is worthless. According to the criteria of orthodoxy, the judgment may be still more severe. But Christianity admits other criteria. There is often more authentic faith and love in the traditional expressions of the poor than in the sophisticated language of the learned classes and orthodoxy. The distinction between acting and speaking must be remembered. For people who are able to speak, action may not be necessary; the poor are unable to speak, but they are often able to act.

Without any doubt, the poor of Latin America have a deep Christian foundation to their way of life, their social relationship, their common life. Even the success of the Protestant preaching in various regions cannot be explained without an understanding of this deep Christian background. Faith and love are always available, and Christian appeals to such a traditional Christianity always succeed. They awaken the deep Christian sense that exists throughout the masses. Even among the growing industrialized classes of the new megalopolises (Buenos Aires, São Paulo, Santiago, Mexico City, and so on), where a tendency to secularization exists, there is evidence that their evolution is not exactly the same process as that which has gone on in the urban masses of Europe; so far they have not disclaimed their heritage of popular Christianity.

This popular Christianity—urban or rural—is more than so-called popular religiosity. The word "religiosity" has been used to express a type of religious folklore—a religious tradition without faith. But popular religion, which is so vital in Latin America, certainly includes faith as well as hope and love.

Granting the existence of this strong popular religion, the strategy of liberation does not try to secularize it or guide it to the elitist religion. It does not want to change popular religion according to the criteria of an elitist sociology, but to liberate it according to authentic theological criteria. The sociological criteria would compel the lower classes to change by assigning to them the problems of other classes. But if the poor are judged (or forced to judge themselves) by the criteria of the upper classes, they are forced to feel their inferiority. The strategy of liberation sees no reason why the poor should be made to feel a false inferiority. It does not want to submit them to the norms and values of the bourgeoisie of the industrialized West.

This strategy, rather, is aimed at achieving several positive tasks of liberating the people. It starts with the premise that Christianity as a whole is a movement toward liberation. Then, concretely, in Latin America today, it sets itself two tasks or goals.

The first task is the liberation of popular religion. Certain patterns and structures of popular religion do contribute to maintaining the peoples in a condition of domination and submission. Such a situation must not be attributed to God; the structures of domination are the products of the manipulation of Christianity by the upper classes and by a clergy controlled by them. The real content of Christianity has been warped and given wrong emphases to suit upper-class ideology. The true meaning of rites, beliefs, words, customs, and social relationships has often been masked by a process of manipulation. Their content of liberation has been hidden or destroyed. Despite their faith (or perhaps because of it), the poor suspect that there is something wrong in the ordinary preaching of Christianity, but they cannot explain what it is. The strategy of liberation intends to explicate the true sense of words, rites, norms, and traditions for the whole liberation of the people. The problem is to come back to the actual meaning of all Christian data. In other words, the first task of the strategy of liberation is to free popular religion from the manipulation of the ruling classes in order to give back to the people its true religion and all its tools.

The second task of the strategy of liberation is to support all true movements for the liberation of people by undertaking their struggles and sufferings, their slavery and hope, their rebellion and martyrdom. It assumes that all true liberation proceeds from the deepest Christian inspiration. It recognizes Christ's salvation in the popular movements. Of course, it does not intend to control or dominate these movements; they have their own dynamics. But it does intend to save and to complete the spiritual impulse behind concrete movements and to give them Christian strength. The strategy of liberation believes that Christian faith and community are a light and a force able to help the people awaken their own consciousness, as a group and as individuals. A church's strategy of liberation is not to substitute for various other types of compatible strategy (economic, political, military, cultural, and so on), but to enlighten them and to stimulate the persons who are called to work with them.

The Catholic social movement in Europe has clearly wanted to be such a strategy since the last years of the nineteenth century. But unfortunately this movement has been more tolerated than accepted by the institutional church; the Catholic Church as a whole has never undertaken its program, or even consented to it with anything but reluctance. In most cases, Catholic workers' unions have grudgingly been allowed to operate as an active minority, but only as a minority submitted to the purposes of the whole. They have been obliged to subordinate their own aims to the general aims and plans of the Roman church and clergy (who follow either the conservative strategy or that of secularization). The institutional church on all levels—the Curia, the diocese, the parishes, the religious institutes—has never adopted the popular strategy.

But today there is a new opportunity for the strategy of liberation in Latin America. In that part of the world there are still Christian people not yet separated from the Christian church as an ecclesiastical system. There is also a popular aspiration and movement to liberation. These peoples want both Christianity and liberation and they believe there is a real connection between them.

Thus a strategy of liberation adopted enthusiastically by the church as a whole could bring together the major part of the nations. On the other hand, if the Christian churches undertake a strategy adjusted to the desires of the small upper classes linked with the imperialist power, they will isolate themselves from the main movement of the peoples. They will become the prisoners of a small Herodian class, dependent upon a foreign culture and foreign interests. Like all national institutions in Latin America today, the church must choose between the vested interests of a small dominating minority and the interests of the people as a whole. There is a place for the Christian church within the popular liberation movements. But assuming that place will require the institutional church to make a concrete commitment to liberation and, therefore, to work out a new strategy of integration with such movements.

STRATEGY AND THE THEOLOGY OF LIBERATION

The theology of liberation tries to enlighten and to guide the church toward pastoral practice, a geopolitics, and a strategy of liberation. It is not a theology for the intellectual elites, nor is it a modernization plan designed for the upper classes along the models of the Western bourgeoisie. It is a theology for a church that has decided to enter the liberation movement of the people.

The world is in a revolutionary period. The Spirit has to tell human beings what Jesus' words mean for those who have to act in this revolutionary world. That is theology now.

Even after reading these pages, many persons will be surprised by this insistence that it is theology that must guide and enlighten the practical and primarily political liberation of the peoples. Grasping this premise requires one to overcome the modern conditioning that theology is all very well in its place but has little connection with the real world of men and women, society and politics, domination and oppression. Therefore, perhaps, the best way to end this book is to recall that it began by calling the analysis of the present condition of the world a theological task.

An Analysis of the Present World

All human beings, no matter what their class or education, have some idea of the world in which they are living, and some opinion as to its process of evolution, its future, its most urgent tasks. We try to understand its more probable issues from its present conditions, and this reflection provides some arguments to justify our action or lack of action. Christians use Christian arguments and Christian ways of reasoning in this process.

Theology does not intend to do anything essentially different from this process of reflection common to all humankind. But theology is more ambitious in the sense of attempting to do it in another, more systematic way. More precisely, in working toward the same goal, theology uses all the methods that the current condition of human knowledge provides. Today this includes the rational data and methods provided by all the human sciences (although it does not stop there).

It is precisely this use of the data, rather than the conclusions, of the human sciences that many persons object to or do not understand. A somewhat oversimplified version of their view runs like this: the analysis of the present condition of the world and society is an exclusively scientific problem and consequently a task prior to and independent from theology. The various human sciences allow us to know and understand today's reality. Theology should simply listen to the conclusions of human sciences and culture, registering them without any further comment or conclusions. After that— and only after that—theology can act by stating God's word as a parallel to the conclusions of science. In other words, theology can offer a superstructure or a supernatural meaning to the processes that occur in the world, but it cannot propose any changes in the conclusions of science, since in doing so its nonrational reasons might produce disturbances in those conclusions.

That is the common opinion of today's scientific culture. It cannot even imagine another problematic. But following this idea to its logical conclusion means that theological work is devoid of serious or sound values: it can only add a simple superstructure to the present establishment of knowledge; it cannot speak with authority about anything in the real world in which humankind lives. This leads directly to a new expression of the problem of the relationship between religion and science. To the theologians themselves, any valid theology must be able to criticize science, especially the human sciences. Otherwise it is unable to define its own subject and, on those grounds alone, would be rejected by the scientific world as a mere symbol.

Of course, theologians have to accept the facts shown by scientific observation; they have to accept everything that is proved to be real by scientific work. But the human sciences, given their starting point, the nature of their subject matter, and their methods, involve ideologies. These ideologies are not present in the form of explicit statements but, rather, as a perspective, a pattern for the selection and analysis of the problems handled by any particular science. Such ideologies involve, as a matter of fact, a concept of humanity and thus implicitly an idea of God. This implicit meaning assigned to God is at the root of the debate between theology and science.

For example, the Western social sciences reject from the area of their considerations any subjectivity, any idea of freedom, and any action of persons on the whole of society. They isolate endless elementary variables of various social phenomena and try to define them in themselves and the connections between them. But historical units do not exist for the social sciences; they are reduced to mere subjective ideas or opinions or feelings covering the play of several objective variables. The human being is considered from the outside; the human objective phenomenon and the subjective form of living those phenomena are radically separated. Such a division is visible, for example, in the analysis of revolutionary facts by human sciences. The whole person can be explained without the idea of freedom, so human sciences are bound to conclude that freedom is not to be found among human phenomena. Freedom is not a scientific or rational datum, so it is expelled from the field of objective knowledge and reduced to the status of metaphysical opinion or subjective belief.

The Western social sciences also seek the permanent structures of human existence and cannot accept the idea that history can bring about new elements or values. Everything that seems new, they think, can be reduced to some previous structure and interpreted as a new manifestation of the permanent constitution of the human being. Such sciences, therefore, never encounter revolution—at least not revolution in the sense of something new that happens in the world. They eliminate it beforehand by screening the elements of human existence for those elements that they will admit as real. For them, revolution can be interpreted only through the categories of anomie, anarchy, disturbance of order, and so on; it has to be explained by the variables that generate these categories. (See, for example, Pitirim Sorokin, the leader of the American sociology of revolution. Sorokin is one of the few authors to at least accept the existence of that phenomenon.)

Of course, these same sciences, which are not able to accept the facts of subjectivity, freedom, and the historical processes, offer a strategy of secularization as the sole future for Christianity. Christianity may function as a response to some religious needs, they say, but for it to attempt to act on the whole society would be irrational.

One cannot help but note that both revolution and Christianity claim as their goal the changing of the whole of society. And both are rejected as nonscientific realities for which there is no room in the rational future of humankind. The reason is that both are based on freedom, and freedom is not a scientific idea. The human sciences offer an interpretation of the world as a system without freedom. But Christian theology thinks that understanding today's world can be important only if it provides the possibility of a world with freedom. Understanding human beings and society without freedom is understanding a system, not human beings and human society.

Thus the point of encounter between theology and Western science is the problem of freedom. If freedom is the central problem of any revolution, the logical conclusion is that revolution is also a privileged point of view for studying the modern world and the relationship between religion and science or for analyzing today's world as a problem of the relationship between religion and science.

Marxism stands in opposition to Western science. The Western sciences justify the established order; they function as a legitimating ideology. In contrast, Marxism is essentially a criticism of the capitalist system in all its aspects. And it begins by criticizing Western science as ideological. Marxism's criticism is exemplified in its treatment of the science that is the empress of all human sciences at the present time: economics. Marx showed how capitalist economics is not a simple science but an ideology underlying and justifying the whole Western system, a whole way of life. Then the various Marxist schools (at least those working in the Western world, the only place that offers conditions for free research) applied the same criticism to the other human sciences of capitalism, and their criticisms were generally successful.

The weakness of Marxism begins when it attempts to build a new society. For the Marxist science believes it is able to understand, in a rational way, not only the old society, but the new as well. In practice, however, the supposed Marxist science of the revolutionary parties (not to mention the Marxism of the Soviet Union that is no longer Marxism) has fallen into a kind of voluntarism. Its so-called new society has no reference to any science: it is the society created by the party. Its "rationality" stems only from the programs of the party. Marxist science is only the ideology of the party, the result of the reduction of any rationality to the voluntarism of the party, a collection of arguments in order to justify the pragmatist decisions of the party.

For Marxist science, revolution is not only an accepted phenomenon, but the central reality in history. On this point, Marxism would be open to a dialogue with Christianity. But Marxists consider each revolution from the viewpoint of the program of the party; for them there is no revolution, no science, and no rationality outside the party. And in practice, the party finds the problem of power more important than the problem of freedom. Consequently, in Marxist revolution there is no freedom for the people, only for the party. The same science that expels freedom from history and revolution expels God from humankind and history. The party is supposed to be sufficient to create a new world, but it ends by creating a new power.

Actually, the ideas of God and freedom are connected and their fate is common. This fate can be considered from inside the basic phenomenon of revolution where these ideas encounter the scientific question. This is a point at which the three units—God, freedom and revolution, and science—confront each other.

Nor is freedom the only point of encounter between Christianity and science. The future is another one. Knowing the world means knowing its relationship not only with freedom, but with the future as well. The world is meaningless if it has no future. It is essentially movement toward the future. Which future? The sciences do not foresee the future. The world cannot be understood without its future, but this future cannot possibly be known. Thus Ernst Bloch said that reality cannot be true. Truth is the future that is not yet a reality; such is the riddle of human existence and the frontier of science as well.

Of course, the human sciences are not devoid of any prospect of the future. In fact, the ambition of any science is foreseeing the future, but the future it foresees is the mere continuation of the same factors that are presently acting and presently known. It is the projection of the past, and as such it is meaningless, not a human future. Of course, a large part of the future will be a continuation of the past or a new combination of the patterns that have existed in the past. But a human future means also a creation of something new; human existence would remain absurd if all endeavors to renew or create something new were useless and vain.

In contrast to the static view of science, Christian revelation is simply a message about the future. But this message is never the mere continuation of scientific knowledge about the past and present condition of humankind; there is no parallel between the two ways of understanding. Between science of the past and Christian eschatology, there is an empty room, and this empty space is of the utmost importance for understanding human existence. Around this empty space, the encounter between eschatology and human science takes place. What is the possible link between them?

That is the subject matter for a theology of revolution, because revolution is one of the most spectacular events to fill that empty space. Revolution moves all the forces and variables considered by the sciences, and it also moves eschatological hope for the future. Revolution is a mixture of scientific rationality, utopia, prophecy, determinism, and freedom; it is a privileged point of encounter between all sorts of determinisms and the possibilities for human freedom. But this is not to say that revolution is far from us; rather, it is the matter of our daily existence. All human beings are waiting for a revolution—some in fear of a revolution made by others, others wishing for their own revolution. Without an idea of revolution, without a correct theology of revolution, no one can understand the deepest feelings of human existence. The analysis of the present world is the analysis of its probable future, of the feared and wished-for future. *Here* is a task for a theology of revolution.

An Analysis of Revolutionary Practice

No one can force another person to join a revolution. We all must make up our own minds, starting from our own ideas, personal experiences, and personal ways of approaching history. Joining a revolutionary (or counter-revolutionary) action is an important act involving one's total existence. Consequently, it is one of the most serious decisions a person can take, and no one can choose for another.

It is also true that no one can make the decision on the basis of personal intuition alone, without consulting all available information. We all have to create a bit of "popular" theology for ourselves in order to justify the position taken. The specific task of scientific Christian theology is to apprise popular theology.

There are four areas that the theology of revolution or liberation must enlighten for Christians: the object or the purpose of revolution; the subject or the agent; the state; and the culture within which a revolution takes place.

The Purpose of Revolution. The primary question of every revolution concerns its object or purpose: What kind of society is to be built? Every revolution is to be judged at first by the kind of society it intends to create. Moreover, the pathway and the steps to a revolution depend on the aim selected. The revolutionary process will be determined by the nature of the future society; the pattern of the future society to be created is present during and within the process. The end is immanent with regard to the means (even classical philosophy still thinks so).

It is evident that humankind's possibilities for selecting tomorrow's society are limited by countless conditions. To ignore these conditions simply leads to the complete inability to act in history. Human beings cannot build the society they imagine; they can certainly build it mentally, but not historically. Real persons can work in history only by means of the forces actually present and active in the world independent of their own will. They can use the forces present in the world, but they cannot create new forces. They cannot change forces that do not exist. And they can direct historical forces only in the sense of their own determinism, their past, without setting them to work up to personal expectations. However, human beings can strengthen certain historical forces, produce or reduce some new combinations of selected forces, interfere in the oppositions of the various antagonisms that are the matter of history. By so doing, they can interfere in the revolutions that history creates.

Human history is the result of an endless searching for itself by means of its various contradictions. How should one act among these contradictions? There are contradictions between social classes, nations, states, and citizens. What is the best balance among these contradictions so that human beings will have the best opportunity for influencing the historical process? Within human civilizations there are three main values: wealth, power, and freedom. Each value produces contradictions. In order to act, one must create certain organizations of diverse groups motivated by very different interests. Each organization produces a society based primarily on wealth, power, or freedom. Here is a problem of selection. Christian faith may help in making it. Christian theology can aid in studying distinctions and foreseeing results.

The Subject of Revolution. In considering the subject or agents of revolution, theology must deal with the question of the masses and the elites. Remember that Christians—like any other human group—may support or discourage trends but they are not able to create totally new ones. Masses and elites act and hope in different ways; they have their own determinants and these cannot be changed by the wishes or ethics or philosophy of anyone. But theology and the church can choose between supporting the aims of the masses or those of the elites. History proceeds as some factors are selected and promoted more than others, some agents more than others.

The behavior of a given church depends, at least partly, on its own social structure and the structure of its pastoral work. There are churches that choose an ecclesiastical figure who fosters the religious expectations of the masses; other churches (or religious movements within a church) favor small groups, giving them the sort of Christianity appropriate for their elitist expectations but worthless for the masses. Elites expect science, efficiency, special language, subjectivity; the masses tend toward externalization of their sentiments and sensitivity. For the elites, efficiency is worth more than justice; for the masses, justice is more meaningful than efficiency. The church can be guided by a pastoral program that will support a revolution made by the elites or prevent a revolution made by the masses; it can be guided by a pastoral program that helps the masses in their claims and limits the projects of elites. The problems are actually much more complicated than they sound here, but to some degree the church does collaborate in selecting the agents of a revolution.

The State. The Christian church seems to understand the problem of the state better than the other problems of revolution. But this is probably a superficial understanding. The essence of the state is not always visible; it becomes more visible in exceptional circumstances, such as a revolution (or the perceived threat of one). The problem of the state is the link between power, violence, security, and order, on the one hand, and law, people, covenant, and authority, on the other. The Bible and history show that Christianity has never been indifferent to the state-church and state-citizen relationships. But present theology remains superficial on the subject. It tends to legitimate the liberal constitutions of the states of the developed West. This may be sufficient for the Christians who live in these countries, but it is not enough for those in countries where the problem of the state is more complicated and immediate.

Theology has to judge the various forces facing each other within the structure of a state. Most states have formal liberal constitutions, the inheritance of the culture of the metropolitan West. But behind this formal liberalism is another reality: the state with all its power and contradictions.

In Latin America just now, the church must find the Christian way of thinking and acting while confronting absolute states based on the principles of national security, national power, and national plan. May the church remain indifferent?

Culture. Finally, the cultural problem is part of the analysis of revolutionary practice. Every culture has some political color. There is no culture that is not at least partly responsible for some type of society. A culture both expresses a society and helps it to exist as a consistent body, as a stable structure. Every social change simultaneously produces and presupposes a cultural change—a change in custom, law, science, education, technology, art, religion, and so on. Every aspect of a culture plays a role in the social structure and acts on the weight of each social factor—on power, on wealth or freedom, on people or elites. Every culture sides with the people or the elites, the common citizens or the powerful, justice or efficiency.

The church influences culture. Since every action penetrates cultural processes that are connected to some revolutionary or counter-revolutionary trends, the church's every action produces results supporting or preventing the revolution.

The same can also be said of education, a sector in which the church is present. There are several ways to educate: one can prepare students for liberty or for power, for justice or for efficiency, for welfare or for prestige. What is the so-called education for liberation in Latin America? The theology of liberation can and should raise this question regarding all levels of education and all places in which the church has any influence on education.

Every cultural pattern can accept or reject the establishment. It has within itself its own dynamics. If it accepts the establishment, it will fight against the future revolution or social change. If it does not accept the establishment it will help the true revolution. Since the church promotes cultural patterns, it is responsible for the political effects of its actions.

Conclusion

In conclusion, it can be said that culture, state, agents of social change, masses and elites, social evolution, and analysis of historical processes are subjects that the church has always spoken about without any necessity for a theology of revolution. Why cannot the church continue doing so?

Is this the answer to that question? The Christian message and ethic are expressed in either a static or a dynamic society. In a static society, theology repeats and makes sacred the traditional rules by which that society is surviving. Each social class or category has its traditional role with its own rules. Everyone is responsible for his or her own role and nothing more. Law does nothing but express and confirm traditional roles and their rules. Justice is done when all play their parts. Ethics legitimatizes, by means of Christian concepts, the traditional roles and rules, nothing more. There is an implicit agreement: all persons are supposed to be practicing justice and love whenever they are being faithful to their vocations or roles. In this condition, any theology of revolution is nonsense. And indeed it is judged as nonsense or worse by all those persons who live mentally in a static society; for them, revolution is the work of the devil because it is the subversion of all their values.

However, if society is considered as a social dynamism and in a continuing process of change, the main moral problem is the change itself and the structure of the newly created society. What counts is not accomplishment of the roles, but distribution of the roles; a new society is a new distribution of the roles. When society is dynamic and changing, everybody is responsible for the structure of the future society because everyone helps to make or prevent social change. In this condition, one cannot define a social ethic without a theology of revolution—without an analysis of the pastoral approach and strategy for the constant change and the particular events of change that make up history and the actual fate of humankind.

Appendix
The Peruvian Military Regime

Since its coup d'état on October 3, 1968, Peru's military regime has significantly altered the image of the new military state. Peru stands in contrast to the national security system on which the present regimes in Brazil, Chile, Uruguay, and Bolivia are based as was the Argentinean system from 1966 to 1972.[1]

The Peruvian model is a combination of the national security system with a reformist program (including some radical social transformations). The basic structure of the new Peruvian state is similar to that of the other military states in Latin America. But this military state has initiated and partly carried out an extensive program of nationalization of foreign corporations, agrarian reform, and collectivization in various economic sectors, especially in the areas of mining, fishing, agriculture, and industry.

Such a dual system is justified by a dual ideology stemming from a combination of the national security ideology and a corporative ideology. The Peruvian system is based on two ideologies. The first is adjusted to the civilian collaborators of the system. (Carlos Delgado was its most representative spokesman until President Velasco was removed in September 1975.) That civilian ideology is strong although subordinated to the military ideology, which is inspired by the national security ideology that all the Latin American officers learn in the American military schools. (The most representative spokesman of the military ideology is General Edgardo Mercado Jarrín, former minister of defense and prime minister of the military regime.[2])

Owing to such a combination, the Peruvian military regime defines itself as a "revolutionary military" government. How is such a combination possible? How is it possible to avoid the apparent contradiction of both terms?

The Peruvian combination is possible by virtue of an important shift of the concept of security. After explaining the classical doctrine on national security and its connection with development, General Mercado Jarrín justifies radically new conclusions derived from the classic principles.

The first change is a new concern with external national security. The classical Latin American concept of national security is based on an extension of the American concept: the postulate of the bipolarity of world power. But the Peruvian generals believe that the bipolarization of world power is coming to an end. They believe that now the tendency is toward multipolarity. The axis of power no longer lies between Washington and Moscow. A new kind of bipolarity is growing stronger.

Today there is a great division between the Northern Hemisphere, with the great centers of political and economic power, and the Southern Hemisphere, with hunger and ignorance. If this abyss continues to grow, a new kind of conflict will arise which could involve the great powers. Therefore it is necessary to achieve unity and solidarity in this divided world.[3]

From this new bipolarity, Mercado Jarrín deduces that Peruvian national security is no longer tied to American national security. In his book *Seguridad, Política, Estrategia,* he attempts to demonstrate that Latin America needs a new security program. Peruvian security requires more independence. The Peruvian revolutionary military government is trying to multiply its international connections and especially to strengthen all its efforts toward promoting a common front in the Third World.

There is an apparent contradiction within Mercado Jarrín's book. The author supposes that the national security ideology transmitted by the American military schools to the Latin American military institutes can be applied to a struggle against American dependency. The ideology seems to be independent from its source.

Probably the ideological contradiction of the Peruvian system is the result of the inner contradiction of its policy. Peru is a part of the American Empire, and such a condition does not allow a very extensive independence. The problem is: What are the limits of independence that the United States is willing to tolerate within its empire in a given situation? No one knows the answer, but so far the Peruvian system has been able to maintain a certain nationalist doctrine that limits the requisites of the American national security system.

The attitude toward internal national security is also somewhat different in Peru. The generals are convinced that the best way to preserve order is through change—social, economic, and political. Their concern with internal security is reflected in the attempts to improve the distribution of increments in Peru's economic resources and to institutionalize an apparatus of political participation over which the military can exercise a permanent control.

Because of such change in its idea of security, the Peruvian military has begun to carry out a program of political and economic reforms. At the moment, the Peruvian government is socially the most advanced on the American continent. The ideal of the military reformers is apparently a system involving full participation of the citizens, namely,

. . . the construction of a fully participatory social democracy, not individualism. . . . The means of property are predominantly social property, under the direct control of those who generate the wealth from their work. . . . The power of decision is diffuse and rests essentially in social, economic, and political institutions which are conducted by the men and women who make them up, with a minimum of intermediaries, or with no intermediaries whatsoever.[4]

The limits of the Peruvian system stem from its inner contradictions. On the one hand, there is its attitude toward external national security, its policy of independence, which depends upon the reality of the new North-South bipolarity. The appeal to the Third World may be, in many circumstances, more rhetorical than real. Political realism suggests a lasting, active presence of the old antagonism of East and West. There is a spontaneous tendency to remain tied with the American power. Even the ties of the Peruvian armed forces to those of the United States will be a permanent argument for subordinating the whole policy to military arguments.

On the other hand, the Peruvian approach to internal security through popular participation has to be reconciled with its military control and the vertical system. A system based on the concept of security cannot tolerate any expression of popular participation and democracy.

The Peruvian military system seeks to solve the problem by establishing a corporative model. Under such a system, citizen participation takes place by means of the communities, local communities. Citizens have full participation in the agrarian cooperative or the industrial community. But their participation is reduced to the communitarian level. Individuals can communicate with the central power only by means of their community. All the communities remain under the control of the central military control. The military power occupies the place of the king in the ancient Spanish corporative state. Hence real participation is limited by the central control. The national security system always tends to limit grass-roots initiatives. This Peruvian pattern of participation also reinforces the military's inclination toward consensus by command. In short, the military accept participation but they retain the initiative.

And indeed, in spite of its officially proclaimed goals, the Peruvian military revolutionary system has not yet been able to create a complete corporative system. Although local participation units (agricultural cooperatives, neighborhood committees, and industrial communities) now exist in several sectors, they involve a very small portion of the total population.

The future of the Peruvian experiment depends upon the capacity for survival of an artificial synthesis between the national security system and a development plan based on a Third World perspective. External national security tends to reduce the scope of a radical change of the whole national structure. Internal national security tends to limit real, active citizen participation. There are two possibilities. Either the Third World perspective will prevail, and the national security system will be rejected; or the national security scheme will prevail, and the Peruvian military system will come back to the "normal" Latin American model.

The strength of the Peruvian model stems from the lack of an alternative.

In the face of the supreme power of the American Empire, the armed forces are the only sector able to present a certain resistance. And when it comes to creating and imposing a general program of internal reforms, there is no united front able to replace the armed forces. The total lack of unity of the Peruvian revolutionary movement has led to its complete failure and made it the victim of organized repression by a united bourgeoisie.

Up to now, the progressive sectors of the church in Peru have supported the military revolutionary government. They are conscious of the total lack of any tolerable alternative. They know that the substitute would be the Brazilian model of the true national security state. They recognize that the purposes of the military revolutionary government are excellent, given the present condition of Latin America within the American Empire.

Nevertheless, given the inner contradiction of the Peruvian system, the church's support of it is critical. Christians remain aware of the possibility and the danger of a shift to the Brazilian model. Their critical support tends to orient the military experiment to stronger citizen participation within the corporative system.

But the presence of the national security ideology in Peru is a threat against the very purposes of the military revolutionary government. Moreover, the frequent attacks against a supposed Peruvian "communism"—attacks from all the organs of the American Empire, including the Christian churches of the United States—show that the support of the church is more than ever necessary.

Notes

Chapter 2   The Theology of Revolution

1. Pierre Bigo, *The Church and the Third World Revolution*, trans. Jeanne Marie Lyons (Maryknoll, N.Y.: Orbis Books, 1976).

2. For those readers who might be interested in present-day reports focusing on this criticism of class development theory, I suggest reading the following books (among others): Gunnar Myrdal, *The Challenge of World Poverty* (New York: Pantheon Books, 1970), and Samir Amin, *Unequal Development*, trans. Brian Pearce (New York: Monthly Review Press, 1977)

3. Bigo, *The Church and the Third World Revolution*, p. 6.

4. See, for example, the part that Latin Americans play in the problematic discussed in a book such as *Discussion sur la "théologie de la révolution"* (Paris: Cerf-Mame, 1972). The original German was published in 1969. It is typical of the period.

5. The major works of Jürgen Moltmann have been published in English: *Theology of Hope* (New York: Harper & Row, 1967); *Man: Christian Anthropology in the Conflicts of the Present* (Philadelphia: Fortress Press, 1974); *The Crucified God* (New York: Harper & Row, 1977).

6. From all contemporary literature on Christian anthropology, I signal out Jacques Ellul, *The Ethics of Freedom* (Grand Rapids, Mich.: Eerdmans, 1976).

7. Note the prominence given to the two themes of liberty and totalitarianism in *Octogesima Adventiens*. But it would be interesting to follow these same themes in Pope Paul's speeches, particularly those of the last few years.

Chapter 4   The National Security System in Latin America

1. Concerning the new American political institutions, see Robert Borosage, "The Making of the National Security State," in *The Pentagon Watchers. Students Report on the National Security State*, Ed. Leonard S. Rodberg and Derek Shearer (Garden City, N.Y.: Doubleday and Co., 1970), pp. 3–63. See also José Comblin, *Le pouvoir militaire on Amérique Latine: l'idéologie de la sécurité nationale* (Paris: J.P. Delarge, 1977); also in Spanish, *El poder militar en América latina* (Salamanca: Sigueme, 1978), and Portuguese, *O poder militar na América latina* (Rio de Janeiro: Civilização Brasileira, 1978).

2. Here is an interesting comment from Senator J. W. Fulbright: "Since 1948 the Industrial College has sent teams of military officers around the country to run two-week programs based on the material used to train students in the regular course at Fort McNair in Washington, D.C. Ostensibly, the courses are for reserve officers,

who get credit for retirement by attending, but the larger number of participants are drawn from the general public, and the sponsors in almost all cases in recent years have been local Chambers of Commerce. The promotion sheet distributed to arouse interest in the seminars says they 'bring to a community an educational program with no counterpart in government, industry, business, or the field of education. It is designed to inform, to enhance understanding, and to encourage participation by the individual in community, State, and national affairs.' The seminars are heavily larded with discussions of foreign affairs covering such topics as Africa, South Asia, Comparative Political Systems, Geopolitics, International Economics, Communist China, and World Agriculture. The contents of those of the lectures that I have reviewed present a simplistic, often outdated, and factually incorrect view of complex world problems. The poor quality of the lectures alone is sufficient justification for abolishing the program. But the real issue is of far more fundamental importance. It is not a proper function of the Department of Defense to educate civilians on foreign policy issues or to teach them to be better citizens, even if the material presented is completely objective, which is frequently not the case" (*The Pentagon Propaganda Machine,* New York: Liveright, 1970, pp. 40–41). In spite of such comments, the ideology is spreading.

3. It is especially interesting to compare the readings of the Industrial College of the Armed Forces of the United States with the readings of similar institutes in the Latin American countries. The connection is more than evident. See the annual *National Security Seminar. Background Readings* (Industrial College of the Armed Forces, Fort Lesley J. McNair, Washington, D.C. 20319).

4. For the problem of the definition of geopolitics, see General Golbery do Couto e Silva, *Geopolítica do Brasil* (Rio de Janeiro: José Olympio, 1967), pp. 164–71; Jorge E. Atencio, ¿Qué es la geopolítica? (Buenos Aires: Pleamar, 1965), pp. 21–75; Augusto Pinochet Ugarte, *Geopolítica* (Santiago de Chile: Andrés Bello, 1974), pp. 42–44. These three authors are the most representative leaders of the Brazilian, Argentinean, and Chilean schools of geopolitics respectively. The first and third received the opportunity to put their theories to political practice in their countries.

5. Pinochet, *Geopolítica,* p. 42.

6. Cited by Golbery do Couto e Silva, *Geopolítica do Brasil,* p. 29.

7. See Rudolf Kjellén, *The State as an Organism* (in Swedish, *States som Liftsform,* Uppsala, 1916).

8. Golbery do Couto e Silva, *Geopolítica do Brasil,* p. 29.

9. Pinochet, *Geopolítica,* p. 69.

10. José Alfredo Amaral Gurgel, *Segurança e Democracia* (Rio de Janeiro: José Olympio, 1975), pp. 83–131. This book is a good example of a formalist, "scholastic" version of the Brazilian National Security ideology. Such a simplistic view of history and politics is presently the new background of public education in Brazil through the new courses on Moral Civics, compulsory on all levels of public and private education.

11. See Golbery, *Geopolítica do Brasil,* p. 160; Pinochet, *Geopolítica,* p. 152.

12. Pinochet, *Geopolítica,* p. 155.

13. Ibid.

14. Ibid., p. 221.

15. Golbery, *Geopolítica do Brasil,* pp. 24ff.

16. Ibid., p. 161.

17. See Osiris Guillermo Villegas, *Políticas y estrategias para el desarrollo y la seguridad nacional* (Buenos Aires: Pleamar, 1969), pp. 33–35. General Osiris Villegas was the ideologist of the military government of General Juan Carlos Onganía in Argentina (1966–1970).

18. Amaral Gurgel, *Segurança,* pp. 69–73.

19. Villegas, *Políticas,* p. 34.

20. Ibid., p. 39.

21. Government of Argentina, Law 16, 920, art. 2.

22. Amaral Gurgel, *Segurança,* pp. 83–89.

23. Ibid., p. 83.

24. Villegas, *Políticas,* p. 109.

25. Ibid., pp. 35–37.

26. Ibid., p. 109.

27. Golbery, *Geopolítica do Brasil,* p. 13.

28. Ibid., p. 14.

29. Ibid., p. 15.

30. Ibid.

31. Villegas, *Políticas,* pp. 28–36; Michel Schooyans, *Destin du Brésil* (Gembloux, Belgium: Duculot, 1973), pp. 62ff. Michel Schooyans published the first critical study of national security ideology in Brazil.

32. Schooyans, *Destin,* p. 62.

33. Villegas, *Políticas,* p. 36.

34. *Declaración de principios del gobierno de Chile,* Santiago, March 11, 1974, p. 28.

35. Letter from Colonel Orlando Jérez Borgues, national director of social communication, to all the ecclesiastical institutions, República de Chile, Junta de Gobierno, Dirección Nacional de Comunicación Social, Santiago, April 24, 1975.

36. Villegas, *Políticas,* p. 253.

37. Schooyans, *Destin,* p. 66.

38. *Declaración de Chile,* p. 38.

39. Golbery, *Geopolítica do Brasil,* pp. 225–257.

40. *Declaración de Chile,* p. 27.

41. Golbery, *Geopolítica do Brasil,* pp. 101ff.

42. Ibid.

Chapter 5   National Security and Christianity

1. There are few studies on the relations between church and state in Latin America after the military coups. See Charles Antoine, *Church and Power in Brazil,* trans. Peter Nelson (Maryknoll, N.Y.: Orbis Books, 1973).

2. For instance, pages 13 to 20 of the *Declaración de principios del gobierno de Chile* were prepared by a theologian. Style and vocabulary are specific. The contents of this part of the document is totally different from the following pages. The members of the military junta thought use of Christian terminology would help to attract the churches; therefore, this Christian explanation for their political purposes was prepared. But immediately following it they state their purposes in their own language —national security system language—and so tell us what they really want to do.

3. Letter from Colonel Borgues, April 24, 1975.

4. There was, for example, a clear connection between the Cursillos de Cristiandad and the military coup that gave power to General Onganía in Argentina in 1966. The connections are also clear between the Opus Dei and the military governments. (Of course, the Opus Dei movement will say that it is not a political movement and that it gives its members complete freedom; by mere "coincidence," the members of Opus Dei are presently supporting the military governments, and none are found in the opposition).

5. See Thomas Bruneau, *The Political Transformation of the Brazilian Catholic Church* (Cambridge University Press, 1974), pp. 218–220.

6. Pinochet, *Geopolítica*, p. 62.

7. Golbery, *Geopolítica do Brasil*, p. 230.

8. Ibid.

9. See R. Havard de la Montagne, *Histoire de l'Action française* (Paris, 1950).

10. See John Eagleson, ed., *Christians and Socialism: Documentation of the Christians For Socialism Movement in Latin America* (Maryknoll, N.Y.: Orbis Books, 1975).

11. See Golbery, *Geopolítica do Brasil*, pp. 7–10.

12. Ibid., p. 9.

Chapter 7   Liberty and Liberation: Principles from Biblical Sources

1. See M. Xhaufflaire, *La "théologie politique,"* Cogitatio Fidei 69 (Paris: Cerf, 1972), with a complete bibliography of J. B. Metz.

2. The young critics of Metz were M. Xhaufflaire, the German group of *Kritischer Katholozismus,* and the Dutch group of *Tegenspraak.*

3. See L. Cerfaux, *La théologie de l'Eglise suivant saint Paul,* 2nd edn. (Paris: Cerf, 1965), pp. 59ff.

4. If we ask why the proletariat is endowed with such a value, Marx has two answers, and we cannot know what his definitive thinking is. On the one hand, the proletariat suffers the deepest alienation; and in virtue of the dialectical law, the highest freedom is to proceed from the lowest alienation. On the other hand, the proletariat is author and agent of work, and work is the origin of all values; consequently all value belongs to the proletariat. In any case the mission of the proletariat stems from its universal feature.

5. See Lucien Cerfaux, *Le chrétien dans la théologie paulinienne* (Paris: Cerf, 1962), pp. 414–421. English edn.: *Christian Theology of St. Paul,* trans. Lilian Soiron (New York: Seabury Press, 1967).

Appendix   The Peruvian Military Regime

1. See Kevin J. Middlebrook and David Scott Palmer, *Military Government and Political Development: Lessons from Peru* (Beverley Hills, Calif.: Sage Publications, 1975), with bibliography; Herbert de Souza, *The World Capitalist System and the Militarism in Latin America: A Comparative Analysis . . .* (Box 673, Adelaide St. P.O., Toronto, Ontario, Canada, 1974).

2. See Edgardo Mercado Jarrín, *Seguridad, Política, Estrategia* (Buenos Aires, 1975).

3. Interview with General Mercado Jarrín, in *Visão* (São Paulo, Brazil, April 24, 1974).

4. Middlebrook and Palmer, *Military Government,* p. 15.

Selected Bibliography of
American National Security Ideology

General

Greenwood, John, comp. *American Defense Policy since 1945: A Preliminary Bibliography,* ed. Geoffrey Kemp et al. Lawrence-Manhattan-Wichita: Kansas State University, for the National Security Education Program, 1973.

Larson, Arthur D. *National Security Affairs: A Guide to Information Sources.* Detroit: Gale Research Co., 1973.

Ideology in Debate

Berkowitz, Morton and Bock, P. G. *American National Security: A Reader in Theory and Policy.* New York: The Free Press, 1965.

Hudson, Winthrop S., ed. *Nationalism and Religion in America: Concepts of American Identity and Mission.* New York: Harper & Row, 1970.

Kissinger, Henry A. *The Necessity for Choice: Prospects of American Foreign Policy.* New York: Harper & Row, 1961.

———, ed. *Problems of National Strategy: A Book of Readings.* New York: Praeger, 1965.

McNamara, Robert S. *The Essence of Security.* New York: Harper & Row, 1968.

National Security State

Ackley, Charles W. *The Modern Military in American Society.* Philadelphia: Westminster Press, 1972.

Barnet, Richard J. *Roots of War: The Men and Institutions behind United States Foreign Policy.* New York: Atheneum Publishers, 1972.

Cook, Fred J. *The Warfare State.* New York: Collier Books, 1964.

Coplin, William D.; McGowan, Patrick J.; O'Leary, Michael K. *American Foreign Policy: An Introduction to Analysis and Evaluation.* Belmont, Calif.: Duxbury Press, 1974.

Horowitz, David. *The Free World Colossus. A Critique of American Foreign Policy in the Cold War.* New York: Hill and Wang, 1963.

Klare, Michael T. *War without End.* New York: Alfred A. Knopf, 1972.

Rodberg, Leonard S., and Shearer, Derek. *The Pentagon Watchers: Students Report on the National Security State.* Garden City, N.Y.: Doubleday and Co., 1970.

Steel, Ronald. *Pax Americana: The Cold War Empire and the Politics of Counter-Revolution.* New York: Viking Press, 1970.

Trager, Frank N., and Kronenburg, Philip S. *National Security and American Society.* Lawrence, Kansas: University Press of Kansas, 1973.

History

Kolko, Gabriel. *The Roots of American Foreign Policy*. Boston: Beacon Press, 1969.

Kolko, Joyce and Gabriel. *The Limits of Power: The World and United States Foreign Policy, 1945–1954*. New York: Harper & Row, 1973.

Williams, William Appleman. *The Tragedy of American Diplomacy*. 2nd edn. New York: Dell Publishing Co., 1972.

Other Orbis Titles

GOD, WHERE ARE YOU?

by Carlos Mesters

Meditations and reflections on significant figures and events in the Bible. "We shall," says Mesters, "try to restore to the word of God the function that it ought to have: to serve as a light on the pathway of life, as a help to our own understanding of present-day reality in all its complexity."

ISBN 0-88344-162-4 CIP   *Cloth $6.95*

THE EXPERIENCE OF GOD

by Charles Magsam

"His range is comprehensive; his orientation is personal, biblical, communitarian; his tone is positive and encouraging: all in all, a one-volume course on how to be free wholesomely for God, for oneself and for others." *Prairie Messenger*

ISBN 0-88344-123-3   *Cloth $7.95*
ISBN 0-88344-124-1   *Paper $4.95*

JESUS OF NAZARETH

Meditations on His Humanity

by Jose Comblin

"St. Teresa of Avila warned her nuns to beware of any kind of prayer that would seek to eliminate all reference to the human aspect of Christ. I think Jose Comblin would agree that her warning also describes the theme of his extremely valuable book that can be read and re-read many times with great benefit." *Priests USA*

ISBN 0-88344-231-0   *Cloth $5.95*

PRAYER AT THE HEART OF LIFE

by Brother Pierre-Yves Emery

"Emery's approach is both realistic and down-to-earth and profound and moving. This book can be recommended to anyone interested in a practical analysis of prayer, particularly the specific relationship between prayer and life itself." *Review for Religious*

ISBN 0-88344-393-7   *Cloth $4.95*

PILGRIMAGE TO NOW/HERE

by Frederick Franck

"Every now and then a true gem of a book appears that fails to get caught up in the tide of promotion, reviews, and sales, and, despite its considerable merits, seems to disappear. Such a book is Dr. Frederick Franck's *Pilgrimage to Now/Here*. His *Zen of Seeing* has been a steady seller, and *The Book of Angelus Silesius* is moving well. What happened to *Pilgrimage*, which in many ways is a more important book? Since Orbis is known as a religious publishing house, many distributors and booksellers are reluctant to stock it. Yet this is a religious book in the most significant sense of that word—in what Frederick Franck would call the search for meaning—for it is an account of a modern pilgrimage by jet, bus, train, and on foot to visit holy places and meet Buddhist leaders and Zen masters in India, Ceylon, Hong Kong and Japan."

East West Journal

ISBN 0-88344-387-2   *Illustrated Paper $3.95*

BIBLICAL REVELATION
AND AFRICAN BELIEFS

edited by Kwesi Dickson and Paul Ellingworth

"Essays by scholars who are themselves both African and Christian and who share a concern that Christian theology and African thought be related to each other in a responsible and creative way. There is no comparable book; this one should be in any library attempting serious coverage of either African thought or Christian theology." *Choice*

ISBN 0-88344-033-4   *Cloth $5.95*

ISBN 0-88344-034-2   *Paper $3.45*

IN SEARCH OF THE BEYOND

by Carlo Carretto

"The book describes an 'aloneness' that draws hearts closer together, a 'withdrawal' that enriches family and community ties, a love of God that deepens human love." *America*

ISBN 0-88344-208-6   *Cloth $5.95*

LETTERS FROM THE DESERT

by Carlo Carretto

"It has been translated into Spanish, French, German, Portuguese, Arabic, Japanese, Czech, and now, gracefully enough (from Italian) into English. I hope it goes into twenty-four more editions. It breathes with life, with fresh insights, with wisdom, with love." *The Thomist*

ISBN 0-88344-279-5   *Cloth $4.95*

THE GOD WHO COMES

by Carlo Carretto

"This is a meaty book which supplies on every page matter for reflection and a spur to the laggard or wayward spirit. It offers true Christian perspective." *Our Sunday Visitor*

ISBN 0-88344-164-0   *Cloth $4.95*

FREEDOM TO BE FREE

By Arturo Paoli

"Full of eye-opening reflections on how Jesus liberated man through poverty, the Cross, the Eucharist and prayer." *America*

ISBN 0-88344-143-8   *Paper $4.95*

SILENT PILGRIMAGE TO GOD

The Spirituality of Charles de Foucauld

by a Little Brother of Jesus
preface by Rene Voillaume

"Sets out the main lines of Charles de Foucauld's spirituality and offers selections from his writings." *America*

ISBN 0-88344-459-3   *Cloth $4.95*

AFRICAN TRADITIONAL RELIGION: A DEFINITION

by E. Bolaji Idowu

"This important book is the first to place the study of African religion in the larger context of religious studies. . . . It includes an index and notes. There is no comparable work; this one should be in any collection on African religion." *Choice*

ISBN 0-88344-005-9   *Cloth $6.95*

THE PATRIOT'S BIBLE

edited by John Eagleson and Philip Scharper

"Following the terms of the Declaration of Independence and the U.S. Constitution, this faithful paperback relates quotes from the Bible and from past and present Americans 'to advance the kingdom and further our unfinished revolution.' " *A.D.*

ISBN 0-88344-377-5   *Paper $3.95*

THE RADICAL BIBLE

adapted by John Eagleson and Philip Scharper

"I know no book of meditations I could recommend with more confidence to learned and unlearned alike." *St. Anthony Messenger*

ISBN 0-88344-425-9   *Cloth $3.95*

ISBN 0-88344-426-7   *Pocketsize, paper $1.95*

UGANDA: THE ASIAN EXILES

by Thomas and Margaret B. Melady

"Takes its inspiration from the announcement in August 1972 by General Idi Amin Dada, President of Uganda, that he was told in a dream to order the expulsion of all Asians from Uganda. Tom and Margaret Melady were there and were witness to the tragic events. The book surveys the gruesome events following the expulsion order and the irrational pattern of Amin's record as well as providing a factual background of the Asian presence in Africa. The historical, economic and social complexity of the African-Asian-European situation in Uganda is made clear. Stories of personal devotion and heroism put flesh on the facts." *Religious Media Today*

ISBN 0-88344-506-9 CIP   *Cloth $6.95*